DISCARDED

An Andrew Marvell Companion

GARLAND REFERENCE LIBRARY OF THE HUMANITIES
VOLUME 1243

An Andrew Marvell Companion

Robert H. Ray

Garland Publishing, Inc.
A member of the Taylor & Francis Group
New York and London
1998

Copyright © 1998 by Robert H. Ray
All rights reserved

Library of Congress Cataloging-in-Publication Data

Ray, Robert H., 1940–
   An Andrew Marvell companion / by Robert H. Ray.
      p.   cm. — (Garland reference library of the humanities ; vol. 1243)
   Includes bibliographical references (p.   ).
   ISBN 0-8240-6248-5 (alk. paper)
      1. Marvell, Andrew, 1621–1678.   2. Poets, English—Early modern, 1500–1700—Biography.   3. Marvell, Andrew, 1621–1678—Bibliography. 4. Marvell, Andrew, 1621–1678—Dictionaries.   I. Title.   II. Series.
PR3546.R39   1998
821'.4—dc21
[B]   97-34073
                                                                                    CIP

Printed on acid-free, 250-year-life paper
Manufactured in the United States of America

CONTENTS

Preface	vii
Research in Marvell: Tools and Procedures	3
A Marvell Chronology	5
Marvell's Life	9
Marvell's Works	15
A Marvell Dictionary	17
Selected Bibliography	177

PREFACE

This book provides for the reader of Andrew Marvell a reference and resource volume similar to the companions, dictionaries, guides, and handbooks existing on several other major writers. I especially have modeled it upon my own *A George Herbert Companion* and *A John Donne Companion*, as well as F.E. Halliday's *A Shakespeare Companion*, Edward S. LeComte's *A Milton Dictionary*, and D. Heyward Brock's *A Ben Jonson Companion*. I am greatly indebted to these works, and, while learning much from their formats, criteria for sections and entries, and decisions on inclusions and exclusions, I institute modifications that seem more appropriate to Marvell's life and work and more pertinent to my primary audience. Throughout the writing I have kept before me the kinds of questions I had when first reading, studying, teaching, and researching Marvell. I attempt, then, a compendium of useful information for any reader of Marvell to have at hand, especially information not easily accessible to the nonspecialist. I include key facts about his life, works, and times, to enhance understanding and appreciation, without being exhaustive. In fact, my citations, bibliography, and suggestions for further research direct the reader to those books, articles, scholars, and critics that can best satisfy curiosity stimulated herein on any topic or work related to Marvell. Therefore, the book should be most helpful to the following groups: (1) general readers or undergraduate students coming to Marvell for the first time for any extensive reading or study, (2) postgraduate students seeking both a basic background in Marvell and some initial guidance to methods and tools for research in primary and secondary materials, and (3) nonspecialist teachers, particularly those teaching Marvell's works commonly found in anthologies and covered in survey courses. The scholar and critic, the Marvell specialist, however, will find in several of my entries on individual poems many explications of structure, words, phrases, and lines, with suggestions of wordplay and multiple meanings, not previously noted. I am assuming that the user of this *Companion*, especially in consulting entries in the "Dictionary" portion, has before him or her either an anthology with selections of Marvell's works or an edition of Marvell. This *Companion* is designed to be especially helpful to those with an edition or anthology having few or no notes or other aids in reading and understanding. I emphasize Marvell's poetry, rather than his prose, as well as the most frequently anthologized poems over the more specialized pieces and the selections of lesser popularity and fame. Specifically selected for concentration are the major poems from *Miscellaneous Poems*, 1681.

    The preceding aims and primary audiences largely determine the precise sections included, as well as their lengths, divisions, content, format, tone, and language. "Research in Marvell: Tools and Procedures" notes the most important tools for further research, as well as a step-by-step method of beginning with the "Selected Bibliography" at the end of this volume and then widening one's net to even more comprehensive and complex matters of criticism and scholarship. These steps allow the general reader to stop at the level most useful for his or her purposes, while the student or teacher eventually might wish to pursue more research into seventeenth-century originals and commentaries or into the complexities of text and scholarship: this brief section provides a way to begin. "A Marvell Chronology" presents an overview of dated highlights of Marvell's life and works in order to provide a perspective for absorbing the larger picture and further details in the succeeding "Marvell's Life" and "A Marvell Dictionary." The section "Marvell's Works" provides a list of his major works by customary titles and groups, and the critical studies listed in the "Selected Bibliography" are largely classified according to these works. The lightly annotated "Selected Bibliography" is divided into major categories (with subcategories), such as editions of primary works, tools for research and reference, biographical studies, studies of Marvell's reputation and influence, and criticism. The books, essays, and articles selected are those of first importance to anyone wishing to explore further the field represented within any given division or subdivision of Marvell's life and works. The coverage of the bibliography extends through 1995. Compact annotations in brackets conclude those items of prime significance that need more description than is given in the titles.

    The major portion of the volume, both in importance and size, is "A Marvell Dictionary." Its entries are arranged alphabetically: they identify, define, and explain the most important and influential *persons* in Marvell's life and works (mainly philosophers, family, friends, and governmental and other public figures); *places* either frequented by

Preface

Marvell or important in his life and works; *characters, allusions, ideas,* and *concepts* in his works and from his time; *words* and *phrases* of most importance and difficulty in his works, as well as those conducive to multiple meanings and puns in their interpretation; the most significant, famous, and frequently anthologized *poems* of Marvell; other important *writers* and *works* that are relevant to understanding portions of Marvell's own life or works or his influence and reputation; and *literary terms* important to or arising from Marvell's writing and influence. Maintaining my focus on the relevance of the content of each entry to Marvell's life and works is uppermost: for example, I resist being led astray into too many details about an individual's life (e.g., Oliver Cromwell's), but rather include only those facts that convey the essence to understand him or her and the role played by that individual in the course of Marvell's career and in the content of his writings. Other reference works, biographies, and histories can provide additional matters for anyone interested in the full details of the lives of such individuals.

The format for the entries in "A Marvell Dictionary" is designed to highlight and distinguish elements. The designation of each entry is capitalized and **Bold**: if it is a prose work or book, it is also ***Italicized***; but, if it is a poem, it is in **"Quotation Marks."** The same system of italics and quotation marks is employed within the content of an entry, but without the boldface. In addition, for any mention that appears elsewhere as an entry, I use ALL-CAPITALS as a cross-reference.

Other principles foster clarity and ease of reading. With the exception of the "Selected Bibliography," I modernize spelling and punctuation for all titles of books, prose works, and poems, as well as for any quotations from Marvell's or others' seventeenth-century original editions, manuscripts, and letters. Through the entire volume I spell out fully the names of Marvell's works, of professional journals, and of scholarly and critical books, rather than employ a lengthy list of abbreviations: for the nonspecialist reader, such abbreviations likely would be cryptic and frustrating, causing one continually to turn back to the key in an early part of the volume.

In writing this book, I have drawn from my own reading, teaching, and research of thirty years, and I feel that some new perspectives in close readings of several of Marvell's poems appear in the entries of the "Dictionary." I must acknowledge the study of works of reference, biography, history, philosophy, theology, scholarship, and criticism that enabled me to accomplish this task. Even though it is impossible to separate one's own readings at every point from the cumulative and mutual debts scholars and critics owe, I attempt to cite noteworthy readings that can be specified without burdening such a work as this with scholarly apparatus. I do, however, want my entire

"Selected Bibliography" to be a grateful acknowledgment of and a granting of due credit to the authors of those works found to be most helpful as sources of knowledge and insight, both in my years of studying Marvell and in composing this volume. In listing them I encourage readers to seek these items for fuller discussions and information on works and topics. Also, *The Oxford English Dictionary*, the *Dictionary of National Biography*, the *Cyclopedia of Biblical, Theological, and Ecclesiastical Literature*, the *Encyclopedia Britannica*, the *Dictionary of Phrase and Fable*, the *Gazetteer of the British Isles*, *An Encyclopaedia of London*, *The London Encyclopedia*, and *The Shell Guide to The History of London*, out of countless resources, have been of primary value and deserve singular mention. If I seem to have slighted or if I have been unaware of some work pertinent to my own readings and provision of information in this *Companion*, I apologize most deeply for the oversight.

I am indebted to many groups and their associated individuals for generous assistance. Garland Publishing has been exceedingly understanding and helpful, especially Phyllis Korper, Senior Editor. For continuing encouragement and generosity in allotting time and research sabbaticals for this work, I thank Baylor University and its administrators, especially James Barcus, William Cooper, Herbert Reynolds, Donald Schmeltekopf, and Robert Sloan. I particularly am grateful to the College of Arts and Sciences Faculty Development Committee for its vital support in granting the summer and long-term sabbaticals necessary to complete this project.

I wish to thank my family, especially my wife, Lynette, for unfailing encouragement.

R.H.R.
Baylor University

An Andrew Marvell Companion

RESEARCH IN MARVELL: TOOLS AND PROCEDURES

Although the "Selected Bibliography" concluding this volume provides key items for further study, researchers might wish to pursue Marvell's life and works more thoroughly. The following discussion directs one in such a task.

An annotated bibliographical guide to excerpts and criticism on Marvell saves labor and time. Dan S. Collins's *Andrew Marvell: A Reference Guide* (1981) covers books, articles, essays, brief comments, and doctoral dissertations published on Marvell between 1641 and 1980, although the 1977–1980 period is rather selective. He arranges the volume chronologically by centuries and years of publication and alphabetically by author within each year. Dissertations, however, are listed separately. Collins also provides an author/title index. Gillian Szanto's bibliographical essay titled "Recent Studies in Marvell" published in the Spring, 1975, issue of the journal *English Literary Renaissance* (Volume 5, Number 2) covers selected works on Marvell from about 1945 to 1972, arranging them by types, works, and topics. Supplementing this bibliographical essay is "Recent Studies in Andrew Marvell (1973–1990)" by Jerome S. Dees, also arranged by types, works, and topics. It appears in the Spring, 1992, issue of *English Literary Renaissance* (Volume 22, Number 2). To survey the dissertations written on Marvell, one should consult *Dissertation Abstracts* and *Dissertation Abstracts International* for the years desired. To find further and more nearly current and complete listings of books, articles, essays, and dissertations, the individual should employ the yearly *MLA International Bibliography*, the *Annual Bibliography of English Language and Literature*, and the *Essay and General Literature Index*.

The preceding references, then, provide ways to research almost everything written about Marvell through the larger part of the twentieth century, and for many topics these will suffice. However, if one wishes or needs to consult books, manuscripts, articles, essays, and specific excerpts commenting on Marvell and his works from 1673 to 1923, another reference tool provides the essentials: to study Marvell's reputation and influence in this span, one should consult *Andrew Marvell: The Critical Heritage* (1978), collected and edited by Elizabeth Story Donno. A useful supplement for surveying the early commentary on Marvell is the "Introduction" in *Marvell: Modern Judgements* (1969), edited by Michael Wilding.

For even more comprehensive research that calls for the use of early editions and manuscripts, further tools are necessary. The various reference volumes known as the *Short-Title Catalogue of Books Printed in England* and the *National Union Catalog* note libraries and collections possessing copies of early editions. (The researcher unfamiliar with these tools should consult a reference librarian for help.) Actually, if one cannot physically hold and examine the original books because of limited access to them, seeing early publications of Marvell's works (and those of writers who refer to and comment on Marvell) is much easier than the researcher might think. Because of some microfilms made of English books by University Microfilms International, many libraries now possess Marvell's works filmed from original editions. Armed with the number assigned to a particular book in the *Short-Title Catalogue*, the researcher can locate which reel of film that book appears on in a set of microfilms by using the reel guides that accompany the collections. (Again, seeking a reference librarian's help in orienting oneself to this search is quite valuable.) If a person needs information on extant manuscripts of Marvell's works (their contents and locations), the primary reference tool is the *Index of English Literary Manuscripts*, compiled by Peter Beal and others. Many of the modern editions of Marvell cited in my "Selected Bibliography" also discuss the early editions of and the manuscript sources for Marvell's works, a rather complex matter in some instances.

The standard edition of Marvell's works is H.M. Margoliouth's *The Poems and Letters of Andrew Marvell* (3rd edition, revised by Pierre Legouis with the collaboration of E.E. Duncan-Jones), 1971. Other important modern editions are listed in my "Selected Bibliography," including some that contain the prose works, other than the letters.

A MARVELL CHRONOLOGY

1621   Andrew Marvell born on March 31 at Winestead-in-Holderness, Yorkshire.

1624   The Reverend Andrew Marvell (the poet's father) appointed Master of the Hull Charterhouse.

1629   Probably attends Hull Grammar School (until 1633).

1633   Matriculates at Trinity College, Cambridge, as sizar.

1638   His mother dies (April). His father remarries (November).

1639   Takes Bachelor of Arts degree.

1641   His father dies by drowning.

1642   Living in London. From 1642 to 1647 Marvell travels in Holland, France, Italy, and Spain. Meets Richard Flecknoe at Rome in 1646.

1647   Sells his property in Meldreth, Cambridgeshire.

1648   "An Elegy upon the Death of My Lord Francis Villiers" published.

1649   "To His Noble Friend Mr. Richard Lovelace, upon His Poems" and "Upon the Death of Lord Hastings" published.

1650	Writes "An Horatian Ode upon Cromwell's Return from Ireland" and "Tom May's Death." Moves to Nun Appleton, Yorkshire?
1651	Tutor to Mary Fairfax, daughter of General Fairfax, at Nun Appleton, Yorkshire, in 1651 and 1652, apparently writing "Upon Appleton House" during this period.
1653	John Milton recommends Marvell as Latin Secretary to the Council of State, but he is not appointed. Becomes tutor to William Dutton, a ward of Oliver Cromwell's, in Eton. Lives there in the house of John Oxenbridge. Probably writes "Bermudas."
1654	Writes "The First Anniversary of the Government under His Highness the Lord Protector."
1655	"The First Anniversary" published anonymously.
1656	At Saumur (in France) with his pupil William Dutton. Marvell is described here as a "notable English Italo-Machiavellian."
1657	Writes "On the Victory Obtained by Blake over the Spaniards." Appointed Latin Secretary to the Council of State.
1658	Writes "A Poem upon the Death of His Late Highness the Lord Protector." Participates in Cromwell's funeral procession.
1659	Elected Member of Parliament for Hull (January). Loses his parliamentary seat when the Rump Parliament is restored (May). Retains his post as Latin Secretary and granted lodgings in Whitehall.
1660	Re-elected Member of Parliament for Hull.
1662	In Holland (until April, 1663) on a political mission.
1663	Travels as private secretary with the Earl of Carlisle (until January, 1665) on an embassy to Russia, Sweden, and Denmark.
1665	Returns to England.

A Marvell Chronology

1667	Writes "Clarendon's Housewarming" and "The Last Instructions to a Painter." Participates in the impeachment of Clarendon.
1671	Writes some epigrams.
1672	In controversy with Samuel Parker, Archdeacon of Canterbury. Publishes (anonymously) *The Rehearsal Transpros'd* (Part 1).
1673	Publishes Part 2 of *The Rehearsal Transpros'd*, with acknowledgment of authorship.
1674	Writes commendatory poem for the second edition of Milton's *Paradise Lost*.
1675	Writes "His Majesty's Most Gracious Speech to both Houses of Parliament."
1676	Publishes *Mr. Smirke*.
1677	Speaks against the bill to secure the Protestant succession. Conceals two bankrupt friends in a house in Great Russell Street. Publishes *An Account of the Growth of Popery and Arbitrary Government* (anonymously).
1678	Visits Hull. Becomes ill on the return trip to London. Dies on August 16 in his house in Great Russell Street. Buried August 18 in St. Giles-in-the-Fields Church.
1681	*Miscellaneous Poems* published (by "Mary Marvell," actually Mary Palmer, Marvell's housekeeper).

MARVELL'S LIFE

Andrew Marvell was born at Winestead-in-Holderness in Yorkshire on March 31, 1621. His father was the rector there. Andrew was the fourth child, but the first son, in the family. A fifth child (a son) was born but died in infancy. The mother was Anne Pease of Yorkshire. In 1624 the father (also named Andrew) moved to Hull as lecturer in Holy Trinity Church and as Master of the Charterhouse (an almshouse). Here the Master was provided a house surrounded by gardens near the River Hull. The younger Andrew apparently was educated at the Hull Grammar School, near Holy Trinity Church.

Andrew's grammar school education ended at the age of twelve, and he matriculated at Cambridge as a sizar of Trinity College on December 14, 1633. Marvell contributed verses to a Cambridge volume of 1637 that honored the birth of the fifth child of the King and Queen. In April of 1638 his mother died, and his father remarried later that year (in November). Apparently during 1639 Marvell came under the influence of Jesuits, left Cambridge, was found in London by his father, and was persuaded to return to Cambridge. He took his Bachelor of Arts degree in 1639 and continued to reside at the University during 1640, apparently planning to proceed to the Master of Arts. But after his father died by drowning in the River Humber in early 1641, the younger Marvell left Cambridge during the latter part of 1641 and is recorded as living in London by early 1642. It is possible that he studied at one of the Inns of Court, since he lived near them and served as witness to some deeds at Gray's Inn.

From some point in 1642 or 1643 until 1647, Marvell was in Holland, France, Italy, and Spain. It appears that his main goal was to learn the languages of these countries. During 1646 Marvell met Richard Flecknoe, a rather impoverished Catholic priest and poet from England who was at the time living in Rome. In a letter Marvell reveals that he took fencing lessons while in Spain. Marvell returned to England probably in late 1647: in November he sold some property in Meldreth, Cambridgeshire, that he had inherited from his grandfather. During 1648 and/or 1649 Marvell was in London. Published during these years were "An Elegy upon the Death of My Lord Francis Villiers," "To His Noble Friend Mr. Richard Lovelace, upon His Poems," and "Upon the Death of Lord Hastings." Marvell was at this time associated with a circle of Royalist friends, writers, and artists. In 1650, however, Marvell assessed Oliver Cromwell and the new England under Parliamentary and Cromwellian power, not without some admiration, in "An Horatian Ode upon Cromwell's Return from Ireland." Later in the same year, interestingly, Marvell reflected early Royalist disgust for Thomas May, who had abandoned the Royalists and become a thorough Parliamentarian, in his "Tom May's Death." In late 1650 or early 1651 Marvell moved to Nun Appleton in Yorkshire, since he had been hired by Thomas Fairfax, the General of the Army who had resigned in July 1650. He served as tutor in languages to Fairfax's daughter (Mary) for a period of two years. "Upon the Hill and Grove at Bilbrough" and "Upon Appleton House" were written during these years: they center upon Fairfax's Yorkshire estates and are both addressed to him.

In February 1653, John Milton wrote a letter to John Bradshaw, who was President of the Council of State. Milton recommended that Andrew Marvell be appointed to serve as Milton's assistant in his post of Secretary for Foreign Tongues (which Milton more narrowly held as Latin Secretary). Milton praised Marvell for his knowledge of languages; for his four years abroad in Holland, France, Italy, and Spain; and for his service as tutor to Mary Fairfax. In fact, Milton argued that Marvell was "fit every way" for the position. Marvell, however, did not receive the post: it was granted to Philip Meadows. Marvell, instead, became the tutor of William Dutton, a ward of Cromwell's, and lived at Eton in the home of John Oxenbridge, a friend of Cromwell's. Oxenbridge and his wife had spent much time in the Bermudas, and he was appointed in 1653 as one of the commissioners for government of the colony. It is quite likely that Marvell wrote his poem "Bermudas" in 1653 with the major stimulus coming from the Oxenbridges. In July of 1653 Marvell wrote a letter to Cromwell to report of his activities in tutoring William Dutton, and he praises the examples and influences of the Oxenbridge household. The Oxenbridges were thoroughly Puritan in background and beliefs. It is interesting that Marvell also became acquainted with John Hales, who lived near Eton in the Anglican community at Ritchings. Hales had been William Laud's chaplain at one time and was Fellow of Eton and Canon at Windsor. The Parliamentarians had evicted him from both positions.

Marvell apparently admired Hales's *Tract Concerning Schisme and Schismatiques* of 1642, since he copied a section of it later into his own *The Rehearsal Transpros'd*. Marvell's own toleration, balance, and tendency to have friends and respected acquaintances in different political and religious camps may be epitomized by the Oxenbridge and Hales attachments while at Eton. In September 1653, an Eton friend of Marvell's, Nathaniel Ingelo, served as chaplain to Bulstrode Whitlocke on an ambassadorial mission to Sweden. This diplomatic effort was to win Sweden's neutrality in the Dutch War. Marvell wrote Latin verses in praise of Ingelo which included lines flattering Queen Christina and Sweden. It is thought that she saw these verses by Marvell and that they could well have been a factor in helping England's cause in winning the friendship of Sweden at this time.

Marvell continued serving Cromwell and his government in various ways. In December of 1654 Cromwell celebrated the first anniversary of the Protectorate. Marvell at this time wrote "The First Anniversary of the Government under His Highness the Lord Protector," a poem extolling both Cromwell and the new England. The poem was published anonymously in 1655. In 1656 Marvell was in France (at Saumur) with William Dutton. James Scudamore in a letter referred to Dutton's presence in France, along with a reference to Marvell as his "governor," whom he also calls "a notable English Italo-Machiavellian," thus reflecting Scudamore's Royalist scorn for both the young ward and the tutor serving Cromwell, the man seen as causing the execution of King Charles I. In 1657 Marvell wrote "On the Victory Obtained by Blake over the Spaniards," a poem praising Admiral Robert Blake's capturing of sixteen Spanish treasure ships, but it also profusely praises Cromwell and suggests that he should accept the role of king. Also in 1657 Marvell was made Latin Secretary to John Thurloe, Secretary to the Council of State. Marvell's duties entailed writing some of the official governmental correspondence, as well as receiving and attending some of the foreign envoys in England. Marvell wrote two songs for the wedding of Cromwell's third daughter, Mary, in November 1657. In August 1658, Cromwell's second daughter, Elizabeth, died. Then Oliver Cromwell himself died on September 3, 1658: his body decomposed so rapidly that he was buried quickly and privately. Marvell took part in the formal state funeral procession for Cromwell, walking beside the empty coffin. Marvell wrote "A Poem upon the Death of His Late Highness the Lord Protector" in late 1658.

Beginning in 1659 Marvell served in Parliament for Hull until his death. Although he continued to serve as Latin Secretary for about a year after Oliver Cromwell's death, his major governmental service for the last twenty years of his life was as a Member of Parliament. He was first elected for Hull on January 11, 1659 (Old Style 1658). Richard Cromwell, however, was forced by the Army to dissolve this Parliament in April, and the Rump Parliament was restored: Sir Henry Vane sat for Hull, rather than Marvell. Marvell retained his post as Latin Secretary, and in July was granted lodgings in Whitehall. In October the Rump Parliament was dismissed by the Army, only to be brought back in late December. In March of 1660 the House was dissolved. In April Hull returned Andrew Marvell and John Ramsden to Parliament. In May Charles Stuart was proclaimed King. Although John Milton was pursued for prosecution, Marvell was not. Indeed, Marvell was able to prevent Milton's trial in court, to secure his release from prison with lesser fines, and to speak for him in the House of Commons. Marvell served in 1661 and 1662 in an increasingly Royalist Parliament and felt more hostility therein. He quarrelled with the Royalist Colonel Anthony Gilby, his fellow M.P. from Hull, and he had an altercation with the Royalist Thomas Clifford. Marvell diligently and frequently reported to Hull by letters that gave accounts of Parliamentary actions, etc., during all his years as M.P.

In May 1662, Marvell accompanied a member of the Privy Council, the Earl of Carlisle, on state business to Holland. He again went abroad from July 1663, to January 1665: he served as Secretary to the Earl of Carlisle on embassies to Russia, Sweden, and Denmark. In 1665, after his return to England, Marvell resumed his position as M.P. From 1665 to 1667 there was increasing dissatisfaction with the policies of the Earl of Clarendon, Lord Chancellor and King Charles's chief advisor. Marvell satirized him in "Clarendon's Housewarming" and "The Last Instructions to a Painter" (1667). Marvell participated in the speeches and proceedings leading to Clarendon's impeachment and eventual Act of Banishment against him in December 1667.

From 1668 on Marvell became increasingly disturbed by the intolerance shown toward Nonconformists by certain Anglicans and members of Parliament. In particular, his disagreement with Samuel Parker, Archdeacon of Canterbury, and Parker's vindictive, anti-Nonconformist writings led to Marvell's satirical *The Rehearsal Transpros'd* of 1672 and 1673 (in two parts). King Charles II read and enjoyed the first part of the work, published anonymously. And the King protected the author from prosecution by ecclesiastical authorities. Some readers of Marvell's anonymously published *The Rehearsal Transpros'd* (first part) had assumed that both Marvell and Milton had written it, but when Marvell acknowledged his authorship with the publication of the second part, it was clear that only he had written it. Marvell illustrated his continuing regard for Milton, however, by writing a commendatory poem published with the second edition of

Paradise Lost in 1674. Milton died in November of 1674, and Marvell quite likely attended his burial in St. Giles Church, Cripplegate.

Despite the area of agreement with the King in regard to toleration, Marvell increasingly became disenchanted by Charles's policies regarding France, Catholicism, and the harm done to the King's relationship with the Parliament by these policies. In 1675 Marvell wrote a parody of King Charles's speech opening a session of Parliament in April.

In 1676 Marvell wrote *Mr. Smirke: Or, the Divine in Mode*, criticizing Anglican persecutions of Nonconformists. In the following year Marvell sheltered Richard Thompson and Edward Nelthorpe from harsh bankruptcy laws, apparently keeping them in a home rented on Great Russell Street in the name of Mary Palmer, his housekeeper. Also in 1677 he opposed a bill to secure the Protestant succession and for Anglican bishops to control church preferment. He also published anonymously *An Account of the Growth of Popery and Arbitrary Government*, criticizing France and its king and the failure of the English Parliament to support financially a war against France in support of the Protestant Prince of Orange.

In 1678 Marvell visited Hull, became ill on his return trip to London, and died on August 16. He was buried in St. Giles-in-the-Fields Church on August 18, the cost of the funeral and of a memorial stone paid for by Hull.

In 1681 was published the volume titled *Miscellaneous Poems* in which "To the Reader" is signed by "Mary Marvell," claiming to be the wife of Andrew Marvell. This woman actually is Mary Palmer, his housekeeper. She was part of an elaborate scheme thought up by the bankrupts concealed by Marvell to be able to claim and protect five hundred pounds that had been deposited with a goldsmith (in Marvell's name) by Nelthorpe. It is ironic that through such subterfuge in publishing a book has been preserved for all time almost all of the important works of a major poet.

(For fuller study of Marvell's life, see the works cited in my "Selected Bibliography," especially Pierre Legouis, *Andrew Marvell: Poet, Puritan, Patriot*; John Dixon Hunt, *Andrew Marvell: His Life and Writings*; and Hilton Kelliher, *Andrew Marvell: Poet & Politician, 1621–78.*)

MARVELL'S WORKS

As customarily classified by titles and/or groups, Marvell's major works are as follows:

A. Poetry

    Clarendon's Housewarming
    The Last Instructions to a Painter
    Miscellaneous Poems [Contains all of the famous lyric poems]

B. Prose

    Letters
    The Rehearsal Transprosed

A MARVELL DICTIONARY

A

A. C. See CLARKE, ANDREW.

Abbot, George (1562–1633). Opposed WILLIAM LAUD.

Abednego. See SHADRACK.

Acklam, George. One of the mayors of Hull to whom Marvell sent letters reporting government matters, since he was a Member of Parliament for the city.

Admire. *Verb*: (1) to wonder or marvel; (2) to view with wonder or surprise; (3) to regard with pleasure or approval or affection.

Admit. *Verb*: (1) to allow to enter, to let in; (2) to permit or allow; (3) to acknowledge; (4) to accept as true, to concede as fact.

Adust. *Adjective*: referring to an assumed dry condition of the body and its HUMORs, according to the GALENISTs. Generally connoting a state of being dried up by heat.

Aesculapius. In mythology, son of Apollo and Coronis. God of medicine and healing. Restored many to health and raised Hippolytus from the dead: ZEUS killed Aesculapius for the latter deed, since Zeus wanted none to have such power.

Aeson. King of Thessaly. Father of Jason. Was restored to youth by Medea.

Aetna. Volcanic mountain in Sicily. In mythology, Jove or Jupiter (ZEUS in Greek mythology) imprisoned the Giant named Enceladus under Sicily, and Mount Aetna's eruptions were said to illustrate the Giant's presence.

Affect. *Verb*: (1) to aspire to or seek to obtain, (2) to like or love, (3) to frequent or inhabit, (4) to influence or act upon.

Affection. *Noun*: (1) emotion or feeling; (2) passion; (3) disposition, inclination, mental tendency; (4) fondness; (5) biased feeling.

Affects the metaphysics. See METAPHYSICAL.

Afford. *Verb*: (1) to perform or accomplish, (2) to grant or bestow or give of what one has, (3) to be capable of yielding, (4) to supply from resources or to yield naturally.

Air. *Noun*: (1) one of the four ELEMENTS, (2) the atmosphere or space just above the earth, (3) breath or sigh.

Ajax. Marvell, in "The Unfortunate Lover," refers to Lesser Ajax (Locrian Ajax), not the more famous Greek hero in the Trojan War (Greater Ajax). This Ajax alluded to by Marvell is, in mythology, the son of Oileus and the leader of the Locrians in the Trojan War. He proudly claimed to have escaped from a storm against the wishes of the gods. Poseidon, who had rescued him, then shattered the rock where Ajax had found shelter and drowned him.

Alarms. *Noun*: calls to arms or battle (with trumpets or drums).

Albemarle, Duchess of. See MONCK, GEORGE.

Albemarle, Duke of. See MONCK, GEORGE.

Alchemy. The "science" or "chemistry" of the Middle Ages and Renaissance that attempted to turn base metals into gold by the use of a "philosopher's stone." Also, these practitioners of alchemy, the alchemists (or "chymists" or "chemics"), wanted to concoct or extract an "elixir" (or "elixir vitae"), a miraculous medicine that supposedly would cure all disease and prolong life. This elixir was also referred to as the "essence" or "quintessence" (or "fifth essence"), an absolutely pure substance that could purge impurities. It was believed by some to be latent in all matter, and it was thought to be what makes up the heavenly bodies. *One must note that many writers commonly do not distinguish between the "philosopher's stone" and the "elixir" and the "quintessence," but use these terms interchangeably.* Chemicals would be combined, heated, and distilled from a larger to a smaller receiving vessel.

Allow. *Verb*: (1) to praise or commend, (2) to approve of, (3) to accept as reasonable or valid, (4) to permit.

Allure. *Verb*: (1) to tempt, entice, charm; (2) to draw to oneself, to draw forth, to elicit.

Amalgamating disparate experience. See DISSOCIATION OF SENSIBILITY.

Amber. *Noun*: (1) ambergris: waxy, oily substance secreted from a whale, used in cooking and in perfumes; (2) yellow translucent fossil resin, used for ornaments, and often found hardened around trapped insects.

Ambergris, ambergreece. See AMBER (1).

Amphion. In mythology, son of ZEUS and Antiope. A musician who built the walls of Thebes by causing stones to move to music.

Anchises. In mythology, a Dardanian king. He was so handsome that Aphrodite (VENUS) came down from heaven to IDA to join him. She became pregnant by him and bore their son, Aeneas. Anchises was saved at the end of the Trojan War by being carried through flames by his son. Father and son went to Italy. Anchises died at the age of eighty in Sicily and was buried on Mount Eryx. The Roman emperors and legendary kings of Britain were said to have descended from Anchises.
 Marvell alludes to him in the "First Song" of "Two Songs at the Marriage of the Lord Fauconberg and the Lady Mary Cromwell," line 30. Anchises here symbolizes Robert Rich who had married OLIVER CROMWELL's fourth daughter (Frances).

Angel. *Noun*: (1) spiritual being, above man and below God in the hierarchy of creation, who attends God and serves as a ministering spirit and a divine messenger (see also HIERARCHY, THE HEAVENLY); (2) an English coin stamped with the image of the Archangel Michael piercing the Dragon (of Revelation).

Antipodes. *Noun*: (1) those who dwell directly opposite to each other on opposing sides of the earth, (2) those who resemble dwellers on the other side of the earth, (3) places on the surface of the earth that are directly opposite to each other.

Apelles. Painter for Alexander of Macedon. Fell in love with Campaspe, Alexander's mistress, while painting her portrait, and Alexander gave her to him.

Apollo. In Greek mythology, son of Zeus and Leto. Regarded as the sun god, as well as the god of fine arts, music, and poetry. Had many women, nymphs, and goddesses as lovers or would-be lovers. Marvell alludes to his pursuit of DAPHNE.

Apothecary. *Noun*: a pharmacist, one who mixes and prepares drugs or medicines.

Approve. *Verb*: (1) to try, (2) to experience, (3) to corroborate or confirm.

Apsley, Sir Allen (1616–1683). Treasurer of the Duke of York's household (see JAMES II).

Aranjuez. Spanish royal gardens near Madrid.

Aretino, Pietro (1492–1556). Italian poet.

Aristotle (384–322 B.C.). Greek philosopher. Studied under PLATO for twenty years. Was tutor to Alexander the Great. Aristotle established a school (the Lyceum) in Athens and taught there for twelve years. His thought survives largely in his and/or his students' lecture notes, and his study covers all realms of knowledge in his time. His influence dominated thought for 2,000 years after him, reaching its height in the Middle Ages when he was idolized as the final word on all knowledge: he was particularly central to the schoolmen. In logic, his development of deductive reasoning held sway until the scientific advances following BACON and the rise of science and induction in the 17th century. Ultimately disagreed with and challenged Plato and

PLATONIC thought, arguing rather for the reality of the physical and material world, and for the duality of body and spirit. In contrast to an idealistic mode of thought, Aristotle tends toward the pragmatic, the practical: *Nicomachean Ethics*, *Politics*, and *Poetics* treat conduct, government, and literature in this light.

Many of the assumptions underlying both NATURAL ORDER and the view of the universe ascribed to PTOLEMY have their sources in Aristotle, especially in his *Metaphysics*. He envisions a ranked, hierarchical nature that leads to the pure Unmoved Mover at the top that is the source of all energy in the universe. His philosophy was ultimately brought into agreement with major Christian conceptions and was embraced by the church.

The ideas of intelligences directing the SPHERES, of the human TRIPARTITE SOUL, and of the four ELEMENTS owe much to Aristotle, and they frequently appear in Marvell and other writers of his time.

Ark. *Noun*: (1) the ark God had Noah build to save himself and his family from the flood: see Genesis 6–9; (2) the Ark of the Covenant, a holy chest eventually containing the Ten Commandments and carried from place to place by the Hebrews in their wanderings and battles, finally being placed in Solomon's Temple, where it is believed to have been destroyed in the Babylonian destruction of the Temple.

Arlington, Earl of. See BENNET, HENRY.

Arminianism. The doctrines formulated and argued for by ARMINIUS and his followers.

Arminius, James (1560–1609). Dutch Protestant theologian who proposed views counter to those of CALVIN. Argued against Calvinistic views of absolute predestination and contended that God is not to be held responsible for evil. The role of free will is uplifted. At the Synod of Dort in 1618–19 Arminian doctrines were condemned, but they gained great influence, nevertheless, in many Protestant churches.

As. Frequently means "that" and "since" (or "because").

Ashburnham, John (1603–1671). Arranged CHARLES I's flight from HAMPTON COURT to the Isle of Wight in 1647. Suspected of betraying the King to the governor of the island. See also CARISBROOKE CASTLE.

Ashley. See COOPER, ANTHONY ASHLEY.

Assay. *Verb*: to test or try, sometimes with the connotation of a man "trying" a woman sexually.

Assume. *Verb*: (1) to adopt or take, (2) to take food or drink into the body, (3) to take upon or put on, (4) to lay claim or usurp.

At sharp. With sharp weapons.

Attend. *Verb*: (1) to pay attention to or consider or listen to; (2) to apply oneself to; (3) to wait upon or serve or accompany; (4) to wait for or expect; (5) to wait or stay.

Augustine, Saint (354–430). Bishop of Hippo in Africa from 396 to 430. Recognized as one of the greatest thinkers, writers, and theologians in Christianity. His mother (Monica) was a devout Christian and continually wished Augustine to become one. He lived a rather dissolute early life, with a mistress and an illegitimate son. At the age of 28 he went to Milan as a teacher of rhetoric where he heard Ambrose preach and was impressed by his use of Neoplatonic philosophy (see PLATONIC). He experienced a mystical conversion in Milan that was confirmed by a reading of St. Paul. He turned more ascetic and philosophical. He was baptized by Ambrose in 387. On his return to Africa his mother died, just after a conversation between mother and son on the ascent to heaven and its glories. After returning to Africa, he became assistant priest to the bishop at Hippo, and, after the bishop's death, Augustine was made Bishop in 395 and remained so until his death during the siege of the city by the Vandals.
    Augustine wrote sermons, commentaries, essays, and letters. Two of his works, however, are his most famous and influential. His *Confessions* detail his early life and conversion, expressing extreme guilt for the sexual and other sins of his youth. *The City of God* proposes that there are two cities in existence vying for man's adherence, Jerusalem and Babylon or the heavenly city and the earthly city or the city of God and the city of man. Although heavily influenced by PLATONIC philosophy and its ability to be reconciled with some facets of Christianity, Augustine increasingly saw the differences. He could agree that looking into himself at his own soul can reveal God and felt that he could find in God the author of all and the illuminator of truth. He is one of the four traditional Doctors of the western church.

Augustine's formulation of the concept of the BOOK OF CREATURES also influenced writers, thinkers, and clergymen of the 16th and 17th centuries.

Aurora. In mythology, goddess of the dawn. Daughter of Hyperion and Thia.

B

B., Mr. See BAXTER, RICHARD.

B. and L. See BERKENHEAD and L'ESTRANGE.

Babel, Tower of. The tower of brick erected by men who wanted its top to reach to heaven. God, seeing their pride, confounded their language so that they could no longer understand each other. They then ceased their building and scattered to various parts of the earth. See Genesis 11:1–9.

Bacon, Francis (1561–1626). Studied and practiced law, served in Parliament, and held the position of Lord Keeper of the Great Seal under Queen Elizabeth. His advancement was even more rapid under King JAMES, serving as Solicitor General, Attorney General, Lord Keeper, and Lord Chancellor. Knighted in 1603, created first Baron Verulam in 1618, and made Viscount St. Albans in 1621, Bacon accumulated many political enemies, and he was tried and convicted by the House of Lords in 1621 on the charge of accepting bribes as a judge. He was barred from holding public office: thus in public disgrace, Bacon retired to his estate to concentrate more on philosophical and scientific speculations and proposals and on writing. His *Essays* had first appeared in 1597, but subsequent editions through 1625 expanded their number. His most influential works are *The Advancement of Learning* (1605) and *Novum Organum* (1620), containing key proposals in his visionary plan to refute Aristotelian and medieval authority and means of reasoning. Bacon proposes the inductive (or scientific) method of arriving at truth, wishing to eliminate the human tendency to be misled by subjectivity. Bacon's works placed him in the vanguard of the rise of science, endorsing both an attitude of objective observation of physical matter outside of the individual and an increase of practicality and utility in outlook in the seventeenth century. His *New Atlantis*, proposing a type of scientific Utopia, appeared a year after his death.

Bait. *Verb*: (1) to stop to refresh and rest, (2) to make a brief stop, (3) to furnish a hook or trap with a bait, (4) to use dogs to bite and annoy other animals (such as bulls or bears) for sport.

Balm. *Noun*: (1) aromatic substance exuding from some trees and valued for fragrance and medicinal qualities, (2) a soothing and healing substance, (3) according to PARACELSUS, the life-preserving fluid existing in every living being, the absence of which means death.

Balsam, balsome. See BALM.

Banneret. Knighthood conferred on the battlefield for brave deeds: CHARLES I revived this type of knighthood at the Battle of Edgehill in 1642.

Banquet. *Noun*: (1) a sumptuous feast of food and drink; (2) sweets, fruit, and wine; (3) dessert; (4) Eucharist or Lord's Supper.

Battery. *Noun*: (1) bombardment by artillery upon a fortress or city, (2) pieces of artillery.

Baxter, Richard (1615–1691). Presbyterian clergyman and prolific writer of prose. Criticized by JOHN BRAMHALL in his *Vindication* and defended by Marvell in *The Rehearsal Transprosed*. Marvell refers to him in this work as "Mr. B."

Bayly, Thomas (died 1657?). Royalist clergyman. Took B.A. and M.A. at Magdalene College, Cambridge. Took D.D. degree at Oxford. Attended CHARLES I on the battlefield. After the death of the King he converted to Roman Catholicism. Then he lived and died in Italy. Wrote *Herba Parietis; or the Wall-Flower* (1650).

Bays, bayes. *Noun*: leaves of the laurel, traditionally depicted as woven into a garland or celebratory wreath, and commonly used to reward poets and poetic achievement. Also see JOHN DRYDEN and SAMUEL PARKER.

Bays, Mr. A character representing SAMUEL PARKER in Marvell's *The Rehearsal Transprosed*. Marvell took the name from the Duke of Buckingham's *The Rehearsal* (see VILLIERS, GEORGE). In Buckingham's play the character so named represents JOHN DRYDEN.

Bearbaiting. See BAIT (4).

Bear-garden. A place of amusement on the south bank of the Thames where dogs were used to bite and annoy bears for sport. See BAIT (4).

Becomes. *Verb*: (1) comes to be, (2) befits or suits.

Bedlam. A hospital in London established specifically as an asylum for the insane. The name is a variant of "Bethlehem": the hospital was Bethlehem Hospital (actually St. Mary of Bethlehem).

Behind. *Adverb*: (1) [spatially] in the back of or toward the rear of; (2) [temporally] following in time, later.

Belasyse, Thomas (1627–1700). Second Viscount Fauconberg. Married MARY CROMWELL at Hampton Court on November 19, 1657. He was related to THOMAS FAIRFAX. After the Restoration of CHARLES II, he became a Privy Councillor and Ambassador. Was made an earl in 1689. Marvell wrote two songs for the wedding.

Bell, book, and candle. To be pursued with bell, book, and candle is to be excommunicated.

Bel-Retiro. Buen Retiro, a royal residence near Madrid, Spain.

Bennet, Henry (1618–1685). Served on Royalist side in the civil war (see CHARLES I). Close to the future CHARLES II and the royal family before the Restoration. Made Keeper of the Privy Purse. Helped to manage the King's mistresses and was particularly allied with Lady Castlemaine (see VILLIERS, BARBARA) in opposition to Clarendon (see HYDE, EDWARD). Made Secretary of State in 1662. Became a member of the cabal (see MAITLAND, JOHN). Created Earl of Arlington in 1672. He began, however, to lose influence in 1674 because of political enemies and other factions. He resigned his secretaryship and was made Lord Chamberlain. He retired to his estate at Euston in Suffolk, where he died and was buried.
Marvell refers to Bennet several times in both "The Last Instructions To a Painter" and in his letters.

Bergamot. *Noun*: a type of pear known for its excellence and called "the pear of kings."

Berkenhead, Sir John (1617–1679). A censor of books for the government. He is referred to by Marvell as the "B." of "B. and L." in *The Rehearsal Transprosed*.

"Bermudas." One of the works in *MISCELLANEOUS POEMS*. The poem probably was written as a result of Marvell's conversations with John and Jane Oxenbridge while he was tutor to WILLIAM DUTTON and living in the Oxenbridge home at Eton. Some PURITANs had fled

England in the early 17th century and settled in the Bermudas. The Oxenbridges, strong Puritans and victims of persecution by Laud, had lived there, and in 1653 John Oxenbridge became one of the commissioners for government of the colony. (For more on the Oxenbridges, see the entry on DUTTON, WILLIAM.) Since the islands were known for rich natural resources and fertility from early travel accounts and then also became one of the Puritan refuges from religious persecution, they were regarded as a kind of earthly paradise, seemingly provided by God for his true followers.

In the poem Marvell imagines a boat of such religious exiles from England (see "English boat" in line 37) rowing near their island home and singing (with "holy" and "cheerful note") their praises to God for his provision. Lines 1–4 and 37–40 give us this context, and these two sets of four lines surround the song itself (lines 5–36).

Lines 5–12 acknowledge that God led them over the ocean to this "isle so long unknown"—it was not discovered until 1515 by Juan Bermudez. This island (Bermuda) is "far kinder than our own [island, England]," because in England they suffer religious persecution. The "sea-monsters" (line 9) are whales that sometimes become stranded on the shore of the island. The singers picture God landing the exiles here and making them "Safe, from the storms' and prelates' rage": they find shelter here from the storms at sea and also from the storms' counterparts in England, the prelates (high Anglican churchmen, such as WILLIAM LAUD, who had persecuted John Oxenbridge).

Lines 13–28 catalogue the natural riches provided for them by God in this earthly paradise. The "spring" season is "eternal" here, and thus God "enamels" the land, colors it brightly, with these varied elements. Birds ("fowls") are provided, along with fruits such as oranges that hang on the green trees like "golden lamps in a green night." Lines 19–20 can be interpreted in two ways: "pomegranates" can refer to the shrub or small tree containing the fruits, or it can refer to the fruits themselves, within which are enclosed juicy red pulp and many seeds. So, the "jewels" within are the fruits themselves contained within the shrubs, or they are the seeds within each fruit. In either instance, Marvell compares "pomegranates" to jewelry cases containing rich natural gems more beautiful than those found in the rich market island of ORMUS. God gives "figs our mouths to meet" and throws "melons at our feet": this is very much like the existence enjoyed by the speaker of "THE GARDEN" in his Adam-like enjoyment of paradise. "Apples" in line 23 refers to pineapples: the sense is that God plants the pineapples there (through the labor of his followers, since they were introduced to the island by the settlers). The pineapples had to be replanted each year, but Marvell makes this a positive action, suggesting that they are so valuable that "no tree could ever bear them twice." God is also seen as providing cedars of Lebanon and AMBERGRIS.

Lines 29-36 conclude the song by praising God for allowing them this island as a Temple and for casting the "Gospel's Pearl upon our coast." The pearl here might allude to one or both of two Biblical passages: (1) Matthew 13:45-46 ("Again, the kingdom of heaven is like unto a merchant man, seeking goodly pearls: Who, when he had found one pearl of great price, went and sold all that he had, and bought it"); (2) Matthew 7:6 ("Give not that which is holy unto the dogs, neither cast ye your pearls before swine, lest they trample them under your feet, and turn again and rend you"). The former passage is quite appropriate in the context of the poem's comparison of the superior riches and "jewels" found in this God-provided paradise, compared to the wealth of "Ormus" and the world outside. However, equally relevant is the latter passage as a comment on the value of this secluded holy place of worship, safe from the trampling swine, the "prelates" and other persecutors in England. Their exalted praise here will arrive at "Heaven's vault" and rebound to echo beyond the "Mexique Bay," beyond the Gulf of Mexico—i.e., the singers' praise will be heard by heathens and Roman Catholics in America, with the missionary hope that they might be converted.

Betray. *Verb*: (1) to reveal or to disclose something or someone, (2) to place into the hands of an enemy by treachery, (3) to expose to punishment, (4) to be false or disloyal.

Beza, Theodore (1519-1604). CALVINIST theologian.

Bilbrough. One of the estates in Yorkshire owned by THOMAS FAIRFAX. Marvell served as tutor to his daughter and probably wrote "Upon the Hill and Grove at Bilbrough" during his residence with the family.

Bill. *Verb*: to peck.

Bill-borow. See BILBROUGH.

Blake, Robert (1599-1657). Graduated from Oxford. Served in the Parliamentary army in the civil war. Appointed in 1649 to share in the chief command of the English fleet as one of the admirals and generals at sea. Made a member of the Council of State in December 1651. In May 1652, a Dutch fleet under the command of Tromp anchored off Dover, did not salute the castle, and exercised with repeated volleys of small arms fire. Blake was sent to meet the threat. As Blake approached on May 19 with his fleet, Tromp attacked. The battle lasted the rest of the day. Tromp withdrew. Another battle was fought in the channel in November 1652, with Tromp's fleet, and Blake was forced to retreat. The Council after this increased the number of ships and the effectiveness of the fleet. It also appointed an old colleague of Blake's, Colonel Deane, and MONCK to join him as admirals and generals of the sea. They engaged Tromp again off Portland in February 1653. The English were victorious, but not decisively. Blake was injured and recovered slowly. He joined the fleet again in battle in June 1653, to help the English to victory, but Deane was killed.

After peace with Holland in April 1654, Blake remained senior commissioner of the Admiralty and was appointed to command the fleet which sailed to the Mediterranean in September 1654. He received reparations and restitution for wrongs committed on English subjects and ships earlier by various countries. He was given orders to proceed off Cadiz and to engage in hostilities against Spain. He was forced by winter and ill health on ships to return to England. But in the spring of 1656 the English began taking Spanish treasure ships. In April 1657, Blake was informed that a large Spanish fleet from America had arrived at Teneriffe (see TENARIFE). Blake proceeded there and attacked the Spanish fleet at anchor near a line of forts along the shore. Every Spanish ship was burned, blown up, or sunk. OLIVER CROMWELL praised Blake highly for this victory and sent him a jewel as a token of appreciation. Blake died on his way back to England on August 7, 1657.

Marvell refers to Blake and the English victory over the Dutch off Portland in "The Character of Holland." He also writes of him in "On the Victory Obtained by Blake over the Spaniards, in the Bay of Santacruze, in the Island of Teneriffe, 1657."

Blast. *Verb*: (1) to blow violently, (2) to wither.

Blood, Thomas (1618–1680). On the Parliamentary side in the civil war. Was a J.P. in Ireland during the Cromwell years, with large payments in land for his services. At the Restoration the land was taken from him. After participating in an abortive plot to take Dublin Castle and the Duke of Ormonde, Blood hid under various disguises and was sheltered by various groups of people. Finally, he left Ireland and went to Holland. Subsequently he returned to England, Scotland, and Ireland. In November 1670, William of Orange came to England, attended by the Duke of Ormonde. Colonel Blood and five others stopped Ormonde's coach and forcibly removed him. The Duke was saved in the ensuing struggle.

In April, 1671, Blood came to the Tower of London disguised as a parson, with a woman posing as his wife. She pretended to become ill and was cared for by the Keeper of the Regalia (Talbot Edwards) and his wife. Over the next several days Blood nurtured the friendship with the Keeper's family to the extent that he said that his nephew wished to marry the Keeper's daughter. An appointment was made for the nephew to meet the intended bride in the early morning of May 9. Blood and three companions came, with concealed arms and rapiers in their canes. Blood asked the Keeper to show them the crown jewels to pass the time while supposedly waiting for Blood's wife. Edwards was attacked, his head covered and his mouth gagged. Since he tried to make noise, they beat and stabbed him. They took the crown, globe, and scepter. They were pursued and captured. Blood refused to confess except to the King himself. CHARLES II agreed to see him out of curiosity to see such a bold ruffian. Blood confessed to the plan being his own. The King returned his Irish estates to him. Blood remained in London and Westminster until his death.

Marvell refers to "daring Blood" in some lines that are printed in some versions of "The Loyal Scot" (lines 178–185). These eight lines also are printed separately in some texts as "Upon Blood's Attempt to Steal the Crown." He also alludes to Blood in "Upon Sir Robert Viner's Setting Up the King's Statue in Wool-church Market."

Bloome, Robert. One of the mayors of Hull to whom Marvell sent letters reporting government matters, since he was a Member of Parliament for the city.

Bonner, Edmund (1500–1569). Served as chaplain to Cardinal Wolsey and later served Henry VIII. Imprisoned under Edward VI and released upon the accession of Queen Mary I. Became Bishop of London. Began condemning and burning numerous people as heretics. Was extremely unpopular. Under Queen Elizabeth I he refused to take the Oath of Supremacy, was deprived of his bishopric, and was imprisoned up to his death.

Book, Eternal. See "Book of Life" under BOOKS OF GOD.

Book of Creatures. See BOOKS OF GOD.

Book of Life. See BOOKS OF GOD.

Book of Nature. See BOOKS OF GOD.

Book of Scriptures. See BOOKS OF GOD.

Books of God. The concept held by many writers, clergymen, and philosophers that God "wrote" two "books" which mankind can "read" and thus learn of God and truth. One is the "Book of Scriptures" (i.e., the Bible or Divine Revelation). The other is the "Book of Creatures" or the "Book of Nature" (i.e., everything God created in the universe). Many writers refer to a third, the "Book of Life" (also called the "Book Eternal") that essentially is the roll or register of the Elect, the individual saved souls known only by God.

Boot. *Verb*: to profit or to be of use or to do good.

Boynton, Katherine. Known as a court beauty during the time of CHARLES II.

Bramhall, John (1594–1663). Archbishop of Armagh. Attended Sidney Sussex College, Cambridge. Took B.A., M.A., B.D., and D.D. degrees. Became chaplain to Tobias Matthew, Archbishop of York. Later went to Ireland as chaplain to Thomas Wentworth. Became Bishop of Derry in Ireland. Made Archbishop of Armagh in 1660. After his death was published his *Vindication*, to which SAMUEL PARKER's *Preface* was attached. Marvell's *The Rehearsal Transprosed* was written in response to Parker's *Preface*.

Brave. *Adjective*: (1) courageous, daring; (2) splendid, showy, beautiful, handsome, grand; (3) finely dressed; (4) worthy, excellent; (5) boastful.

Break. *Verb*: (1) to separate forcefully into parts; (2) to divide or part; (3) to wreck [a ship]; (4) to burst the surface; (5) "break the heart": to overwhelm with sorrow; (6) to demolish or ruin; (7) to dash against an obstacle [especially water or waves against a bank or wall, etc.]; (8) to cease or end; (9) to discipline, train, tame [especially animals, such as horses]; (10) to violate; (11) to penetrate; (12) to disclose, reveal, utter; (13) to escape confines, to emerge.

Brideoak, Ralph (1613–1678). Chaplain to CHARLES II.

Bright. *Adjective*: (1) shining, (2) beautiful, (3) of vivid or brilliant color, (4) glorious or splendid.

Brooke, Lord. See GREVILLE, FULKE.

Brume. *Noun*: winter.

Buckingham, Duke of. See VILLIERS, GEORGE.

Bullace. *Noun*: a wild plum.

Bushy points. Tasselled fasteners used to hold up hose.

Buttery, buttry. *Noun*: a storeroom for provisions of food and drink.

C

C., T. See CORNEWALL, THEOPHILA.

Cabal. See CLIFFORD, THOMAS.

Cabinet. *Noun*: (1) a small chamber or room; (2) a case in which to keep jewelry, letters, documents, or other valuable items; (3) a picture gallery.

Calvin, John (1509–1564). Jean Cauvin, French theologian and Protestant reformer. Studied law, logic, Latin, Greek, and Hebrew. After accepting many of LUTHER's beliefs, he was forced to flee Paris during a royal proscription of Lutherans. In 1536 he published *Institutes of the Christian Religion* in which he criticizes many facets of Roman Catholicism and promotes reformed Protestantism. Soon after its publication he took up residence in Geneva, Switzerland. The beliefs of Calvinism emphasize human depravity resulting from original sin, salvation only through God's grace (Calvin agreeing with Luther concerning the inability of good works to gain salvation, but emphasizing God's grace more than the individual's faith emphasized by Luther), and the doctrine of the Elect (those predestined by God for salvation). Calvin argues that Christ "imputes" righteousness to the believer. Calvin argues that the two sacraments are Baptism and the Lord's Supper. These beliefs of Calvin, along with his insistence upon the church being governed largely by individual congregations (rather than by an episcopal hierarchy) and upon the Bible as the true and authoritative one of the BOOKS OF GOD, became most important in the thinking and practices of the English PURITANs of the 16th and 17th centuries.

Calvinism. The doctrines and practices of the Calvinists, following John Calvin. See CALVIN.

Calvinist. A proponent of Calvinism, the doctrines and practices subscribed to by John Calvin and his followers. See CALVIN.

Cambridge University. See TRINITY COLLEGE.

Carew, Thomas (1594?–1640). "Carew" is pronounced "Carey." Poet and courtier. Took his B.A. at Oxford in 1611, studied law, served as secretary to Sir Dudley Carleton (ambassador to Venice and later to the Netherlands), served as secretary to Edward Herbert, and eventually held some positions at Court under CHARLES I. Most of his poetry was published after his death.

Carew is primarily a follower of JONSON and the CLASSICAL line in poetry (and is usually grouped with the "Cavalier Poets"), but he also reveals some influences from DONNE and the METAPHYSICAL strain. He is one of the most polished and impressive literary craftsmen of the minor poets during the first half of the 17th century. His "An Elegy Upon the Death of the Dean of St. Paul's, Dr. John Donne" was first published in the 1633 edition of Donne's poems, along with several others contributed by other poets. Carew's is by far the best of them and indeed is one of the most perceptive critical assessments of Donne ever written. His own poem is carefully crafted, at points imitating Donne's own style. Among many of his memorable comments on Donne's contributions to English poetry are the following: (1) Donne "purged" the Muses' garden of its "pedantic weeds," (2) Donne's "imperious wit" caused the "troublesome language" to bend in "awe" of it, (3) Donne exiled the "goodly train of gods and goddesses" from noble poetry, and (4) Donne was like a king that ruled the "universal monarchy of wit."

Carisbrooke Castle. Castle on the Isle of Wight. CHARLES I fled to this castle from HAMPTON COURT in 1647. Here he was treated as a prisoner by the governor. In March of 1648 Charles attempted to escape but was apprehended. A rumor persisted at the time that OLIVER CROMWELL engineered Charles's flight from Hampton Court in order to further damn Charles later, but the rumor seems to have no basis in fact. See also ASHBURNHAM, JOHN.

Carlisle, Earl of. See HOWARD, CHARLES.

Carousel. *Noun*: tournaments participated in by knights.

Cartwright, Thomas (1535–1603). PURITAN clergyman. Became major fellow at Trinity College, Cambridge, in 1562. Went to Ireland in 1565. Returned to Cambridge in 1567 and made Lady Margaret Professor in 1569. Began to criticize the hierarchy of the Church of England. Deprived of his Professorship and fellowship in 1570–71. Went to Geneva. Returned to England in 1572. Wrote "A Second Admonition to Parliament," leading to a warrant for his arrest. Fled to the continent where he continued writing for the Puritan cause. Returned to England in 1585 and was allowed to remain. Served the Earl of Leicester, continued to write, and died at Warwick.

A Marvell Dictionary   C   35

Cassowar. The cassowary, a bird that devours anything.

Castlemain(e), Countess of. See VILLIERS, BARBARA.

Catherine of Braganza, Queen of England. See CHARLES II.

Cawood Castle. Seat of the Archbishop of York until he fled from it in 1642. Two miles southeast of Nun Appleton. See "UPON APPLETON HOUSE," stanza 46.

Celebrate. *Verb*: (1) to perform publicly [a marriage or funeral or other ceremony]; (2) to proclaim publicly; (3) to praise, to extol.

Cell. *Noun*: a small dwelling or cottage.

Center, centre. *Noun*: (1) in some contexts, the center of the earth; (2) in some contexts, the center of the universe.

Chain(ed) shot. Cannon balls chained together.

Chammish. Referring to Cham (also known as Ham), one of Noah's three sons who repopulated the world after the flood. Cham's descendants were believed to dwell in Africa. He also revealed the nakedness of Noah (when Noah was drunk) to his brothers Shem and Japhet (see Genesis 9 and 10).

Charing Cross. A part of London named after a large cross originally erected in this area by King Edward I. The cross was removed in 1647, but the area retains its name. THOMAS OSBORNE, Earl of Danby and Lord Treasurer, in 1675 erected on the site of the old cross a bronze statue of CHARLES I on a horse, a statue that had been cast in 1633. The long delay in putting up the statue helped make Danby's project the butt of such ridicule and satire as Marvell's "The Statue at Charing Cross," in which he refers to Danby as "the Treasurer." The statue still stands on the site today.

Charles I (1600–1649). Charles Stuart, King of England, 1625–1649. Son of JAMES I and father of CHARLES II and JAMES II. Increasing conflicts between King and Parliament, as well as among factions in the Church, developed into the Great Rebellion (English Civil War) with Parliamentary and PURITAN forces pitted against those of the King and Court. Charles surrendered and eventually was beheaded. Also see CROMWELL, OLIVER; FAIRFAX, THOMAS; HYDE, EDWARD; and CHARING CROSS.

Charles II (1630–1685). Charles Stuart, King of England, 1649–1685. Son of CHARLES I. Although officially King after the beheading of his father in 1649, Charles II had fled from England and the threat of Parliamentary and PURITAN victory under CROMWELL in the English civil war. Cromwell and Parliament essentially ruled England without a king during the Interregnum of 1649 to 1660. During this time Charles resided primarily in France, Germany, and the Netherlands. In 1660 he was restored to the English throne, after concessions were made and agreements reached between Charles and the powers in England at that time, especially through GEORGE MONCK. EDWARD HYDE, Earl of Clarendon, was Lord Chancellor under Charles, and Hyde's daughter, Anne, married Charles's brother, James, Duke of York. (James eventually became King JAMES II of England.) In the matter of the Church, Charles disappointed those Puritans who felt that he would enact principles and policies of toleration. Instead, in 1662 was passed the Act of Uniformity which caused many clergymen to be ejected from their positions (see NONCONFORMIST). Charles married Catherine of Braganza, the daughter of John IV of Portugal. Charles's illegitimate son, known as James Scott, was in 1665 made Duke of Monmouth by Charles (against the advice of Clarendon). By 1667, as a result of intrigue from some factions and the dissatisfaction of Charles himself, Clarendon left both his office and England. Charles then began to court France and to accept money from Louis XIV, showing increasing intentions of alliance with France and Roman Catholicism. Eventually, popular and Parliamentary antipathy caused Charles to withdraw from and hide many of his plans to ally with France. Political intrigue, war with the Dutch, and the question of the royal family sympathizing and even embracing Catholicism continued as problems to the end of his reign. Some wanted the Catholic Duke of York (James, Charles's brother) to be king, while others, playing on this fear, wanted the Duke of Monmouth (Charles's illegitimate son) to be declared the proper successor. When Charles died in 1685, his brother James succeeded to the throne.

Marvell served in Parliament from the time of Charles's Restoration to Marvell's own death. The King and the political, religious, and social issues of his reign figure greatly in Marvell's satirical poetry and prose of this time. Charles is referred to in "The Last Instructions To a Painter," "The Loyal Scot," *The Rehearsal Transprosed*, "His Majesty's Most Gracious Speech to Both Houses of Parliament," and several other works.

Chemist, chymist. See ALCHEMY and PARACELSUS.

China clay. Porcelain. It was believed that the Chinese made porcelain by burying clay for many years.

Choler. See HUMOR.

Chymick, chemic. See ALCHEMY and PARACELSUS.

Cicero, Marcus Tullius (106–43 B.C.). Roman orator, statesman, and prose writer. Studied philosophy, literature, rhetoric, and law. Practiced law. Elected Consul in 63 B.C. He discovered Catiline's conspiracy to overthrow the government and suppressed it. After the assassination of Julius Caesar, Cicero made speeches attacking Antony. After the Second Triumvirate of Antony, Octavian, and Lepidus assumed power, Cicero was killed by Antony's army. Speeches, treatises, and letters by Cicero survive. He is influential in the rhetoric, politics, and philosophy of his prose works, as well as the primary model for the polished, lengthy clause or sentence known as Ciceronian prose style. He is commonly called "Tully" or "Tullie."

Circe. In Greek mythology, the sun god's daughter who was exiled to the island of Aeaea after murdering her husband. She was an evil enchantress. The companions of Odysseus were changed into swine when they visited her island. Odysseus himself was not changed, having been given an herb by Hermes to resist Circe's power. After seeing Odysseus unchanged, Circe transformed the men back to their normal state, entertained them and Odysseus lavishly as her guests for a year, and bore Odysseus a son. See SIRENS.

Circean. See CIRCE.

Circle. Frequently used in the Renaissance as the symbol of perfection, infinity, immortality, and God.

Civic crown. A garland of oak leaves granted to one who saves a citizen's life in battle.

Clarendon, Earl of. See HYDE, EDWARD.

Clarke, Andrew. A London publisher referred to by Marvell in *The Rehearsal Transprosed* as "A. C."

Clary. *Noun*: drink made of wine and honey.

Classical. As used in this "Dictionary," "classical" refers to the particular style and content of poetry stemming from "classicism," especially as viewed and practiced by BEN JONSON and his followers in the late 16th and early 17th centuries. The assumptions of such classical verse arise from similar assumptions in works of ancient Greece and Rome that provide the major models for Renaissance classicism. The term "classical" is extremely complex and is applied in numerous ways, but the following working definition, albeit a greatly simplified one, may serve to illustrate the major characteristics of it, especially those that differ in important respects from those of much METAPHYSICAL poetry.

As far as content, many classical poems are complimentary in nature, praising certain individuals. Praises for the country life and for good food and drink also are common. The *carpe diem* theme (literally, "seize the day": urging one to live and love fully and actively now, for time is passing rapidly and death is approaching) is a recurring one. Epitaphs (compact poems memorializing individuals who have died) appear frequently in classical verse. In many (especially in JONSON) the poet is in a public role as a social, moral, and ethical critic. Generally the speaking voice is rather formal and polite in word choice and tone, with emotion kept restrained.

In style and structure a classical poem is overtly well organized, displaying strict divisions, logical progressions, and stages clearly defined from beginning to end. The structure and style of the poem, stanzas, and lines employ careful balance, parallelism, and symmetry. The metrics generally are regular, avoiding excessive variations. Frequently the classical poet writes in couplets, many of which have carefully placed and clear caesuras. All in all, clarity is valued in syntax, word choice, and thought. Some relevant examples of classical poetry in which one can see these characterisitics are the following by Ben Jonson: (1) the song beginning "Still to be neat," (2) the song beginning "Come, my Celia, let us prove," (3) No. 4 of "A Celebration of Charis," (4) "To William Camden," (5) "To Penshurst," (6) "On My First Son," and (7) "Inviting a Friend to Supper."

Although Marvell traditionally is classified as a metaphysical poet, one should be alert to the great extent to which he actually fuses the classical with the metaphysical.

Cleveland, Duchess of. See VILLIERS, BARBARA.

Cleveland, John (1613–1658). Poet who was educated at Christ's College, Cambridge. Served the Royalist cause in the civil war. Was imprisoned in 1655 on trumped-up charges and died soon after his release. Popular poet and satirist. Wrote an anti-PURITAN satire titled

"The Rebel Scot" during the war. Marvell plays against this poem in his own "The Loyal Scot," in which Marvell has "Cleveland's ghost" in the Elysian Fields repent for his own satire and now to praise a loyal Scot (see DOUGLAS, ARCHIBALD) and to denounce Anglican clergy, in contrast to Cleveland's own denunciation of Scottish Presbyterians in "The Rebel Scot."

Clifford, Thomas, Lord Clifford of Chudleigh (1630–1673). Royalist Member of Parliament. He and Marvell came to physical blows early in the Restoration, and a hostile speaker and House required that Marvell confess to giving the first provocation in the altercation. He was advanced dramatically in the government under the favor of Royalists around CHARLES II. In 1666 he was appointed Comptroller of the Household and placed on the Privy Council. Clifford was much in the King's confidence in 1669 when an intrigue with France was furthered by Charles to break the Dutch treaty. Clifford became one of the five (along with BUCKINGHAM, ASHLEY, LAUDERDALE, and ARLINGTON) that made up the so-called "Cabal." The name was taken from the coincidence that their first initials formed the word. For three years this group was the most powerful administrative force and determiner of foreign affairs under the King. (One should note that Marvell uses the term "Cabal" in line 121 of "The Last Instructions to a Painter," but this refers more loosely to a plotting faction and not to the specific cabal formed with Clifford included in 1669 and after. Marvell's poem was written prior to this.) In 1672 Clifford was made a baron, Lord High Treasurer, and Treasurer of the Exchequer. With the passage by Parliament of the Test Act in 1673, in opposition to Clifford's strongly expressed wishes, the Cabal was dissolved. Clifford resigned his offices, left London, and died shortly thereafter.

Marvell does allude to Clifford in "The Last Instructions to a Painter." In line 17 he refers to "the new Comptroller," who is Clifford in his position as Comptroller of the Household. In line 18 he is made analogous to a "tall louse" who brandishes "the white staff." He also refers to him by name in some of his letters.

Cloister. *Verb*: (1) to enclose; (2) to place in a monastic house or cloister. *Noun*: (1) an enclosure; (2) a place of religious seclusion, such as a nunnery, convent, monastery.

Clonmell. During OLIVER CROMWELL's Irish military campaign, he unsuccessfully attacked and placed under siege the city of Clonmell. The Irish, however, were forced to evacuate the city in May 1650.

Clora. Female character addressed in "The Gallery" and referred to in "Mourning." The name also appears in a reference to the "matchless Clora" in "An Elegy upon the Death of my Lord Francis Villiers." Some scholars argue that in the "Elegy" the reference is to Mary Kirke, daughter of the poet Aurelian Townsend. Some scholars suggest that one or both of the other poems also suggest that she is Clora.

Closes. *Noun*: enclosed fields.

Cocles. Publius Horatius Cocles, Roman hero who defended a bridge by himself.

Collins, James. A London publisher.

Colossus. The Colossus at Rhodes (Rhodian Colossus) was a huge statue of Apollo, the legs of which stretched across the harbor on the island of Rhodes in the Aegean Sea. It was cast of bronze and constructed about 280 B.C. with a height of 120 feet and became one of the Seven Wonders of the ancient world. It was destroyed by an earthquake in 224 B.C.

Combination of dissimilar images. See METAPHYSICAL CONCEIT.

Come. *Verb*: (1) to move towards or to approach, (2) to be derived [from], (3) to arrive [in course of time], (4) to happen, (5) to approach for sexual contact, (6) to experience sexual orgasm.

Complexion. *Noun*: (1) the type of physical appearance, personality, disposition, and temperament resulting from the dominance of a particular HUMOR in the body: choleric, sanguine, phlegmatic, or melancholic. Also see ELEMENT and GALEN; (2) the color and appearance of the skin, especially in the face.

Conceit. See METAPHYSICAL CONCEIT.

Conjunction. See "THE DEFINITION OF LOVE."

Contignation. *Noun*: a joining or framing together of boards.

Conventicles. Meetings of DISSENTERs for the purpose of worship.

Conventicles Act. Act passed in 1664 which made religious meetings of DISSENTERs illegal.

Cooper, Anthony Ashley, Earl of Shaftesbury (1621–1683). Attended Oxford and Lincoln's Inn. Served CHARLES I in the civil war as a colonel of a regiment of horse and captain of a troop of foot. In 1664 he gave up all commissions under the King and went over to the Parliamentary side. Served as field-marshal and commander-in-chief of Parliamentary forces in Dorsetshire. In 1649 he was appointed justice of the peace for Wiltshire and Dorsetshire. Was made a member of the Council of State. At first a supporter of Cromwell, but by 1656 had broken with him. Elected as a Member of Parliament for Wiltshire. Supported the Restoration of CHARLES II. Appointed to the Privy Council. Created Baron Ashley in 1661. Appointed Chancellor of the Exchequer. Became one of the Cabal (see CLIFFORD, THOMAS). In 1672 Cooper was made Earl of Shaftesbury. Made Lord Chancellor in November 1672. Dismissed from this position in 1673. In early 1674 Shaftesbury made himself the head of parliamentary opposition to the court. In 1679 Charles made him president of a new Privy Council. Shaftesbury continued many of his views, however, and supported the Duke of Monmouth, Charles's illegitimate son, as successor to the throne, rather than James, Charles's Roman Catholic brother. In late 1679 Monmouth returned to London with Charles's permission and was hidden in Shaftesbury's house. In 1681 Charles told Shaftesbury that he would never yield on the Monmouth question. In July Shaftesbury was arrested and committed to the Tower on the charge of high treason in conspiring for the death of the King and the overthrow of government. Ultimately he was acquitted. Other charges were concocted by the court party, and they were ready to arrest him again. Shaftesbury fled to Holland in November 1682, and he died there in January 1683.

Marvell frequently refers in his letters to Shaftesbury. He also is seen as the supporter of Shaftesbury in 1677 with his writing of the prose pamphlet *An Account of the Growth of Popery, and Arbitrary Government in England*.

Copernican. Referring to Copernicus and/or his concept of the universe. See COPERNICUS.

Copernicus, Nicolaus (1473–1543). Polish astronomer. Studied in Poland and Italy. Well-versed in astronomy, mathematics, law, medicine, and theology. Increasingly disagreed with the theories of PTOLEMY, and he formulated a heliocentric theory for the structure of the universe (i.e., one with the sun as the center, rather than the earth). Argued that the earth and other planets move around the sun in orbits. His work profoundly influenced later astronomers such as KEPLER and GALILEO and others of the "NEW PHILOSOPHY."

Cordial. *Noun*: a medicine, food, or drink that invigorates the heart.

Corn. *Noun*: (1) grain, (2) seed. [Does not designate Indian corn, as in later American usage.]

Cornewall, Theophila. The apparent subject of "THE PICTURE OF LITTLE T. C. IN A PROSPECT OF FLOWERS." Theophila Cornewall was a young girl born in 1644 whose parents were Humphry and Theophila Cornewall, the mother being the former Theophila Skinner, of a family well known to Marvell and his father. The Theophila Cornewall born in 1644 ("little T. C.") had an older sister, in fact, with the same name, who had been born in 1643 but who had died after living only a few days. [For more information on these families, see the article by H.M. Margoliouth in *Modern Language Review* 17 (1922), pp. 351–61.]

"Coronet, The." One of the works in *MISCELLANEOUS POEMS*. Marvell's METAPHYSICAL characteristics appear in this poem, especially in the employment of a METAPHYSICAL CONCEIT. The conceit of weaving a garland of verses, like flowers, with its becoming a crown, a coronet, gives the essential structure to the poem. Some comparison can be made to a previous metaphysical poem ("A Wreath") by GEORGE HERBERT, who, like Marvell, attended TRINITY COLLEGE.

The speaker acknowledges in lines 1–4 that he has previously sinned and, in doing so, has made Christ suffer. It is as if he personally is responsible for contributing to the crown of thorns placed on Christ's head at the Crucifixion: see Matthew 27:29 ("And when they had platted a crown of thorns, they put it upon his head, and a reed in his right hand: and they bowed the knee before him, and mocked him, saying Hail, King of the Jews!"). In the phrase "When for the thorns," *for* can be taken in two senses, "because of" and "in place of," with both meanings relevant here. It is because of the past pains he has inflicted on Christ through his sins that he now wants to substitute a new garland, a new crown, for the crown of thorns. In line 4 the speaker says that he wants to "redress that wrong": this also is deliberately used in two senses by Marvell. He is literally "re-dressing" Christ by discarding the crown of thorns and putting a new crown on him, but he also is "redressing" in the sense of repenting, making up for the painful wrong he has previously inflicted on Christ. In line 1 Marvell uses effective stress variation and sounds in "long, too long": the heavy stresses and the *o* sounds in all three syllables add length to their pronunciation and convey the speaker's awareness of the great period of time that he has spent wronging Christ with his own sins.

Lines 5–8 show the speaker in the act of constructing his garland or crown. It seems to be a garland of "flowers" that he searches in every garden and meadow to gather. He dismantles the tall headdresses of flowers ("fragrant towers") that he once made for his "shepherdess" (his secular lady love, described in PASTORAL terms). But when he parenthetically says "my fruits are only flowers," the suggestion is that these "flowers" are metaphors for poems, the fruits of the labor of the poet. He is likely alluding to Christ's statement in Matthew 7:16 ("Ye shall know them by their fruits") and repeated in Matthew 7:20 ("Wherefore by their fruits ye shall know them"). The speaker is criticizing the secular products of his own past creativity: he has been writing poems that are *only* flowers, merely flowers. Apparently he has created poems of a pastoral and PETRARCHAN nature and glorifying a lady, rather than Christ. His new flowers and new garland will be to glorify Christ.

Lines 9–12 picture the poet looking over all that he has accumulated (his "STORE") in order to weave this new garland. He wants to weave a "chaplet," a coronet, of a kind that Christ never wore before: we feel his sense of pride, his ego, here, and this explains why he acknowledges his own deception of himself in parentheses. Indeed, paradoxically, at the very moment he wishes to atone for his past sins against Christ, he actually is committing a sin, the sin of pride!

He discovers his own sin, significantly in line 13, the middle line and turning point of the poem. Lines 13–16 present his discovery of the old "Serpent," as old as his appearance in the Garden of Eden where he tripped up Adam and Eve through pride. So, the "Serpent" here is Satan, pride, and sin all in one. He is entwined ("twining in") among the "flowers" and is camouflaged ("speckled") and hard to see. But the poet does discover him among the flowers of this poetic garland: he discovers his own pride in creating these verses supposedly to glorify Christ but which actually are working for his self-glorification. The garland, with its intricate wreathings of flowers (verses), is one of "Fame and Interest," of self-glorification and self-interest. Even in attempting to write a Christian poem, the speaker/poet discovers that it is tainted with his own sense of proud creativity and doing good works. Cleverly Marvell has the poet's pride in his own wreathing of words and lines reflected by the image of the serpent also wreathing among those very poetic "flowers." Pride can be interwoven in the very fabric of whatever the human does, and it is difficult to perceive. The structure and style of this poem itself, composed of subtle transitions between lines and clauses, along with varying line lengths, convey quite well the activity of weaving and the product of such weaving, a poetic coronet.

Lines 17–26 conclude the poem with self-condemnation and then a turn outwardly from self and self-accomplishment to Christ and his available help. Lines 17–18 address "foolish Man" in general, but certainly mainly center on the speaker himself as the immediate example of "foolish Man." He would have debased "Heaven's diadem," Christ's crown, with "them" ("Fame and Interest" of line 16) and "mortal [rather than heavenly] glory." Significantly, these lines (17–18) make up the first couplet encountered in the poem: this couplet punctuates an important turn through self-recognition by the poet and his rejection of failed means to glorify God. He then turns to Christ ("thou") in line 19 for necessary help. It is interesting and appropriate that the first eighteen lines of the poem are filled with occurrences of the personal pronoun "I," reflecting his self-interest and self-glorification. But lines 19–26 contain no occurrence of "I" and instead focus on Christ, "thou," and "thy," a focus necessary through humility to receive help and grace. Line 19 acknowledges that it is Christ ("thou") who alone ("only") can conquer Satan. Lines 20–22 ask that Christ either remove Satan and all of his sinful wiles or destroy the speaker's own "curious FRAME": this phrase suggests destruction of the garland, the chaplet, the coronet that the speaker has made, but it also suggests the poem itself as this intricate, "CURIOUS" structure. Line 23 asks Christ, then, to "let these [the flowers, the elements of verse] wither so that he [Satan, the serpent, the sin inherent in the garland proudly made] may die." In line 25 "they" are these flowers. Lines 25–26 seem to allude to Genesis 3:15 in which God says to the serpent, "And I will put enmity between thee and the woman, and between thy seed and her seed; it shall bruise thy head, and thou shalt bruise his heel." Christ is the seed that ultimately treads on the head of Satan and who also will tread on the coronet of poetic flowers suffused with sinful pride. Paradoxically, then, the coronet could not crown Christ's head because of its sinful pride on the part of the speaker/poet, but with the poet's own penitence the coronet can now be an offering made of humility and be an appropriate instrument for crowning Christ's feet. His coronet for Christ only becomes worthy through humility. It is possible that Marvell also alludes here to Luke 7:37–38 in which a sinful woman (traditionally interpreted as MARY MAGDALENE) wept at the feet of Christ, washed his feet with her tears, wiped his feet with her hair, kissed his feet, and anointed them with ointment. The humble, repentant sinner at Christ's feet is relevant to the speaker/poet's situation, certainly.

Corposant. *Noun*: a ball of fire appearing on the masts and rigging of ships in a storm. Word comes from Portuguese sailors calling such manifestations the "bodies of saints"—i.e., *corpos santos* or *corpus sancti*.

Courage. *Noun*: (1) spirit, vigor, energy; (2) boldness or bravery; (3) sexual desire or lust.

Cowslip-water. *Noun*: (1) the juice of the cowslip plant, which grows wild in pastures and has fragrant yellow flowers; (2) a lotion made from the juice of the cowslip plant, which is used for cleansing and removing wrinkles from the skin.

Creature. *Noun*: (1) a created being, animate or inanimate; (2) an animal; (3) a human being; (4) anything created; (5) a person who owes his or her position, wealth, or power to another person [including a patron] and who is willing to carry out the will of the benefactor.

Croft, Herbert, Bishop of Hereford. See SMIRKE, MR.

Cromwell, Mary (1637–1712). Third daughter of OLIVER CROMWELL. Marvell wrote two songs for her wedding in November 1657, to THOMAS BELASYSE, second Viscount Fauconberg, at Hampton Court.

Cromwell, Oliver (1599–1658). Attended Sidney Sussex College, Cambridge, but left after his father's death. Resided in Huntingdon and elected as Member of Parliament for Huntingdon in 1628. Sold his property in 1631. Moved to Ely in 1636 upon the death of his uncle, who made him his heir. In 1640 Cromwell was one of the Members of Parliament for the town of Cambridge. Served on many committees. In 1642 in the conflict with CHARLES I and the Royalists, Cromwell joined Essex's army as a captain. He disarmed the Royalists at Huntingdonshire. During early 1643 he transformed his troop into a regiment, and he saw to it that they were strict PURITANs of his own kind. He became one of four colonels of horse in the new army to be raised by the Earl of Manchester. He was in the forefront of the combined armies of the Earl of Manchester, Lord Willoughby, and Sir THOMAS FAIRFAX at the victory of Winceby in October, 1643. In early 1644 Cromwell was named lieutenant-general in the Earl of Manchester's army. In the Battle of Naseby Fairfax entrusted to Cromwell the command of the cavalry in the entire army.

With the surrender of Oxford in 1646 the war was almost over. Cromwell then returned to his duties in Parliament. Cromwell was forced to be a mediator in the growing conflict between Parliament and the Army. Finally he had to again take control of the Army and restore discipline and authority to it. In the Council of War then set up, Cromwell was predominant. Fairfax was not an influence of significance in it. Cromwell and the Council carried on negotiations with the King, but eventually Charles fled to the Isle of Wight. Cromwell sought to quell dissatisfaction in the Army and to redress their military grievances. By December 1647, many dissensions and conflicts had been resolved. By January 1648, Cromwell believed that Parliament should govern the kingdom, since Charles had refused the compromises and bills that Parliament had offered him. He stated also that the Army would stand by Parliament against all opposition. Parliament then voted to make no further addresses to the King. Cromwell was at this point convinced that only this course could secure the foundation of the cause for which they had fought.

In 1649 Charles I was beheaded. Cromwell was chosen by the Council of State to command in Ireland, and he was there from August 1649, to January 1650. By June 1650, Cromwell had been appointed captain-general and commander-in-chief of all Commonwealth forces. To prevent a Scottish invasion of England, Cromwell took a large force into Scotland. His victories over Scotland completed, Cromwell was granted (as a country residence for him) HAMPTON COURT by Parliament in 1651. In 1653 Cromwell was made Protector, who held executive power in the new government, while Parliament retained legislative power. Parliament's acts became law without approval by the Protector, unless the law was contrary to the constitution. While Parliament was in abeyance, the Protector could make ordinances with the force of law until Parliament said otherwise.

In 1657 many urged Cromwell to accept the title of king, but Cromwell refused to do so. He was installed again as Protector and now had the right to appoint his own successor. Also in 1657 he concluded an alliance with France.

Cromwell became ill in the summer of 1658 and died on September 3. He was buried in Westminster Abbey. His son was RICHARD CROMWELL. In Parliament after the restoration of CHARLES II, it was moved and agreed to that the body of Oliver Cromwell (and some others) be exhumed and hanged on the gallows. His body was disinterred in January 1661, and placed on the gallows at TYBURN on January 30, 1661, the twelfth anniversary of the execution of Charles I. His head was then set on a pole on the top of Westminster Hall. The body was buried under the gallows.

Both Marvell and MILTON served as Latin secretaries under Cromwell. Marvell also served as tutor to WILLIAM DUTTON, a ward of Cromwell's. Marvell wrote "The First Anniversary Of The

Government Under His Highness The Lord Protector, 1655" and "A Poem upon The Death of His Late Highness The Lord Protector." He also participated in Cromwell's funeral procession. His most important poem concerning Cromwell is "An Horatian Ode upon Cromwell's Return from Ireland."

Cromwell, Richard (1626–1712). Was proclaimed Protector on the day of his father's death (September 3, 1658) but resigned the title in April 1659. See CROMWELL, OLIVER.

Curious. *Adjective*: (1) carefully or skillfully made, (2) ingenious, (3) inquisitive, (4) fastidious, (5) exquisite.

Curtana. *Noun*: ornamental sword worn at the coronation.

Cymar. *Noun*: a loose-fitting woman's robe or bishop's gown.

Cynthia. (1) Goddess of the moon, hunting, and chastity; (2) the moon. Same as Diana. Loved ENDYMION upon LATMOS.

D

Damon. Main character in the four "Mower Poems." See "THE MOWER AGAINST GARDENS," "DAMON THE MOWER," "THE MOWER TO THE GLOWWORMS," AND "THE MOWER'S SONG."

"Damon the Mower." One of the works in *MISCELLANEOUS POEMS*. This is the second in the sequence of poems referred to as the "Mower Poems" (also see "THE MOWER AGAINST GARDENS," "THE MOWER TO THE GLOWWORMS," AND "THE MOWER'S SONG").

This second poem reveals that the mower's name is Damon, a fact not given in the first poem of the series ("THE MOWER AGAINST GARDENS"). He is a pastoral figure, cutting the grassy fields with his scythe. The first poem in the series establishes his association with unspoiled, unfallen nature, from which perspective he severely criticizes fallen "man" and his unnatural, sinful, lustful ways and values. Ironically, the first stanza shows the mower having been struck by love of the beautiful ("FAIR") Juliana. But this "love" obviously is passion, since it is described as parallel to the "scorching" day. It is in the heat of summer, in July, we learn in the third stanza. The play on "July" in "Juliana" becomes apparent at that point: the heat of passion from Juliana is parallel to the heat of summer in July, then.

In the second stanza Damon comments on the "unusual heats" in this summer that affect the vegetation (withering the grass, the "meadows") and most animals, such as grasshoppers and frogs. The "hamstringed" (lamed in the leg) frog has to cool off by wading, and grasshoppers retreat to the shade. Only the "snake" stays out in the sun and heat, shedding its old skin and thrives with a new one. At this point one begins to feel some rather sinister connotations lurking beneath the seemingly innocent surface of Marvell's lines. The snake's archetypal association with Satan in the Garden of Eden and its common symbolic import as a phallic symbol become extremely important. The snake is thriving in the environment in which Damon has fallen to passion in the form of Juliana. The parallel to Adam, Eve, and Satan in the Garden of Eden becomes clear at this point and central to the rest of the poem and to the series of "Mower" poems. Without yet realizing it, Damon, the representative of unfallen humanity and nature, has been tempted and has fallen in his own "garden."

Stanza 3 acknowledges that this extreme heat is caused by more than just the heat of the sun. It comes from a "higher beauty" (at least one higher than the sun in Damon's own mind!), in the form of one Juliana: the heat she generates burns "the fields and mower both," since her heat is that of passion. Damon notes that this heat is not from the "DOG-STAR," Sirius: this star in the constellation Canis Major (Greater Dog) was believed to cause heat on earth when it is ascendant and when the sun is in Leo, during the hot "dog-days" of summer. Marvell's allusion to PHAETON in the context of the sun, heat, and passion actually is quite humorous in wordplay. Phaëton in mythology was the son of the sun (the sun-god, Phoebus or Helios). So, Marvell, in one sense, has Damon say that the *sun* becomes hotter than the sun's own *son* who almost burned up heaven and earth with his father's chariot! The couplet ending this stanza recognizes the true source of the heat.

In stanza 4 Damon, like the grasshopper and frog, needs relief from this heat; but he not only needs relief from the "fires" of the "hot day," as do the animals, but also from the "fires" of his own "hot desires." A "cool cave" or a "GELID" (cold, chilly) fountain (spring or stream) might, he first thinks, provide relief. But then he recognizes the futility of seeking these kinds of relief because, with this extreme heat, the only moisture left unevaporated or unexhausted is that in his own tears, and the only cold left is in the "icy breast" of Juliana. This reveals that Juliana has behaved as the "Petrarchan lady" (see PETRARCHAN) in her unresponsiveness to Damon.

Stanza 5 presents Damon addressing Juliana ("fair shepherdess") indignantly, resenting her lack of esteem for Damon himself and the presents he has given her (a *supposedly* "harmless" snake, but the connotations of Satan and a phallus are subtly there; some chameleons that *change* color, as he wants her to do and as he himself already has; oak leaves tipped with honeydew, sweetness to appeal to her but which symbolizes also his own tongue and sweet utterances). He calls her "ungrateful" and especially resents Juliana's lack of interest in "who them brought." At this point the pattern of Eden and Adam, reflected in Damon, is developed further. We see not only passion but also now pride reflected in his nature and in his own fall. [It is interesting to recall that, in the first poem in this series of "Mower" poems, Damon railed against "luxurious" (lustful) "man" and against "man, that sovereign thing and proud." Now he himself is subject to passion and pride.]

Stanza 6 pictures the proud Damon, crowing and preening. He sees himself as the darling of the gods and nature. The morning provides him with dew, and the sun evaporates ("licks off") his "sweat." The evening bathes his feet in "COWSLIP-WATER": i.e., he literally has the natural juice of the wild plant on his feet as he walks, the same juice used by women in a skin lotion. So, Damon sees himself as identified still with Adam before his fall and with innocent nature that cares for God's central creation, man. But the dramatic irony from our perspective is that Damon naively does not yet realize how his own pride and passion have disrupted this pre-fall harmony with nature. He actually is like Adam *after* the fall, not before it.

Stanza 7 furthers our sense of Damon's egotistical nature when he compares himself to the shepherd. He uncovers ("DISCOVERS") more ground with his scythe than the shepherd's sheep cover. He also pictures the hay he accumulates by mowing the grass as equivalent to Jason's golden fleece, wittily playing this against the common fleece of the sheep that the shepherd has. He is proud of himself and his riches within his "CLOSES."

His vanity is also quite apparent in stanza 8. He holds up his scythe (with its blade shaped like a "crescent moon") as if it were a mirror in which to view his own face, in a way parallel to NARCISSUS. He is so proud of himself that he equates himself with the "sun," paradoxically seen reflected in the "crescent moon." He again mistakenly associates himself with the *unfallen* Adam and asserts that the immortal fairies have him join them in dancing and singing, as if he were in harmony with them and participated in their "deathless" nature. The "ring" in which he is enclosed is the traditional "fairy ring," literally a circle of contrasting color on the ground caused by fungi. Indeed, the unfallen Damon might once have sensed these spirits permeating nature and once could transform the mundane (like the ring of fungus) into something far greater. But, alas, Damon is now like the *fallen* Adam, and his story of these enjoyments speaks of matters already in the past, a fact finally acknowledged by him in the next stanza.

Stanza 9 conveys Damon's lament for his lost happiness, ending his innocent life in his Edenic garden because of the entrance of "Love" and its "thistles." Through passion he now is in pain. Marvell cleverly enforces the Adam and fall pattern by echoing explicitly in these lines Genesis 3:17–19 as follows: "And unto Adam he said, Because thou hast hearkened unto the voice of thy wife, and hast eaten of the tree, of which I commanded thee, saying, Thou shalt not eat of it: cursed is the ground for thy sake; in sorrow shalt thou eat of it all the days of thy life; Thorns also and thistles shall it bring forth to thee; and thou shalt eat the herb of the field; In the sweat of thy face shalt thou eat bread, till thou return unto the ground; for out of it wast thou taken: for dust thou art, and unto dust shalt thou return."

Stanza 10 pictures the Mower using his scythe, not just cutting grass, but "depopulating all the ground": this echoes the Genesis passage quoted above, in that it reflects the curse of death on fallen man, with his own returning to dust. Damon, fallen and aware of sin and death, projects and applies that death to nature itself now. Adam's fall brought death to all humanity and affected all of nature. Damon is reenacting this. Humorously ironic, but also quite serious, is Marvell's having Damon carelessly swing the scythe into his own ankle and fall down: symbolically, Damon has caused his own fall by yielding to pride and temptation. As Adam sinned through free will, so has Damon. The last line of the stanza ("By his own scythe the mower mown") certainly attributes responsibility to Damon as Adam as man in general. Also significant is the fact that Damon is cutting both grass and flesh, since this alludes to the Biblical statement, "All flesh is grass" (Isaiah 40:6) and to "[evildoers] shall soon be cut down like the grass" (Psalms 37:2).

In stanza 11 Damon says that his physical wounds can easily be treated with "shepherd's purse" (a weed used to stop bleeding) and "clown's all-heal" (a nettle used to heal wounds). But his wounds given by "Love" and by Juliana's eyes have no cure. The only end to this hurt, he says, will come with "Death." So Damon sees himself subject to passion as an inescapable element of human life in the fallen world. In calling Death a "mower too," Damon again echoes the passages from Isaiah and Psalms quoted above. As he cuts the grass, so will Death eventually cut him and all humans, all flesh. Eden and physical immortality have been forfeited. The last line also cleverly plays on the traditional image of Death as the Grim Reaper with his scythe, the ultimate mower.

Danae. In mythology, daughter of King Acrisius and Aganippe. Mother of Perseus by ZEUS, who came to her in the form of a golden shower.

Danby, Earl of. See OSBORNE, THOMAS.

Daphne. In Greek mythology, a NYMPH who was the daughter of the river god Peneus. She was a devotee of Artemis, vowed to chastity. APOLLO was struck by passion for her and chased her. She prayed to her father that her beauty be changed so that Apollo would not embrace her. She was immediately transformed into a laurel tree (her name in Greek means laurel), and Apollo adopted the laurel as his sacred tree and wore its branches in his hair. For Marvell's unique adaptation of this incident, see "THE GARDEN," lines 29–30.

Davenant, John (1576–1641). Bishop of Salisbury. Moderate CALVINIST.

De Ruyter. See RUYTER, MICHEL ADRIAANS-ZOON DE.

Declaration. The Declaration of Breda in 1660. CHARLES II promised liberty of conscience in religion to his subjects.

Declaration of Indulgence. Issued by CHARLES II in 1672. Suspended penal laws against DISSENTERs and Roman Catholics.

"Definition of Love, The." One of the works in *MISCELLANEOUS POEMS*. Many of Marvell's METAPHYSICAL characteristics appear in this poem, and the influence of JOHN DONNE is particularly strong. Marvell's geometrical, geographical, cartographical, and astronomical METAPHYSICAL CONCEITs might be compared to those in Donne's "A Valediction: Forbidding Mourning" and "A Valediction: Of Weeping." The many paradoxes of Marvell's poem also relate it to characteristics of the verse of both Donne and GEORGE HERBERT.

Stanza 1 begins his definition of his personal love for someone else: the "birth" (or origin) of his love is as rare as the object, the woman, toward whom this love is directed. Both the origin of his feeling of love and the woman loved are unique, then. The speaker portrays "Despair" as the father of this love and "Impossibility" as the mother ("begotten by Despair upon Impossibility").

Stanza 2 elaborates on the last statement made in stanza 1. "Magnanimous Despair" is an oxymoron, seemingly contradictory, but is explained in its context by the implication that Despair here indeed is nobly generous in the way it discourages his hope (and thus his ultimate disappointment) that such an ideal love (a "divine," PLATONIC one) as the one he feels could ever be consummated physically. "Hope" is like a "feeble" bird that can only flap beautiful "tinsel" wings that do not function for flight. So, paradoxically, his Despair is magnanimous in not raising his hopes, his expectations for any physical fulfillment in this intellectual, spiritual, divine, ideal love.

The speaker says in stanza 3 that his soul reaches out (is "extended") and is "fixed" (established) in the spiritual being of the woman he loves. He would quickly join the woman physically, but "Fate" intervenes to prevent the fulfillment of the love physically: metaphorically, Fate drives powerful "iron wedges" between the two lovers, erecting some insurmountable barriers that prevent their spiritual love from also being expressed with physical togetherness and consummation. The great power of "Fate" is indicated with the images of powerfully hammering these "iron wedges" and also of crowding, pushing itself between the two lovers.

Stanza 4 indicates why personified "Fate" takes such actions. Fate sees that the two lovers have perfect love for each other, and Fate jealously wants to guard any challenge to its own power and reputation. So, Fate will not allow the two people to "close," to come together, to unite physically. This "union" would depose the power of the tyrant Fate, since it would allow complete spiritual and physical fulfillment in love, a perfection that Fate (in its ordinarily perceived role in this world and life) cannot allow. Paradoxically, then, a "definition" of love as perfect in this world would destroy the "definition" of fate in this world. Therefore, a "definition" of love this perfect cannot be allowed. Marvell also seems to be using "definition" in its sense of "restriction." Love, as *defined* (in both senses) by Fate in this world is that love has to be limited: love cannot reach complete fulfillment and perfection in this world.

Stanza 5 explains the consequences of such determination by the tyrant Fate. Fate's ("her") "decrees of steel" recall her "iron wedges" alluded to earlier and further attest to her power. The two lovers have been placed *physically* apart, seemingly as distant as the North Pole and the South Pole, doomed never to touch each other ("Not by themselves to be embraced"). The speaker parenthetically inserts (line 19 of the poem) that, however, "Love's whole world on us doth wheel": the axis of the earth between the two Poles is the axis upon which the whole world turns, and Marvell makes this a conceit to convey the idea that the spiritual axis between the two lovers' souls is the defined perfect spiritual bond around which the whole world of love must turn (and, by clear implication, the lesser love found in the whole world will be inferior to that perfect spiritual love of the center, the axis). In a sense, the two lovers define the center for all worldly lovers that must revolve around them. (This idea about two lovers might profitably be compared to Donne's presentations in "The Good-Morrow," "The Sun Rising," "The Canonization," "A Valediction: Forbidding Mourning," and several others.)

In stanza 6 the speaker poses the only possible conditions under which he and his beloved might be joined physically—but, of course, these conditions are all impossible (and make us recall "Impossibility" in the first stanza). They could be joined if the "heavens fall" or if an earthquake convulses and collapses the earth or if the earth is compressed from a globe into a flat plane ("planisphere"), with the two Poles brought together in the center, one side representing the northern hemisphere and the other side representing the southern hemisphere.

Stanza 7 assumes resignation to the impossible conditions of the previous stanza. The speaker uses a geometrical conceit that contrasts two different types of lines ("oblique" and "parallel") in order to contrast two types of loves. The speaker and his lady have loves that are like parallel lines: no matter how far parallel lines are extended, they never cross, never come together. This represents the fact that their spiritual loves will never come together, never "meet," never "close," never be fulfilled physically in this world. Their loves are parallel and equal for each other and extend into infinity, eternity. In contrast, "oblique," non-parallel lines extended will eventually cross, come together. These lines represent loves possessed by those who do not have the spiritual love on the level of the speaker and his lady. "Oblique," in fact, suggests imperfection, inferiority, and deviation in love. These loves are physical and are consummated physically in this world.

The last stanza summarizes the poem and poses the final "definition" of this love. He gives a two-part definition of the "Love" that he and his beloved possess: it is (1) the "Conjunction of the mind" and (2) the "Opposition of the stars." The primary conceit here is from astronomy and astrology. "Conjunction" refers to the apparent proximity of two planets or other heavenly bodies when viewed from the earth (and, in astrology, it refers to the coming together of two bodies in the same sign of the ZODIACK); therefore, he means that the minds of the two lovers are in proximity and union (i.e., their intellectual and spiritual love unites them, as already implied in earlier conceits of the poem). "Opposition" refers to the position of two heavenly bodies when exactly opposite to each other, as viewed from the earth. But the implication also is that the "stars" are a symbol of "Fate" (especially in astrological interpretation), and Fate "debars" the two lovers, prevents their physical proximity and union (as already implied in earlier conceits). Marvell also seems to be playing seriously with another common meaning of "conjunction" in his time: "conjunction" was also used to mean sexual union, copulation. So, the word serves paradoxically to enforce the idea that this is precisely what they *cannot* experience. Their only intercourse is one of the "mind," not of the body.

Denham, Lady. One of the mistresses of James, Duke of York. Several persons were accused of poisoning her, but no trace of poison was found. See JAMES II and DENHAM, SIR JOHN.

Denham, Sir John (1615–1669). Royalist, dramatist, and poet. Appointed Surveyor-General of the Works at the Restoration of CHARLES II. Best known for his poem titled "Cooper's Hill." Became a member of the Royal Society in 1663. Went insane near the end of his life, an occurrence that many attributed to the fact that his young wife became the mistress of the Duke of York (see JAMES II and DENHAM, LADY). Marvell, in "Clarendon's Housewarming," implies that his madness was due to a brick falling on him.

Deodand. *Noun*: a thing forfeited or to be given to God: specifically, in English law, a personal chattel which, having been the immediate cause of the death of a person, was given to God as an expiatory offering (i.e., forfeited to the Crown to be used for such pious purposes as being sold or distributed for alms). See "THE NYMPH COMPLAINING FOR THE DEATH OF HER FAWN."

Descrey. See DESCRY.

Descry. *Verb*: (1) to declare, make known, reveal; (2) to reveal something hidden or secret; (3) to cry out against or denounce; (4) to see or perceive; (5) to explore or investigate.

Destiny. *Noun*: (1) whatever is fated to happen, (2) the power or agent that determines events, (3) supernatural or divine preordination, (4) God's divine providence, (5) mythological goddess of destiny.

"Dialogue between the Resolved Soul and Created Pleasure, A." One of the works in *MISCELLANEOUS POEMS*. One of the "Dialogue Poems" (also see "A DIALOGUE BETWEEN THE SOUL AND BODY"). The first stanza of ten lines (spoken by the narrator, the individual who is urging his own resolute soul to easy resistance against "Nature" and its created pleasures) begins a major motif of the poem, the military one. The Soul is urged to arm itself and do battle against the approaching "army" of pleasures. In telling the Soul to take its "immortal shield," its "helmet," and its "sword," the speaker immediately alludes to Ephesians 6:11 ("put on the whole armor of God, that ye may be able to stand against the wiles of the devil") and 16–17 ("Above all, taking the shield of faith, wherewith ye shall be able to quench all the fiery darts of the wicked. And take the helmet of salvation, and the sword of the Spirit, which is the word of God"). The divine Soul's power lies in its weapons of the Christian faith as embodied in the Bible. The army of worldly pleasures that the soul faces has "silken banners," suggesting its beautiful luxuriousness that seriously tempts any but the most resolute ("resolved") soul. The temptations are not only "FAIR" (beautiful), but "strong." But this "thing Divine," the resolute Soul, will have no problem in categorically rejecting every temptation offered, and this lack of conflict and the weakness of worldly temptations in the face of a resolute soul are clearly foreshadowed here. The rest of the poem supports these implications. "Nature" truly "WANTS" (lacks) any art to conquer this determined Soul.

In lines 11–16 Pleasure offers its first temptation with flattery of the soul. Specifically offered is appeal to taste and smell, two of the five senses, with "fruits and flowers." Understanding the reference to "souls" of fruits and flowers depends upon the concept of the TRIPARTITE SOUL (or that of the three souls). Fruits and flowers (any vegetation) were believed only to possess one of the three souls, the vegetative (or vegetable) soul, as opposed to animals possessing two and humans possessing three. The one possessed by fruits and flowers is the lowest of the three and is associated with growth and reproduction. Since the human possesses all three souls (or parts of a soul), the implication here is that the lowest soul of the individual human can be stimulated by that corresponding soul in vegetation. The Soul (lines 17–18) gives a short answer stating that it is interested in heavenly, spiritual food, and pictures itself on a journey to heaven. The soul has no time to "BAIT," to stop for mere physical food on this spiritual journey. This first interchange between Pleasure and the Soul sets the pattern for the rest of the poem: Pleasure speaks at length, building up to a temptation, and then the Soul gives a short, curt answer in contrast. This reflects the absolute conviction of the Soul and its ease in rejecting worldly temptation.

In lines 19–22 Pleasure offers soft pillows, appealing to touch, to feeling. This is the third of the five senses thus brought into play. The Soul rejects this gentle physical rest for the "gentler" comfort of spiritual and ethical purpose. Lines 25–28 again bring in smell but add sight (the fourth sense) also, with the sweet smell and beautiful color of "Perfumes." Secondarily, there is a foreshadowing of the temptation to be like God that becomes more important later in the poem. This appeal is again easily rejected with the implication that the sight and smell of a humble soul is sufficient perfume.

The next interchange (lines 31–36) more specifically develops the appeal to sight and combines it with an appeal to pride and self-esteem. Pleasure tells the Soul to look at its own face in a "crystal," a mirror. The Soul responds that no earthly sight compares to God's level of spiritual reality and creativity.

The final conversation before the intervention of the Chorus (lines 37–44) appeals to the fifth sense, hearing, through music. This is the highest temptation that can be offered through the senses: it was a Renaissance commonplace that hearing is the loftiest of the senses and most closely approaches the intellectual and spiritual planes above it. And this feeling is reflected in the Soul's statement that this appeal is the one that might tempt it, but resistance still prevails with the assertion that the Soul has no "time to lose" in its spiritual journey, even on music's power. So, the Soul has overcome physical temptation from all five senses. With the Soul's saying, "None can chain a mind / Whom this sweet chordage cannot bind," one sees a METAPHYSICAL characteristic in Marvell's wordplay on "chordage," suggesting musical chords, but also "cordage," ropes with which one may be bound.

After this victory of the Soul over the senses, Chorus steps in to mark an important turning point (lines 45–50). Chorus asserts that the Soul "does fence the batteries," does ward off the attacks, thus picking up the earlier military imagery (see BATTERY). But Marvell again seems to be engaging in wordplay with the use of "FENCE": it not only suggests to ward off, but also "to fence off," to erect a barrier against. In addition, relevant also is furthering the sword imagery from the first stanza: i.e., the Soul has been in a fencing match with the senses and has been successful in its ability to fence in this contest with weapons. The Chorus then urges the Soul to persist against new "charges," continuing the military motif.

The first of the new attacks is made by Pleasure in lines 51–54: it offers a composite of all things beautiful ("fair"), soft, and sweet in the form of feminine beauty, a beautiful woman. So, all of the previous offers of appealling things are concentrated and made more impressive by their being embodied in one human. The Soul easily rejects this offer with sarcasm: if this woman is a physical "heaven," then the true Heaven not now available to sight must be far greater and worth the resolute spiritual journey that the Soul refuses to veer away from.

Pleasure next (lines 57–60) offers wealth and then (lines 63–66) the whole world. The Soul easily rejects these appeals that lead up to the climactic one in lines 69–72: Pleasure here offers all knowledge, even including seeing into the future and into the very center of the earth which is itself the center of the universe (see CENTER and PTOLEMY). This appeal to have Godlike knowledge plays on human pride and was the cause of the falls of Adam and Eve. The Soul's answer, in turn, upholds humility, not pride and proud knowledge, as the way to climb to Heaven. This is the final triumph by the Soul. Like Christ resisting the temptations of Satan (see Luke 4:1–13 or Matthew 4:1–11), the Soul is victorious over worldly temptations. Attaining Heaven and its pleasures await the resolved Soul. These pleasures are all beyond the realm of this world, beyond either fixed point, north or south pole, around which the stars seem to revolve. In having the Chorus say that these pleasures beyond earth are "thine everlasting STORE," Marvell surely has in mind a portion of the Sermon on the Mount: "Lay not up for yourselves treasures upon earth, where moth and rust doth corrupt, and where thieves break through and steal. But lay up for yourselves treasures in heaven, where neither moth nor rust doth corrupt, and where thieves do not break through nor steal. For where your treasure is, there will your heart be also" (Matthew 6:19–21). The resolved Soul does indeed have its heart with heavenly treasure: as the Chorus says at the poem's beginning, "Nature wants an Art / To conquer one resolved heart."

It also is quite significant that Marvell has the temptation of the Soul parallel that of Christ and then to echo the Sermon on the Mount. In Matthew the temptation of Christ by Satan occurs in Chapter 4, and the Sermon on the Mount comes immediately thereafter (in Chapters 5, 6, and 7). So, the overall structure of this poem and some of its major themes parallel this portion of the Bible.

"Dialogue between the Soul and Body, A." One of the works in *MISCELLANEOUS POEMS*. One of the "Dialogue Poems" (also see "A DIALOGUE BETWEEN THE RESOLVED SOUL AND CREATED PLEASURE"). This poem reflects the renewed seventeenth-century interest in a medieval tradition of debates between the soul and body. This tradition stems primarily from Galatians 5:17 ("For the flesh lusteth against the Spirit, and the Spirit against the flesh: and these are contrary the one to the other: so that ye cannot do the things that ye would"). In contrast to "A DIALOGUE BETWEEN THE RESOLVED SOUL AND CREATED PLEASURE," this poem is not one of temptation but of equal debate between the two entities. There is more balance in the opposing claims and more dramatic conflict. What is interesting is that Marvell gives the Body the last word and breaks the previous equality of 10-line stanzas assigned to each speaker by giving the Body four more lines in the last stanza. In addition, this poem has more of what are regarded as METAPHYSICAL characteristics than the other dialogue.

In the Soul's first speech in the opening 10-line stanza, Marvell develops an extended comparison, a METAPHYSICAL CONCEIT, of the body as a prison in which the Soul is confined. Actually, the basic comparison is a traditional one, used many times previously by writers, but Marvell gives it fresh life and uniqueness with the extended intellectual, witty, METAPHYSICAL elements in his. For example, Marvell compares feet to fetters (paradoxical, in that captives' feet are usually themselves placed in fetters, but, from the Soul's perspective, the feet themselves, being physical, are indeed fetters placed on the Soul). Similarly, Marvell compares hands to manacles, whereas captives' hands are usually placed in manacles. In addition, wittily and paradoxically, Marvell portrays the "bones" of the feet and hands as the "bolts" holding together the parts of the fetters and manacles. The alliteration of the *b* in "bolts of bones," along with the plosive sound and heavy stress, conveys the sense of disgust and outrage felt by the Soul concerning these physical restraints placed on it by the Body. Extremely paradoxical and witty also is the next complaint of the Soul in lines 5–6: the Soul feels "blinded with an eye" and "Deaf with the drumming of an ear." Ordinarily one thinks of an eye being the means to sight (rather than to blindness) and an ear being the means to hearing (rather than to deafness). But, of course, the paradox is explained by the fact that, from the Soul's perspective, these physical elements hinder the spiritual. Emphasis on the physical causes spiritual infirmities. The Soul goes on in this extremely detailed conceit that takes us far beyond the old traditional treatments of this basic comparison: the nerves, arteries, and veins threading through the Body are pictured as the chains which bind and hold up the Soul, like a captive in prison chained against a wall as a part of the torture administered during imprisonment. The last two lines of the first stanza make the idea of torture very explicit: the Soul does feel "tortured" from all the previously named elements of the Body, as well as from being bound within a "vain head" and "double heart." The head and heart are appropriate as parts of the Body within which the Soul is held prisoner, and "double heart" is literally true as a physical entity with two chambers, two ventricles. But Marvell also uses "double heart" to imply duplicity, hypocrisy, deception. Also "vain head" plays on multiple meanings of "VAIN": specifically relevant are the implications of the head being empty, thoughtless, futile, and proud.

In the second stanza the Body responds in kind and makes its complaint against the Soul. It feels that, in fact, it is the one taken captive, restricted, and tortured by the Soul. The question it asks ("Oh, who shall me deliver whole / From bonds of this tyrannic soul?") echoes in a witty reversal St. Paul's question in Romans 7:24: "O wretched man that I am! Who shall deliver me from the body of this death?" The Body feels that the Soul has impaled him like a stake or spear thrust up through him, unnaturally holding and torturing the Body in an upright posture (see IMPALE, meaning 2). The Soul's straining upward to Heaven forces the Body into this unnatural position. So, in the first stanza the Soul wanted to be "raise[d]" from a dungeon, and here the Body complains about being raised by the Soul. The Body feels that this upward thrust of the Soul makes the Body "mine own precipice." This whole image plays on the Christian idea that the human's superiority to other animals is indicated by his erect position given by God, because of his divine soul. But the Body emphasizes that this is what creates the possibility of man's fall: the theological concept of the Fall is placed wittily in the literal image of the Body being forced to totter with instability on two feet, always in danger of falling from the proud "precipice" that the Soul has forced it to be placed upon. In lines 15–16 the Body states that this "FRAME," the body itself, is needlessly animated by the soul. Lines 17–18 accuse the Soul of making the Body live only in order that it will die. The Soul, by implication, wants the Body to die, since the Soul will be released from its prison and thus achieve Heaven. Adam's (man's) fall originally introduced death for the

Body, and here the Body is complaining that indeed the Soul wants the Body's inevitable death, since it is by this means that the Soul will achieve its own life. In lines 19–20 the Body accuses the Soul of torturing the Body (comparable to the accusation by the Soul at the end of the previous stanza) by never letting the Body rest: the Soul (paradoxically) is pictured as a demonic spirit that possesses and animates the Body.

Stanza 3 begins (lines 21–22) with the Soul throwing back the Body's statement about demonic possession: the Soul, in contrast, pictures itself as a good spirit being imprisoned by a witch's magic within the Body. This is analogous to the good spirit Ariel being imprisoned within a tree by the witch Syrocax in Shakespeare's *The Tempest*. In lines 23–24 the Soul pictures itself being forced to experience the griefs of the Body. The Soul in itself has no senses through which to feel, but it is tied to the Body and has to suffer the pain that the Body suffers: thus, the paradox that the Soul must "feel, that cannot feel, the pain." Lines 25–26 convey the Soul's feeling that the Body quite audaciously uses the very resources of the Soul ("my care"), such as its rational and intellectual nature (see TRIPARTITE SOUL), to preserve itself—i.e., the Body preserves its own physical nature which is inimical to the Soul's welfare, since the Soul seeks the destruction, rather than the preservation, of the Body in order to obtain its own release: the preservation of the Body, then, "destroy(s)" the Soul. The Soul further complains (lines 27–28) that it not only has to suffer the Body's physical diseases and their associated pains, but (paradoxically) even worse is to endure the "cure" of those diseases—i.e., the cure of the disease means a restoration to health of the Body, a preservation that is destruction for the Soul's nature and purposes. Marvell takes this "cure" and develops it into a witty metaphysical conceit in the concluding lines of this stanza (lines 29–30). The "cure" becomes a shipwreck that cuts off the Soul's journey toward the "port," the port being death or Heaven or both, from the Soul's perspective.

Stanza 4 concludes the poem with the Body's last speech, and the Body here is given four additional lines, in contrast to the ten lines in each of the previous stanzas. The Body again (as previously) answers in terms and ideas analogous to the ones just employed by the Soul in its complaint. Here the Body uses health and suffering of pains, just as did the Soul. But from the Body's perspective, the Soul is the source of ill health and suffering. The Body says that the maladies caused by the Soul are not even able to be treated by PHYSIC (medical science or medicine). Hope, fear, love, hatred, joy, and sorrow are these "maladies" catalogued through this stanza. Here it is assumed that the "Soul" encompasses all of the emotions and thoughts of the human, all those psychological, intellectual, and spiritual manifestations beyond the mere physical. By being tied to the Soul, the Body must endure these, in a way parallel to the physical ills that the Soul complained of having to endure because it is connected to the Body. The last four lines of this stanza (and of the poem itself) take the dichotomy and conflict of the Soul and Body into much larger dimensions, into philosophical and Christian ones. The Body blames the Soul for creating the possibilities of sin for the human—i.e., for causing the Body to fall. This implies that Adam's original fall was caused by the Soul building up pride through its emotional and intellectual nature. This interestingly echoes the Body's earlier statement (lines 13–14) that the Soul causes the Body to totter with instability, in great danger of falling from the "precipice" of itself which the Soul has created. The last two lines create the conceit of the Soul being like "architects" who cut down and shape into square lumber the once-thriving and natural "green trees." So, the Body pictures the Soul as going against and destroying something natural (i.e., the Body itself). The Soul, just as the architect, destroys according to its own design and purposes. In the Renaissance a square shape is unnatural, not occurring in nature, and is usually associated with something bad (see also "THE MOWER AGAINST GARDENS"). So, the Soul is pictured as causing the unnatural and artificial to supersede the natural. The sympathy with nature and its association with something innocent, pristine, and fertile recurs in significant ways through much of Marvell's work. Also recurring in association with nature and its connotations is Marvell's favorite color, "green." The "green trees" here are living embodiments of this innocent life, and the Soul is made to be its destroyer. Certainly Marvell alludes here to the idea that Adam's fall in the Garden of Eden (analogous to the "forest"?) introduced death to the body, a state that did not previously exist for Adam and Eve. So, the Body claims that it was once innocent and flourishing but that the Soul causes it to be hewn, to fall and die.

This poem illustrates to some extent the fusion of the METAPHYSICAL and CLASSICAL in Marvell, the combination of influences from both DONNE and JONSON. The conceits, paradoxes, wordplay, and combination of seriousness and humor are quite metaphysical, but the balance in lines, stanzas, and overall structure, as well as the use of octosyllabic couplets, argue for a classical strain.

Diana. See CYNTHIA.

Discover. *Verb*: (1) to uncover, (2) to disclose or reveal, (3) to show, (4) to manifest or display, (5) to find out, (6) to see.

Discovery of occult resemblances in things apparently unlike. See METAPHYSICAL CONCEIT.

Disparate experience. See DISSOCIATION OF SENSIBILITY.

Dissenter. In general, the term is synonymous with NONCONFORMIST. However, more specifically, sometimes distinguished from the latter by designating one who not only refuses to conform to the state church but who also disagrees with the principle of state churches.

Dissociation of Sensibility. A famous phrase used by the poet and critic T.S. Eliot in a 1921 *London Times Literary Supplement* review of H.J.C. Grierson's 1921 volume entitled *Metaphysical Lyrics and Poems of the Seventeenth Century*. Eliot says that later in the 17th century (after DONNE and the other major METAPHYSICAL poets) a "dissociation of sensibility set in." He apparently means a separation of thought and feeling or thought and experience in verse, since he praises Donne by saying that "a thought to Donne was an experience." He also asserts, "When a poet's mind is perfectly equipped for its work, it is constantly amalgamating disparate experience." He also calls sensibility "the feeling" in verse.

Divertisement. *Noun*: amusement.

Do, doe. *Verb*: (1) to put forth action or effort; (2) to perform or carry out; (3) to accomplish or finish; (4) to copulate, have sexual intercourse.

Dodona's Grove. The seat of ZEUS.

Dog Days. See DOG-STAR.

Dog-star. Sirius, supposed to cause heat on earth when it is ascendant and the sun is in Leo (during the "dog days" of summer) and to bring ill health and fever.

Donative. *Noun*: a donation, gift, or present.

Donne, John (1572–1631). Poet, prose writer, clergyman. Attended Lincoln's Inn and then served as a soldier briefly. Became a secretary to Sir Thomas Egerton, Lord Keeper of the Great Seal, but lost this position after secretly marrying Egerton's niece, Ann More. By 1608 he enjoyed financial support and respect from two patronesses, the Countess of Bedford and Magdalen Herbert, the mother of GEORGE HERBERT. Donne sent his *La Corona* series of sonnets to Mrs.

Herbert. Donne also was acquainted with BEN JONSON and other respected writers and titled people of his time.

Donne's wishes for secular employment eluded him, ultimately because King JAMES I wanted Donne to serve in the English church. In 1615 Donne was ordained. Subsequently he became Reader in Divinity at Lincoln's Inn, a chaplain serving King James, and Dean of St. Paul's Cathedral. In 1624 was published Donne's prose work *Devotions Upon Emergent Occasions*, following a serious illness at the end of 1623. In the summer of 1625 Donne visited the home of Magdalen Herbert, now Lady Danvers, at Chelsea. He was forced to stay there much longer than originally planned because of an outbreak of plague in London. Donne refers in one of his letters to the fact that George Herbert was also here at the time. Donne preached a memorial sermon after Lady Danvers's death in 1627: according to Izaak Walton, Donne did "weep and preach" the sermon. After a serious illness in late 1630 and early 1631, Donne died on March 31, 1631.

Many of Donne's sermons were published some years after his death, and these sermons and his *Devotions* have assured his reputation as a great preacher and prose writer. However, his reputation as a great poet rests primarily on his secular *Songs and Sonnets*, although his *Holy Sonnets* and other *Divine Poems* are not to be ignored by any means.

Donne is now regarded as the first METAPHYSICAL poet, and Marvell generally is seen as one of his major followers in this group. He does use many of the characteristics regarded as typical of Donne and the metaphysicals in certain poems and in parts of poems; however, debts to Ben Jonson and the CLASSICAL strain appear strongly in Marvell's work, as well. Fusion of the influences from Donne and Jonson is integral to understanding and appreciating the work of Marvell and others after Donne.

Donne, for not keeping of accent, deserved hanging. See JONSON and METAPHYSICAL.

Doubt. *Verb*: (1) to be undecided, (2) to mistrust, (3) to fear, (4) to suspect.

Douglas, Archibald (died 1667). Captain on the *Royal Oak* when the Dutch fleet under de RUYTER came up the Medway to Chatham in 1667. He refused to desert his ship and died in the flames as it was burned. Apparently he was a land officer sent with a detachment of soldiers to defend the ship. He was not in a naval position. Marvell praises him in both "The Loyal Scot" and "The Last Instructions To a Painter."

Drummond, William, of Hawthornden (1585–1649). Born near Edinburgh, Scotland, at the family estate of Hawthornden. Studied law before inheriting his father's estate and title as laird of Hawthornden. He then spent much time reading and collecting many volumes of books for his library before he began writing poems himself. After a poem in 1617 celebrating a visit to Scotland by King JAMES I, Drummond became better known among English poets and readers, including Michael Drayton. In 1618 BEN JONSON walked from London to Edinburgh, met Drummond, and stayed with him for two weeks. Drummond invented several military and other mechanical devices, including different types of pistols, pikes, telescopes, and measuring instruments. He supported the Royalists and CHARLES I and wrote some political prose and poetry in their support.

Drummond's own poems and prose pieces are minor, and his renown rests mainly on his recording of Jonson's comments during the latter's visit to Scotland. This prose account usually is referred to as Jonson's *Conversations with Drummond* (or simply as *Conversations*). Some of the most famous and influential comments about DONNE and METAPHYSICAL poetry (as well as other writers) are those attributed to Jonson by Drummond in this work. For example, Drummond records Jonson saying the following (among other remarks on Donne): "that Donne, for not keeping of accent, deserved hanging," "that Donne said to him he wrote that epitaph on Prince Henry . . . to match Sir Edward Herbert in obscureness," "he esteemeth John Donne the first poet in the world in some things," "affirmeth Donne to have written all his best pieces ere he was 25 years old," and "that Donne himself for not being understood would perish."

Dryden, John (1631–1700). Poet, dramatist, and prose writer. Was made poet laureate in 1668. Dryden was portrayed by the Duke of Buckingham (see VILLIERS, GEORGE) in *The Rehearsal* (1671) as BAYS (or Bayes). Marvell, in *The Rehearsal Transprosed* appropriates the name "Bays" to symbolize SAMUEL PARKER. Dryden wrote his satire *Absalom and Achitophel* in 1681 and his *Religio Laici* (defending the Anglican compromise church) in 1682. But after JAMES II became king, Dryden converted to Roman Catholicism. The relationship between Marvell and Dryden was generally antagonistic, largely because of their political, religious, and literary differences. In "ON MR. MILTON'S *PARADISE LOST*" Marvell mockingly refers to Dryden as "the Town-Bays" who relies on rhyme and other poetic ornaments to uphold his own poetry, in contrast to MILTON's poetry. Dryden, in some of his writings after Marvell's death, refers to Marvell as "Judas" and compares him to "Martin Mar-Prelate" who was "the first

Presbyterian Scribler." But Dryden seems influenced to some extent by Marvell: see FLECKNOE, RICHARD. Also see METAPHYSICAL.

Duchess of York. See JAMES II.

Duke of York. See JAMES II.

Dull. *Adjective*: (1) slow of understanding; (2) lacking keenness in senses and feelings, unresponsive; (3) sluggish or stagnant; (4) depressed, gloomy, melancholy; (5) tedious or uninteresting; (6) lacking sharpness.

Duncalfe, Humphrey. One of the mayors of Hull to whom Marvell sent letters reporting government matters, since he was a Member of Parliament for the city.

Dutton, William. Ward of OLIVER CROMWELL. Marvell became his tutor in 1653, living with him at Eton in the home of John Oxenbridge, a friend of Cromwell's. Oxenbridge and his wife (Jane) had spent much time in the Bermudas, and he was appointed in 1653 as one of the commissioners for government of the colony. It is likely that Marvell wrote "BERMUDAS" in 1653, stimulated by the Oxenbridges. The Oxenbridges were thoroughly PURITAN in background and beliefs, and Marvell praises their examples and influences for Dutton in a letter of 1653 to Cromwell. Oxenbridge, a NONCONFORMIST, in 1669 went to Boston, preaching and living there until his death in 1674. In 1656 Marvell was with Dutton in France at Saumur. JAMES SCUDAMORE refers scornfully to Marvell as Dutton's tutor at this time.

E

Earth. *Noun*: (1) one of the four ELEMENTs; (2) the world on which humanity dwells, envisioned in the PTOLEMAIC concept as the center of the universe; (3) the land on this world, as opposed to the seas; (4) the ground and soil; (5) place for burial; (6) the body; (7) anything mortal; (8) personified "Mother Earth," fertile and bringing forth life.

Eccentric. *Adjective*: (1) elliptical or non-circular, (2) deviating.

Echo. See NARCISSUS.

Elagabalus (205–222). Roman emperor who lived a life of unmitigated pleasures.

Elected. In its special theological sense, chosen by God to receive salvation.

Element. *Noun*: (1) in Ancient, Medieval, and Renaissance thought, one of the four simple substances [from lightest to heaviest: fire, air, water, and earth] out of which all material bodies are made: anything composed of any one or more of the four elements is mortal and therefore subject to decay and death [see also HUMOR, COMPLEXION, GALEN, and NEW PHILOSOPHY]; (2) more generally, any constituent substance out of which a more complex substance is made.

Eliot, T.S. See DISSOCIATION OF SENSIBILITY.

Endymion. In mythology, the beautiful young man, a shepherd, who was kissed by and made love to in his dreams by CYNTHIA upon LATMOS. He is said to be asleep there immortally and eternally, never conscious, and visited by Cynthia night after night. She had fifty daughters by him.

Engine. *Noun*: (1) a plot or snare; (2) a mechanical apparatus or tool; (3) an instrument of warfare; (4) an instrument of torture, such as the rack; (5) an instrument or means.

Enow. Enough.

Essence. See ALCHEMY.

Eternal Book. See "Book of Life" under BOOKS OF GOD.

Examine. *Verb*: to test.

Exhalation. *Noun*: (1) action of breathing forth; (2) evaporation; (3) that which is exhaled, breath, vapor; (4) vapor from damp ground; (5) meteor.

F

Fain. *Verb*: (1) to be glad, (2) to make glad, (3) to rejoice in, (4) to pretend (feign). *Adjective*: (1) glad or content, (2) obliged or necessitated, (3) willing or eager. *Adverb*: (1) gladly, (2) willingly. Also see FEIGN.

Fair. *Adjective*: (1) beautiful; (2) having light complexion or having light or blonde hair; (3) free from blemish, clean; (4) impartial, equitable.

Fairfax, Mary (Maria). See FAIRFAX, THOMAS, and VILLIERS, GEORGE.

Fairfax, Thomas (1612–1671). Third Lord Fairfax. Born in Yorkshire. Matriculated at St. John's College, Cambridge, in 1626. Went to Low Countries three years later to learn the art of war under Sir Horace Vere. Returned to England in 1632. Married Anne Vere, the daughter of Sir Horace, in 1637. Was a commander in the war against the Scots and knighted in 1640. From the beginning of the civil war he was one of the important supporters of Parliament in Yorkshire. Served in battles during 1642 and in the recapture of Leeds in January 1643. Also captured Wakefield in 1643. In 1644 he was wounded at the siege of Helmsley Castle. While he was recovering, Parliament reorganized the army. Fairfax was chosen to be the chief commander. CHARLES I expressed confidence that he could beat Fairfax and the new army. On June 14, 1645, Fairfax and his army defeated the King at Naseby. OLIVER CROMWELL and others praised Fairfax for his personal bravery in this battle. The remainder of 1645 and 1646 saw a succession of victories and successful sieges. In November 1646, he was in London receiving the thanks of Parliament.

In 1645 Parliament had stipulated that Fairfax be created a baron and endowed with land. After the capture of the King, Fairfax urged tender treatment of him and his family and expressed his wish for moderation and lasting peace. He continually urged Parliament to provide for the pay of the soldiers and restored some of the lost military discipline. After the King and Royalists surged forth again with military actions that had to be quelled with battles that cost lives, the army and Fairfax were not as temperate toward Charles as before. Fairfax himself seems to have approved of the trial and deposition of the King but did not even consider executing him. Fairfax himself says in writing, "My afflicted and troubled mind for it [the execution] and my earnest endeavours to prevent it will sufficiently testify my dislike and abhorrence of the fact."

In 1649 Fairfax was reappointed commander-in-chief of all forces in England and Ireland. In the summer of 1650 war with Scotland was imminent, and the Council of State wanted to invade Scotland. Fairfax was willing to fight against the Scots if they invaded England, but he was not willing to invade and attack them. He resigned his position on June 25, 1650. At this time he retired to his country estates in Yorkshire. One of these was Nun Appleton, and the other was Bilbrough. The home that the family lived in was Nun Appleton House which, at this time, was likely a portion of the original nunnery on the site. The original was acquired by the Fairfax family from a Cistercian priory at the dissolution of the monasteries and nunneries in 1542. The house in 1650 probably was rather small and humble, in contrast to the later home built on the site which was much larger and grander. It was in late 1650 or in 1651 that Marvell moved to Nun Appleton and became the tutor for Fairfax's daughter Mary (Maria). He served in this capacity during 1651 and 1652. Marvell probably wrote "Upon the Hill and Grove at Bilbrough" and "UPON APPLETON HOUSE" at this time. (At this writing, the prevailing scholarly opinion is that Marvell lived there before the new house was built and that the new one was begun shortly after Marvell left. However, others contend that the new house had already been built before Marvell's arrival.)

Later in the decade Fairfax served in Parliament and also played an influential role in achieving the Restoration of the monarchy with certain conditions imposed upon the King (CHARLES II). In his later years he retired to Nun Appleton and spent much of his time reading and writing. His wife preceded him in death, and both are buried in the church of Bilbrough.

Falchion, fauchion. *Noun*: a short, broad sword with a sharp point. Also see KNOTS.

Falling sickness. Epilepsy.

Fame. *Noun*: (1) public talk, report, rumor; (2) reputation or character; (3) celebrity, renown.

Fancy. *Noun*: (1) imagination, (2) things imagined or unreal or illusory, (3) a whim or mood, (4) individual taste or liking.

Fantastic. *Adjective*: (1) imaginary, unreal; (2) impulsive, capricious, odd; (3) grotesque.

Fashion. *Noun*: (1) form or shape; (2) a particular shape or pattern; (3) a certain (and usually current) style of clothing, attire; (4) a prevailing custom or mode; (5) showy outward form.

Fast. *Adjective*: (1) firm, secure; (2) strong; (3) rapid.

Fatal. *Adjective*: (1) destined, decreed by fate; (2) doomed; (3) prophetic; (4) ominous; (5) deadly.

Father. *Noun*: (1) male parent; (2) ancestor, forefather; (3) one of the "Fathers of the Church": early Christian writers, usually those of the first five centuries; (4) title by which God is addressed or referred; (5) title for a Roman Catholic priest.

Fauconberg, Lord. See BELASYSE, THOMAS.

Favour, favor. *Noun*: (1) friendly regard, (2) exceptional kindness, (3) something given out of kindness or regard, (4) aid, (5) beauty, (6) charm.

Fawn. *Noun*: a young deer. See "THE NYMPH COMPLAINING FOR THE DEATH OF HER FAWN."

Feake, Christopher. One of the FIFTH MONARCHY men who preached sedition against OLIVER CROMWELL and was imprisoned in 1654.

Feign, feigned. *Verb*: (1) to pretend [sometimes spelled as "fain"], (2) to form or fashion deceptively. *Adjective*: (1) pretended [sometimes spelled as "fained"]; (2) done or said deceptively, dissimulated. Also see FAIN.

Fence. *Verb*: (1) to practice the use of the foil or sword; (2) to ward off, repel; (3) to fence off, to keep off by a barrier erected against something outside of it.

Fenwick, Roger. Colonel who died in the Battle of the Dunes on June 4, 1658.

Fifth Monarchy. A religious sect that anticipated an establishment of a kingdom of the saints which would come after the four kingdoms prophesied in Daniel 7:17–18.

Fifth Scepter. Reference to FIFTH MONARCHY.

Figure. *Noun*: (1) form or shape, (2) statue (3) representation or emblem, (4) diagram.

Finch, Heneage (1621–1682). Solicitor-General. Supported measures to oppress DISSENTERs.

Fire. *Noun*: (1) one of the four ELEMENTs; (2) the operative principle in combustion; (3) a flame; (4) in some contexts, ardor or enthusiasm; (5) in some contexts, passion or emotion.

Firmament. *Noun*: (1) generally, the realm of the created universe above the SPHERE of the moon, according to the PTOLEMAIC concept of the universe: firmament is regarded as immortal and unchanging, as opposed to the SUBLUNARY realm; (2) more specifically, the SPHERE of the fixed stars in the PTOLEMAIC concept, also regarded as permanent and unchanging, until the discoveries of GALILEO began to prove otherwise.

First Mover. According to the PTOLEMAIC view of the universe, the outermost SPHERE is the one called the "First Mover" or "Prime Mover" or "Primum Mobile." Its function is to give the initial motion to all of the spheres and to keep all of them revolving in perfect harmony. As they thus revolve, they create a perfect music called the music of the spheres (see discussion under SPHERE).

Five Mile Act. Act that forbade any NONCONFORMIST minister who had refused to take the oath of non-resistance to go within five miles of a town where he had earlier preached.

Flattery. *Noun:* (1) pleasing praise; (2) insincere or false praise; (3) self-pleasing, consoling deception or accepted idea.

Flecknoe, Richard (died 1678?). English writer and priest (Roman Catholic). Marvell visited with him in his small living quarters in Rome, probably in 1646. Flecknoe was impoverished, malnourished, and extremely thin. As a result of this visit Marvell wrote "Flecknoe, an English Priest at Rome," a critical and somewhat unfeeling satire. Since Marvell did not publish the poem and it remained unpublished until after Marvell's death, perhaps he perceived his own youthful insensitivity in it. He says that the communion host has "more flesh and blood than he [Flecknoe] can boast." He comments on Flecknoe's cramped living quarters and his bad reading of bad verse.

In 1682 DRYDEN published a poetic satire on the writer Thomas Shadwell which he titled "MacFlecknoe." In it he pictures Flecknoe as the ruler of the kingdom of dullness, to which Shadwell is heir. The fact that Marvell's poem on Flecknoe was published in *MISCELLANEOUS POEMS* in 1681 suggests its influence on Dryden's poem of 1682.

Flora. In Roman mythology, goddess of flowers and gardens.

Fly. *Noun*: any winged insect, such as a moth.

Fob. *Noun*: pocket.

Fond. *Adjective*: foolish.

Forbear. *Verb*: (1) to endure, submit to; (2) to dispense with, spare; (3) to give up, part with; (4) to avoid, shun: (5) to abstain or refrain from.

Forswear. *Verb*: (1) to deny or repudiate on oath, (2) to swear falsely or break an oath or forsake previously sworn allegiance.

Forward. *Adjective*: (1) early or well advanced, (2) ready or prompt or eager, (3) presumptuous, (4) extreme.

Fountain. *Noun*: (1) a spring or source of water flowing out of the earth, (2) the source of a stream or river.

Fox, Sir Stephen (1627–1716). In charge of the household of CHARLES II, beginning in 1654.

Foxley, William. One of the mayors of Hull to whom Marvell sent letters reporting government matters, since he was a Member of Parliament for the city.

Frame. *Verb*: (1) to shape, form, create; (2) to direct something to a certain purpose; (3) to attempt; (4) to adapt oneself or conform; (5) to form in the mind, to conceive, to imagine; (6) to cause or produce. *Noun*: (1) a structure consisting of parts put together, (2) heaven or earth regarded as a structure, (3) a structure that provides support, (4) the human body as a structure of parts.

Franke, Richard. One of the mayors of Hull to whom Marvell sent letters reporting government matters, since he was a Member of Parliament for the city.

Front. *Noun*: (1) forehead, (2) face.

G

Gain both the wind and sun. In a battle at sea, to gain the doubly advantageous position of having both the wind and sun at one's back. See Marvell's "The Fair Singer."

Galen (about 130–200). Greek physician and writer who eventually lived, lectured, and wrote in Rome. His experience in anatomy contributed significantly to knowledge of the circulatory and nervous systems. In the Middle Ages and Renaissance his writings were most influential in proposing a theory of HUMORs and COMPLEXIONs, all related to the four ELEMENTs. His work was particularly popularized and made available in English by Sir Thomas Elyot in the early 16th century, most notably in *The Castle of Health*. See also GALENIST and contrast to PARACELSUS.

Galenist. *Noun*: one subscribing to the teachings, theories, or medicine proposed by GALEN, particularly the idea that to combat an imbalance in HUMOR and COMPLEXION, one ingests food and substances of opposite qualities. See also GALEN and ELEMENT. Contrast to PARACELSUS.

Galileo [Galileo Galilei] (1564–1642). Italian mathematician, astronomer, and physicist. Studied and made fundamental discoveries about gravitation and laws of motion. One of the major proponents of the basic truths of the theory of COPERNICUS and thus (with KEPLER and others) one of the developers of the NEW PHILOSOPHY, as opposed to the older cosmology of PTOLEMY.

Galileo developed the first telescope that could be used for astronomical observation. In 1609 and 1610 he announced some discoveries and published *Sidereus Nuncius* (1610). He noted that the surface of the moon is irregular, that the Milky Way is a galaxy of distant stars, that the planet Jupiter has satellites, that there are spots on the sun, and that the planet Venus has certain phases. In 1613 Galileo asserted that Copernicus was right and Ptolemy wrong. Opposition to him from universities and the Roman Catholic Church began to develop from the fact that his arguments appeared to contradict the Bible. In 1616 the Church declared Copernicanism "false and erroneous." Galileo and others were told that the Copernican theory could only be debated noncommittally as a mathematical supposition. For many years Galileo studied and wrote a book published eventually in 1632 as a

"Dialogue." Individuals and groups of the Church, notably the Jesuits, convinced the Pope that the work was not in fact an objective appraisal of the Ptolemaic and Copernican theories, but a dangerous, destructive argument for Copernicanism. The Church developed a case to prosecute Galileo for "suspicion of heresy," and he was tried. He was found guilty of holding and teaching the Copernican theory and was ordered to recant. He did so, and the Pope ordered house arrest (rather than imprisonment) for him. He made further discoveries with the telescope until he became blind a few years before his death, and he continued his studies of the laws of motion until his death.

"Garden, The." One of the works in *MISCELLANEOUS POEMS*. Generally regarded as one of the best of Marvell's works. It embodies many of the assumptions found in other poems by him, especially in those concerned with the natural world.

With both humor and seriousness, Marvell's speaker in the first stanza establishes a contrast between the passive, contemplative life and the active, struggling, fame-seeking life. The speaker comments that some people strain themselves and, in a sense, literally put themselves through a maze (playing on "amaze") to achieve recognition and reward in fields of endeavor: winning the "palm" signifies achievement in the military, "oak" signifies government, and "BAYS" signifies poetry. Sprigs of each plant reward achievement in each area. But the speaker says that men commonly strive for these recognitions "vainly," playing on two senses of the word, indicating both futilely and arrogantly (see VAIN). So, a critical, ridiculing tone toward anyone obsessed with worldly achievement in the active realm of existence is present from the very beginning of the poem. Lines 3–4 enforce this feeling: those who labor incessantly for such achievement are rewarded ("crowned") only with a sprig of leaf from some "single" plant. Wittily driving his point home that this is very little reward for a lot of work, the speaker takes the stance that the reward is a literal one, rather than a symbolic one, and says that such a frantic achiever only gets very little shade from such a sprig of plant ("short and narrow-verged shade"). In fact, pushing matters even further, he says that actually the little shade criticizes and ridicules (does "upbraid") the waste of labor to achieve such an insignificant and unimportant recognition. Those who expend such great energy and time to gain worldly recognition are only accomplishing useless tasks and currying their own egos. In fact, the use of "prudently" (wisely, exercising sound judgment) adds the implication that this little reward is indeed all they deserve for such insignificant pursuits. Then, in the last two lines, the speaker—or Marvell, if we wish to assume so—is ready to emphasize the far greater rewards awaiting the person who chooses to forego the "rat race" and live the contemplative life, especially such as that enjoyed in the natural world, the natural garden. (One should note that the "garden" in this poem is not like the experimental garden condemned by the mower in "THE MOWER AGAINST GARDENS.") In this natural garden all of the trees and flowers come together, unite ("close") to be a true, full garland that gives the reward of complete shade to the person retreating here. So, the reward for the one who chooses the passive, contemplative life is far greater than the puny "rewards" given the toiling achiever in the active, success-oriented life. The fullness of the reward for the one of "repose" is emphasized by the repetition and parallelism in "all flowers and all trees." The repetition of "all" enforces the contrast with "single" in line 4. This technique of parallelism and repetition and the octosyllabic couplets used in this poem reveal some of Marvell's CLASSICAL characteristics that are fused with the METAPHYSICAL in many of his poems.

In stanza 2 the speaker notes the quietness and innocence that he finds in the garden, in contrast to their absence in the active, social world: he was mistaken in trying to find these values in the "busy companies of men." If any plants symbolizing quietness and innocence are to be found at all on this earth, below heaven ("if here below"), then they will only be found growing among the natural plants of the garden. This statement consciously contrasts these plants to those sprigs taken from plants (and thus no longer growing) and used to symbolize the "incessant labors" suggested in the previous stanza. So, if there are rewards of quietness and innocence available for one in this earthly life, they are to be found in the natural world. In contrast, the speaker finds "society" to be "rude," compared to the "delicious solitude" of the garden. Marvell is playing paradoxically with the ordinary idea that society is sophisticated, not rude.

Stanza 3 compares the "white" and "red" of a lady's complexion with this "lovely green" of the natural world and argues that the "green" is much more "amorous"—i.e., nature is more worthy to be loved and more loving than a woman. The speaker even says that those male lovers who carve their mistress's name in a tree are foolish ("FOND"), because they do not realize how much more beautiful than their mistresses are the trees in which they are cutting women's names! In addition, they are "cruel," since they are destroying the beauty of the tree itself. Pushing his argument wittily and humorously, Marvell has his speaker say that if he carves any names of his lovers in trees, they will be the names of the trees, since they are such superior lovers to and much more beautiful than women. This witty, metaphysical exaggeration does emphasize the great value placed on the contemplative life of innocence found in the natural realm, despite the tongue-in-cheek manner in which it is conveyed.

Stanza 4 begins with the assertion, from a definite male perspective, that when "we" (men) have matured beyond mere youthful, sexual passion for women ("run our passion's heat"), then we turn to the garden, the natural world, truly to find love. This, of course, wittily continues his previous argument that trees are superior to women as lovers. Marvell also is having a bit of fun with "run our passion's heat," because it also conjures up associations with a literal race, in which a runner participates in a course, a "heat." This ties in very nicely with the humorous exaggeration of his argument in the rest of the stanza that the gods chased human beauties so that they turned into trees! Marvell is thinking of such events recounted in mythology. He says that APOLLO chased DAPHNE "only that she might laurel grow": the key word to Marvell's fresh and unique treatment of this mythological story is "only," since Marvell implies that this is the only reason Apollo chased her, so that she would be transformed into a laurel tree! This supports his contention that the tree is preferable to a woman as a lover. He then cites the story of PAN chasing SYRINX who was transformed into a reed, but again with the added touch that Pan really wanted her to be so changed: again, support for the idea that the plant is a preferable object of love! An added subtlety in Marvell's creative uses of these myths is the fact that Apollo adopted the laurel as his sacred tree and wore its branches as a wreath in his hair. This garland of leaves is referred to as "BAYS" and became symbolic of achievement in poetry: it is this achievement alluded to by Marvell in the second line of the poem. Thus, by implication, the Apollo and Daphne story is another way that Marvell can contrast the striving for success in the ordinary world against the beauty of the tree itself, the contemplative life in nature, symbolized by "bays" stripped from the tree against the laurel tree itself. So, both human passion for competitive worldly success and human passion for sexual love (two concerns of the poem to this point) are played against innocent contemplation in nature.

Stanza 5 is the first of three stanzas that make up a logical unit cataloguing the ultimate pleasures enjoyed in the garden by the body (stanza 5), the mind (stanza 6), and the soul (stanza 7). The speaker focuses on the sensuous, physical pleasures enjoyed by the body in the rich abundance of the garden. In fact, the speaker depicts the fruits and flowers literally offering themselves to him and even actively making love to him. The apples drop off the trees for him, the grapes ("luscious clusters of the vine") kiss him ("Upon my mouth do crush their wine"), the nectarine and peach put themselves into his hands, and the flowers embrace him ("Ensnared with flowers"). In the second line of the stanza, Marvell effectively uses sounds to convey the sense: the line is full of plosives ("b" and "p") that convey the force and sound of apples dropping to the ground. The speaker enjoys passive, effortless love, with the fruits and flowers as the active partners. This implication actually follows from his argument in the previous two stanzas (3 and 4) that the best lovers are the plants in the natural world, as opposed to women. He is experiencing this superior love enjoyed among the elements of nature. This stanza also shows life as quite different from that of the "incessant labors" depicted in man's competitive, ambitious existence in stanza 1. Indeed, the speaker is recapturing the kind of pleasure enjoyed by Adam in the *Garden* of Eden before his fall, because after his fall Adam was doomed to labor, to the "sweat" of his "face" (Genesis 3:19). These pleasures are those loving ones enjoyed by Adam before he was given Eve to love. These are innocent pleasures of Adam that each man can recapture briefly by a retreat into nature, into the "Garden." Marvell cleverly plays off the "fall" on grass at the end of this stanza against the fall of Adam that comes to Adam after Eve is introduced into Eden. This "fall on grass" is utterly innocent, as opposed to Adam's later fall and to the resulting fall to which all succeeding humans are subject.

Stanza 6 proceeds to a higher level of pleasure enjoyed in the garden—i.e., higher than on the level of bodily pleasure. In saying that the "mind" withdraws into its happiness "from pleasure less," the speaker means from lesser pleasure: sensuous, physical pleasure of the body is on a lesser plane than intellectual, imaginative pleasure of the mind. Marvell employs a METAPHYSICAL CONCEIT in which he compares the mind to an ocean: there was an old belief that the ocean contains counterparts for everything found on land. Just so does the mind contain counterparts or replicas of everything outside of it through sense impressions recorded in the mind. But the speaker notes that the mind does not only record sense impressions, since it goes further through its *creative* power. It "transcends" the worlds recorded by sense impressions, because it creates worlds of its own by the power of imagination. In fact, it paradoxically annihilates "all that's made" (the physical creation recorded as sense impressions) in order to create imaginative, vibrant, "green" thoughts that are experienced in this "green shade" of the garden. The unhampered creative mind is in perfect harmony with its vibrant natural suroundings. This is the mind not crippled by passion and "incessant labors." The implication again is that this is a pleasure Adam enjoyed in his unfallen state and that someone can briefly recapture a sense of in the natural world. One can recover the innocent creativity of the human mind before the fall.

Stanza 7 moves to an even higher dimension in man's nature, with the focus on the soul's pleasure in the garden. The untrammeled soul in the passivity of nature can escape the restraints of the body briefly, like a bird escaping from a cage. By flying into the boughs of the trees, it reaches toward heaven, anticipating that "longer flight" to heaven after death. It enjoys a brief respite from the body, the world, sin, and death with the sense of spiritual ecstasy found in the garden. So, the ultimate in pleasures bodily, intellectual, and spiritual in this world can be experienced briefly in the garden retreat.

With stanza 8, Marvell makes explicit the analogy that already has been implied: the experience in this garden is analogous to that of Adam ("man") before the introduction of Eve into Eden. Humor is again injected into the serious philosophical bent of the poem when the speaker implies that "no other help could yet be meet" after a place so pure and sweet as Eden was before Eve. Marvell is playing here on God's statement (in Genesis 2:18) that he "will make him [Adam] an help [Eve] meet for him." But the speaker implies that she was not much help after all! The speaker is again endorsing the preference of the garden itself over the woman, just as earlier in the poem. The speaker then argues that Adam just had it too good before Eve was created: no mortal can enjoy such happiness as having both the Garden of Eden ("Paradise") and solitude. This is like having two paradises (Eden and solitude). So, God took one paradise away from Adam when he took away his solitude by giving him Eve as a mate.

The final stanza (9) returns to the concrete physical sense of this particular garden to which the speaker has retreated. The garden has been planted in the shape of a sundial ("this dial new"). The intensity of the sun is moderated by the effects of the trees and plants as its light is filtered through them: it is thus "the milder sun." The references to the sundial and the sun introduce strongly the theme of time, appropriate in connection with the return in this last stanza to the sense of the real world, the fallen world in which every human is indeed doomed to suffer finite life and the power of physical death, our own inheritance from the fall of Adam in the original Garden. Obviously, Marvell puns on "time" in this stanza, playing on the thyme plant, one of the "herbs and flowers" of the garden among which the "industrious bee" works. Cleverly Marvell reminds us of and takes us back to the first stanza and the idea of man's "incessant labors." The bee is indeed now an appropriate symbol for fallen man: it works, labors just as man was doomed to after Adam's fall. The bee computes its thyme, as man computes his time. One optimistic note, however, is the one sounded in the final couplet: if man, like the bee, is condemned to time and labor, then his most valuable existence is also like the bee's—in the garden, where he can at least temporarily recapture the sense of his unfallen state and thus transcend the world of time, labor, sin, and death.

Gelid. *Adjective*: cold, chilly, refreshingly cold.

Genius, genious. Attendant or protective spirit given everyone at birth to govern one's fortune, determine one's character, and conduct one out of the world (from classical, pagan belief). More generally, a guardian spirit of a person or place.

Get. *Verb*: (1) to obtain or receive or acquire or earn; (2) to capture or win; (3) to beget, propagate.

Giddy. *Adjective*: (1) dizzy; (2) whirling rapidly; (3) easily excited, frivolous, inconstant.

Gilby, Colonel Anthony. Royalist Member of Parliament representing Hull, along with Marvell, for a time. He had been imprisoned and had served as a spy for the Royalist cause. In a letter of June 1, 1661, Marvell speaks of serious differences between the two. In later letters Marvell praises him highly after their quarrel apparently had been resolved. Marvell refers to him numerous times in his letters.

Gill, Alexander (1565–1635). High Master of St. Paul's School.

Glass, glasses. *Noun*: (1) substance made by fusing sand and used for windows, vessels, and containers; (2) a mirror ("looking glass"); (3) hourglass; (4) microscope (e.g., Marvell's "multiplying glasses" in line 462 of "UPON APPLETON HOUSE"); (5) containers used by alchemists ("chemists")—see ALCHEMY and PARACELSUS.

Go. *Verb*: (1) to move or travel; (2) to walk; (3) to be in a certain condition habitually; (4) to pass or happen; (5) to issue or result; (6) to depart, move away, leave; (7) to turn [to] or be transformed [into]; (8) to die.

Godfrey, Sir Edmund (1621–1678). Justice of the Peace for Westminster.

Goth. *Noun*: any individual of a Germanic tribe that overran the Roman Empire in its latter stages and destroyed many marks of its civilization, art, culture, and history. The word variously connotes anyone or anything barbaric, rude, uncivilized, lacking culture or taste, ignorant, passionate, violent, or destructive. Usually associated with VANDAL.

Greedy. *Adjective*: (1) excessively longing for food or drink, (2) excessively longing for wealth or material possessions, (3) excessively longing or desiring in general.

A Marvell Dictionary   G   81

Greville, Fulke, Lord Brooke (1554–1628). Courtier and poet. FLECKNOE wrote verses complimentary of Brooke's works, and Marvell satirically refers to Flecknoe as deriving himself from Lord Brooke: see line 4 of "Flecknoe, an English Priest at Rome."

Grudge. *Verb*: (1) to complain, to grumble; (2) to be unwilling to give or allow, to begrudge; (3) to envy; (4) to trouble mentally.

Guilford, Earl of. See MAITLAND, JOHN.

Gules. The color red in heraldry.

Gwyn(n), Nell (Eleanor, Ellen) (1650–1687). Actress and one of the mistresses of CHARLES II. Was maintained at lavish expense by the King. Her first son by Charles was Charles Beauclerk, born in 1670. King Charles made him Earl of Burford in 1676 and Duke of St. Albans in 1684. A second son, James, was born in 1671. In 1681 both Nell and another mistress, the Roman Catholic Duchess of Portsmouth (see KEROUALLE, LOUISE RENEE DE) were at Oxford. It is told that the popular Nell was mistaken by the people for the unpopular Duchess, and they attempted to mob her. Nell put her head out the window and said, "Pray, good people, be civil; I am the Protestant whore." Charles's dying request to his brother (see JAMES II) was "Let not poor Nelly starve." James II paid her debts and granted her some sums of money and land. She was buried in St. Martin-in-the-Fields Church.

    In his letters Marvell refers to Nell Gwynn as "Nell" and "Nelly." He comments on money given annually to her children by the King and groups her with Rochester (see JOHN WILMOT) and others as part of "the merry gang."

H

Halcyon. *Noun*: the kingfisher, a crested, brilliantly colored bird supposed to be able to calm the sea.

Hales, John (1584–1656). Took B.A. at Oxford in 1603. Took M.A. in 1609. Was ordained. Lecturer in Greek. Admitted fellow of Eton. Watched the proceedings of the synod at Dort in which the five points of CALVINISM were formulated. Was influenced by the arguments concerning ARMINIUS enough to modify some of his own Calvinistic beliefs. Wrote *Tract Concerning Schisme and Schismatiques*. Was made one of LAUD's chaplains. Made a Canon of Windsor. Under Parliamentary rule he was dispossessed of these positions. He then served as a tutor. Was respected by people of differing factions for his great learning and reading, as well as his tolerant attitudes. He was also known for his charity and sense of humor.

When Marvell was living at Eton while a tutor to WILLIAM DUTTON, he became acquainted with Hales and visited him. He admired Hales's *Tract Concerning Schisme and Schismatiques* and copied a section of it into *The Rehearsal Transprosed*. Marvell refers to him in this work as a "most learned divine, and one of the Church of England, and most remarkable for his sufferings in the late times, and his Christian patience under them." He also calls him "one of the clearest heads and best-prepared breasts in Christendom."

Halt. *Verb*: (1) to limp, (2) to proceed with uncertainty, (3) to stop or pause.

Hampton (Court). Royal palace. CHARLES I escaped from here and went to CARISBROOKE CASTLE on the Isle of Wight in 1647. See also ASHBURNHAM, JOHN.

Harley, Sir Edward (1624–1700). Served in the Parliamentary army in the civil war. Opposed many of OLIVER CROMWELL's actions, however, and was made one of the Council of State in the restored Parliament of 1659. Met CHARLES II at Dover upon his Restoration. Appointed Governor of Dunkirk. Sat in all of the parliaments under Charles II. Opposed all acts for persecuting NONCONFORMISTs.

Marvell wrote several of his letters to Harley.

Harmless. *Adjective*: (1) free from guilt, innocent; (2) causing no harm, inoffensive; (3) free from harm, unhurt.

Hastings, Henry (1630–1649). Henry, Lord Hastings, was the oldest son of Ferdinando, Earl of Huntingdon. He died of smallpox at the age of 19 (in June 1649). Marvell's "Upon the Death of Lord Hastings" was published in *Lachrymae Musarum* (1649), a collection of funeral elegies for Hastings.

Heavenly hierarchy. See HIERARCHY, THE HEAVENLY.

Heliades. In mythology, the daughters of the sun god Helios (or Phoebus). After the death of their brother PHAETON, they grieved extremely and were transformed into poplar trees, with their tears becoming drops of amber from the bark of these trees.

Herb John. St. John's wort. The phrase proverbially designates something indifferent.

Herbert, George (1593–1633). Son of Magdalen Herbert and brother of Edward Herbert (Lord Herbert of Cherbury). Attended Westminster School. Took B.A. and M.A. degrees at TRINITY COLLEGE, Cambridge. Held post as University Orator at Cambridge from 1620 to 1628. In 1625 Herbert was at his mother's home in Chelsea at the same time that JOHN DONNE was there, during a time of plague in London. He served in Parliament briefly but was ordained as deacon in 1624 and later made canon of Lincoln Cathedral and prebendary of Leighton Bromswold. He married Jane Danvers in 1629, became rector of Bemerton in 1630, and was ordained as priest later in the same year. He served in St. Andrew's Church at Bemerton conscientiously and with a reputation for piety, humility, and charity until his early death from (apparently) tuberculosis.

Since Herbert's mother was an important patroness and close friend of Donne, Herbert likely grew up reading Donne's works. Although Herbert was much younger than Donne, they obviously would see one another at times and would converse. Donne wrote the Latin poem "To Mr. George Herbert" that comments on Donne's adoption of a cross and anchor for Donne's seal, and Herbert responded with Latin verses. Donne's writing is also linked to Herbert's by the fact that Herbert's Latin and Greek poetry to the memory of his mother was published with Donne's commemorative sermon for her (1627). Herbert had indicated, as early as 1610 in two sonnets sent to his mother, that he wished to dedicate his poetic talent to the service of God and to the celebration of God's love, rather than to secular love. This dedication resulted in his major work, a book of Christian poems published (a few months after his death) as *The Temple*. He also wrote a prose work called *The Country Parson* (or *A Priest to the Temple*) that finally was published in 1652. He collected and translated proverbs from other countries that also were published posthumously.

Herbert today is regarded as the most important follower of Donne in poetry, one of the METAPHYSICAL poets, along with Marvell. He does employ many of the characteristics regarded as typical of Donne and the metaphysicals, but his debts to BEN JONSON and the CLASSICAL strain appear strongly in Herbert's work, just as in Marvell's. Fusion of the influences from these two major poets is integral to understanding and appreciating the work of Herbert, Marvell, and others. The balanced mixing of characteristics may be seen in such poems as Herbert's "Virtue" and "The Windows."

Hercules. In mythology, Roman name for Greek hero Heracles. A son of ZEUS. Known for his courage, strength, and destruction of various animals and monsters. As an infant he squeezed two serpents to death. His Twelve Labors included such feats as killing the Nemean lion and the nine-headed Lernean Hydra. Among other weapons and armor, he carried a club of bronze.

Heterogeneous ideas are yoked by violence together. See METAPHYSICAL CONCEIT.

Hewel. *Noun*: green woodpecker.

Hierarchy, the heavenly. The supposed nine ranks or levels or orders of angels, especially as proposed by Dionysius the Areopagite, a Christian Platonist (more strictly, Neoplatonist) in the 5th century. His work *On the Heavenly Hierarchy* designated the highest division to be composed of Seraphs, Cherubs, and Thrones. The second division contains Dominations, Virtues, and Powers. The third has Principalities, Archangels, and Angels. The highest are the most contemplative, and the lowest are the most active. Those in the third division, in fact, mediate between man and the realm of God and the angels by delivering messages to man and carrying out God's bidding. The nine orders are also analogous to the nine SPHEREs, and, in fact, these orders were believed to be the INTELLIGENCES that were assigned to the spheres, enabling the creation of the music of the spheres. Most of the angels that fell with Lucifer were of the Seraphs (Seraphim).

Highgate. Marvell's cottage at Highgate, a village in the London suburbs. Marvell refers to it in his letters. It was demolished in 1869: the site is now part of Waterlow Park. The location of the cottage is indicated by a tablet in the main-road wall of the gardens of Lauderdale House.

His. In many contexts, possessive pronoun for "its."

Hoare, Daniel. One of the mayors of Hull to whom Marvell sent letters reporting government matters, since he was a Member of Parliament for the city.

Holland, Philemon (1552–1637). Master of the free school at Coventry. Known as a translator of works by Livy, Plutarch, Suetonius, Xenophon, and PLINY. Translated Pliny's *Natural History*. Marvell probably read this translation: see "THE MOWER TO THE GLOWWORMS."

Holy-Island. Lindisfarne, an island off the coast of Northumberland, which was the first Celtic Christian establishment in England.

Honest. *Adjective*: (1) honorable, respectable; (2) truthful, fair; (3) chaste, pure.

Honor, honour. *Noun*: (1) high respect or admiration; (2) high reputation; (3) exalted rank or position; (4) title of respect given to a person of rank or quality [i.e., "your honor"]; (5) a source of or cause of high respect; (6) chastity, purity [of a woman]; (7) vagina.

Hooke, Robert (1634–1703). Fellow of the Royal Society. In his *Micrographia* (1665) he drew a louse climbing on a human hair, as viewed through a microscope. Marvell alludes to this drawing in "The Last Instructions to a Painter" when he compares the "new Comptroller" brandishing his "white staff" (symbol of his office) to this louse. The Comptroller was THOMAS CLIFFORD.

Hooker, Richard (1554–1600). Born in Exeter. Took B.A. and M.A. at Corpus Christi College, Oxford. Took holy orders in 1581. Appointed Master of the Temple and entered into controversy with the Puritan lecturer Walter Travers. Hooker began writing *Of the Laws of Ecclesiastical Polity* while Master. He then requested a country benefice and was granted the rectory of Boscombe, Wiltshire. Here he completed half of his massive work. Later he moved to a better living

(Bishopsbourne) near Canterbury and continued his writing. He died there in November 1600, and was buried in the chancel of the church.

Howard, Charles, Earl of Carlisle (1629–1685). Married in 1649. In 1650 he was appointed High Sheriff of Cumberland. Bought Carlisle Castle and became governor of the town. In 1653 he was Member of Parliament for Westmoreland and was appointed a member of the Council of State. Represented Cumberland in Parliament in 1654 and 1656. Captain of the Lord Protector's bodyguard in 1654. After the Restoration he became a privy councillor. Created Earl of Carlisle in 1661. Went on state business to Holland in May 1662, and Marvell accompanied him. Was made Ambassador Extraordinary to Russia, Sweden, and Denmark from July 20, 1663, to December 1664. Marvell accompanied him and served as his secretary on visits to these countries during this period. In 1668 Carlisle was sent as ambassador to Charles XI of Sweden. From 1677 to 1681 he was Governor of Jamaica. Died in 1685 and buried in York Minster with a monument erected for him.

Hull. City in Yorkshire where Marvell probably attended grammar school and which Marvell represented in Parliament from 1659 to the end of his life.

Humber. River in Yorkshire upon which the city of HULL, Marvell's own city, is situated. Marvell's father drowned in this river. Marvell refers to this river in "TO HIS COY MISTRESS."

Humor (humour). *Noun*: (1) any fluid or juice of an animal or plant; (2) one of the four major fluids of the body, according to ancient and medieval physiology (primarily from GALEN): blood, phlegm, choler (red choler), and melancholy (black choler). The predominance of one humor over the others or the proportions in which the humors were mixed in the body were believed to determine a person's COMPLEXION—i.e., physical appearance, personality, and disposition (e.g., a dominance of choler causes anger). The healthy, well-balanced individual supposedly has all humors mixed equally. The four humors correspond to the four ELEMENTs (choler determines a choleric complexion and corresponds to fire with its hot and dry qualities; blood determines a sanguine complexion and corresponds to air with its hot and moist qualities; phlegm determines a phlegmatic complexion and corresponds to water with its cold and moist qualities; melancholy determines a melancholic complexion and corresponds to earth with its cold and dry qualities). To correct imbalance, one would take food or substances of the opposite qualities or decrease the one in excess; (3) the temperament or disposition exemplified by a person as a result of the proportion of the fluid humors within the body; (4) the particular style, tone, or spirit of a piece of writing or other artistic composition; (5) temporary mood or whim; (6) a disposition toward a certain action; (7) odd or quaint trait.

Husbandry. *Noun*: (1) agriculture; (2) cultivation of crops; (3) economy, thriftiness, careful management of resources.

Hyde, Anne, Duchess of York. See JAMES II.

Hyde, Edward, Earl of Clarendon (1609–1674). Took his B.A. at Oxford and became a member of the Middle Temple. Practiced law and was appointed Keeper of the Writs and Rolls of the Common Pleas in 1634. Served in Parliament in 1640 and after. Supported and worked for CHARLES I in his conflict with the Puritans and Parliament. When civil war began, he raised money for the King. Expelled from the House of Commons in 1642. Appointed by Charles to be one of the council charged with the care of the Prince of Wales (the future CHARLES II). Resided in Jersey and later joined the Prince at the Hague. Began his *The History of the Rebellion* during his time in Jersey. Resided later with the Prince in Paris, becoming his most trusted advisor. Hyde was formally declared Lord Chancellor in 1658. Hyde returned to England when the King was restored and took his seat in the Court of Chancery in June 1660. Charles granted him titles of nobility, one of which was Earl of Clarendon. Clarendon's daughter married the Duke of York (see JAMES II). Clarendon's position seemed to be quite firm under Charles II, but Clarendon wished to restore the English constitution to its pre-war state, while Charles was more attracted to the French monarchy as a model. Clarendon also wanted to restore the English Church to its previous position.

Clarendon was held responsible by the public for the bad turn of events in the war with the Dutch. When the Dutch attacked Chatham, a mob cut down trees in front of Clarendon's house and broke his windows. His attempts to restrict Parliamentary power also led to ill feeling. Members of the court, including some of the mistresses of Charles, were increasingly hostile to Clarendon. Charles himself felt that Clarendon's feelings and ideas had grown to be impossible to support and that they prevented smooth working with Parliament. Charles asked his brother James to urge Clarendon to retire. Clarendon refused to do so, and Charles had to call for his surrender of the Great Seal in August 1667. The King then told Parliament that he hoped the dismissal of Clarendon would foster greater confidence between Parliament and himself. Charles also promised never again to employ

Clarendon in public afairs. But this did not satisfy Clarendon's enemies, and they wanted to arraign him for high treason. Faced with this danger (and at the secret urging of Charles), Clarendon left England. Parliament passed an act banishing him, making any return by him high treason. The rest of his life was spent in exile. He completed *The History of the Rebellion* during this time. After his death in France he was buried in Westminster Abbey.

Clarendon's penchant for lavish and magnificent living caused much of the resentment against him by individuals and the public at large. His expensive home built in 1664 fostered general criticism of him and led to Marvell's fullest satire of him: see "Clarendon's Housewarming." Marvell also mentions him at several points in "The Last Instructions to a Painter," including a comment on "Hyde's avarice" (line 129).

Hymeneus. Hymen, god of marriage. Traditionally depicted as clothed in a saffron robe and carrying a torch.

I

Ida. Mountains near Troy where, in mythology, Aeneas (son of ANCHISES) was born. Also known as one of the homes of the MUSEs.

Idalian Grove. A mountain and a city (Idalium) in Cyprus, sacred to Venus.

Ignatius of Loyola (Ignatius Loyola) [1491–1556]. Founder of the Society of Jesus: see JESUITS. Born in Spain to a noble and wealthy family. Served as a soldier. Founded the Society of Jesus in Paris, the members taking vows of poverty, chastity, and obedience. Was canonized by the Roman Catholic Church in 1622, thus becoming St. Ignatius of Loyola. He wrote a volume entitled *Spiritual Exercises*, a book of devotion, meditation, and prayer.

Immure. *Verb*: to confine or enclose.

Impale. *Verb*: (1) to enclose with pales or posts, to fence in; (2) to thrust a pale or stake through.

Impute(d). In a theological sense and according to CALVIN, one may be "imputed" to be righteous or may secure "imputed grace" only as freely attributed and given by Christ to his chosen ones from his store of grace, since no one can gain salvation by good works or merit.

Indifferent. *Adjective*: (1) impartial or unbiased; (2) unconcerned or apathetic; (3) of neutral quality, neither good nor bad; (4) unimportant or immaterial; (5) nonessential. Also see INDIFFERENT THINGS.

Indifferent things. A phrase originating in the late sixteenth century and increasingly common during the seventeenth century to refer to such matters of worship as various ceremonies, clerical vestments, discipline, order, and trappings that are not essential to salvation. Some writers prefer the phrase "things indifferent," and some use both phrases. The PURITANs, especially, wished to rid the English church of what they saw as unnecessary Roman Catholic elements.

Innocent. *Adjective*: (1) harmless, doing no harm; (2) free from moral wrong, sin, or guilt; (3) simple, unsuspecting, without guile, naive.

Intellectual Soul. See TRIPARTITE SOUL.

Intelligence. *Noun*: a specialized sense refers to an angel assigned to move one of the SPHERES, according to the PTOLEMAIC concept of the universe. See also HIERARCHY, THE HEAVENLY.

Isle of Candy. Canvey Island, in the estuary of the Thames River.

J

J. M. See MILTON, JOHN.

J. O. See OWEN, JOHN.

James, Duke of York. See JAMES II.

James I (1566–1625). King of England, 1603–1625. The son of Mary Queen of Scots of the Stuart family, he was James VI of Scotland prior to succeeding his cousin Elizabeth I on the English throne. Well educated and a lover of the arts, James himself wrote on religion, government, witchcraft, and demonology. He commissioned a group of English theologians and scholars to produce a new translation of the Bible that was published in 1611 as the Authorized Version, now more commonly called the "King James Bible." James argued for the divine right of kings and insisted on absolute power and abuse of privilege in some matters that increasingly alienated factions in Parliament. His dependence upon and granting of rewards and power to favorites further alienated many of his subjects. Father of CHARLES I and grandfather of both CHARLES II and JAMES II.

James II (1633–1701). James Stuart, King of England, 1685–1688. Created Duke of York soon after his christening. Brother of CHARLES II. In 1648 he escaped from England (during the captivity of his father CHARLES I and the year before his father's execution). He lived at the Hague with his sister, the Princess of Orange. Subsequently, he lived in Paris, Brussels, and other places. For some periods he served in the French and Spanish armies as a volunteer. In November 1659, James contracted a secret promise of marriage with Anne Hyde, daughter of EDWARD HYDE. He returned to England with his brother and was named Lord High Admiral. His marriage to Anne Hyde occurred in 1660. She thus became Duchess of York. Anne bore eight children, exercised control over the Duke's finances, and supported Sir Peter Lely in his painting. In 1670 Anne became a Roman Catholic, a fact not made public until after her death. She died of breast cancer in 1671.

In the late 1660's James apparently also embraced Catholicism, although not publicly. In late 1672 James refused the Anglican rite of communion and resigned from the Admiralty. In 1673 James married Mary Beatrice, sister of King Louis XIV of France. Opposition to this marriage was loudly proclaimed by the anti-French House of Commons. James refused to be reconverted to the Anglican Church but did permit his daughters to be brought up in the English Church. He also approved of his daughter Mary marrying the Protestant Prince of Orange in 1677. Demands were made for James's removal from public affairs and governmental councils. Finally, he did agree to his brother's order that he absent himself from England, going to the Hague in 1679. However, later in the year he was appointed High Commissioner in Scotland. Through political agreements, James's succession to the throne was assured, and he was again given positions and power. He returned to England in 1682 and succeeded upon Charles's death in 1685. He ruled until driven from England in 1688 by the power of William of Orange.

Marvell devotes lines 49–78 of "The Last Instructions to a Painter" as commentary on James and Anne, Duke and Duchess of York. Here he refers to Anne as "Her Highness" and paints her with a "wide mouth" and large "rump." James is portrayed as having several mistresses of which Anne is jealous. Marvell implies that she might even have poisoned one of them, LADY DENHAM, and had an affair herself with HENRY SIDNEY, Groom of the Bedchamber to the Duke and Master of the Horse to the Duchess.

Janus. Roman god with two faces looking in opposite directions. God of doorways, beginnings and endings, before and after, past and future.

Marvell refers to the door of the temple of Janus (in line 234 of "A Poem upon the Death of His Late Highness The Lord Protector") as "Janus' double gate": when the gate of this temple was closed, it was a promise of peace, but when opened, a signal of battle.

"Janus' double gate." See JANUS.

Jermyn, Henry (1636–1708). Master of the Horse for the Duke of York at the Restoration of CHARLES II. Became one of the lovers of BARBARA VILLIERS, Countess of Castlemaine, a favorite mistress of the King. Was a Roman Catholic. Under JAMES II he was made Lord Dover.

For Marvell's comment on his involvement with the King's mistress, see lines 79–104 of "The Last Instructions to a Painter."

Jesuits. Members of the Society of Jesus, an order founded by IGNATIUS OF LOYOLA in 1533 to support and defend the Roman Catholic Church in the Reformation of the sixteenth century and to spread Roman Catholicism. The aggressive and secret nature of the order led to plots and schemes to undermine Protestant governments and to assassinate Protestant rulers, particularly during the time of Elizabeth I and JAMES I.

Johnson, Samuel. See METAPHYSICAL.

Jones, Frances (1633–1672). Subject of Marvell's "An Epitaph upon Frances Jones," a poem very much in the vein of JONSON's epitaphs. She was the daughter of Katherine Boyle, Lady Ranelagh, who visited MILTON frequently. She is buried in the crypt of St. Martin-in-the-Fields Church, London, with Marvell's verses inscribed. (See Brogan's "Marvell's 'Epitaph on ____' " under "Miscellaneous and More than One Type of Poem" in my "Selected Bibliography" for this discovery of the subject's identity in 1979.)

Jonson, Ben (1572–1637). Dramatist, actor, and poet. Jonson's turbulent life included some time as a soldier, imprisonment, and killing a man in a duel. After many years as a Roman Catholic, Jonson reverted to Anglicanism about 1610, draining the whole cup of wine at communion to signify his embracing of the state religion. Some of his best plays are *The Alchemist* and *Volpone*, satiric comedies. He published his plays, masques, and poetry in a volume of *Works* in 1616, containing his "Epigrams" (including epitaphs on some of his children and friends) and another group of poems in a section entitled "The Forest" (with the poem "To Penshurst" included). Jonson is the primary exemplar of CLASSICAL ideals in Renaissance drama and poetry, both in content and style, and he influenced younger dramatists and poets (the "sons of Ben" and, later, "cavaliers") to follow his examples. King JAMES I granted Jonson a pension for life in 1616. Two years later Jonson spent some time in Scotland with WILLIAM DRUMMOND of Hawthornden, who recorded many of Jonson's comments on himself and others. In 1623 Jonson's tribute to the memory of his friend and fellow dramatist and poet William Shakespeare was published in the opening pages of the *First Folio* (Shakespeare's *Works*, his plays, collected and published seven years after his death). Jonson suffered a paralytic stroke in 1628, with subsequent decline physically and artistically. He is buried in Westminster Abbey.

Some of Jonson's remarks made in his commonplace book *Timber* and some of those reported by Drummond reflect the friendship and respect but also some differences in poetic principles between the CLASSICAL Jonson and the METAPHYSICAL DONNE. Jonson writes denigratingly of a "rough and broken" style, of farfetched metaphors that "hinder to be understood," and of "obscurity." It is, then, interesting that Drummond reports Jonson as saying that Donne, in one poem, wanted to match Sir Edward Herbert in "obscureness" and that Donne's work would not last because of not being "understood." Jonson also told Drummond that "Donne, for not keeping of accent, deserved hanging," the classicist's criticism of the metaphysical's irregular metrics. Ironically, some of the characteristics of these two become fused in such younger and later poets as GEORGE HERBERT, HENRY VAUGHAN, THOMAS CAREW, and Marvell.

In "Tom May's Death" Marvell refers to Jonson as "Ben."

Joseph. In the Old Testament, son of Rachel and Jacob. He was loved by Jacob as his favorite child, and Jacob made Joseph a coat of many colors. Joseph's brothers hated him, and, when he came to them one day, they stripped him of his coat and sold him for twenty pieces of silver to the Ishmeelites to be taken as a slave to Egypt. The brothers then took Joseph's coat and dipped it in the blood of a kid goat they had killed. They took the coat to Jacob, who recognized it as Joseph's and assumed that he had been devoured by a wild animal. Jacob mourned a long time for Joseph. Joseph was sold in Egypt to Potiphar, one of the Pharaoh's officers. Joseph was adept at interpreting dreams and was called on to interpret some that the Pharaoh had. Joseph said that the dreams predicted seven years of plenty followed by seven years of famine in Egypt. He advised the Pharaoh to store grain during the bountiful years to use during the lean years. Joseph was appointed to oversee all of Egypt on behalf of Pharaoh. The years of plenty and famine did occur as Joseph had foreseen. Eventually Joseph was reconciled with his brothers and reunited with his father. During the years of famine Joseph, in exchange for food, bought all the land in Egypt for the Pharaoh, except for the land of the priests, who were already assigned provisions by the Pharaoh. See Genesis 37–50.

Jove. See ZEUS.

Jubal. In the Bible, one of the sons of Lamech and Adah. Genesis 4:21 calls him the "father of all such as handle the harp and organ," and he is thus taken as the inventor of musical instruments. See Marvell's "Music's Empire."

Jupiter. See ZEUS.

K

Keeper. The Lord Keeper of the Great Seal, who also presided over debates in the House of Lords.

Kepler, Johannes (1571–1630). German astronomer. Studied and extended the ideas of COPERNICUS. Corresponded with GALILEO. Developed many of Tycho Brahe's observations more fully. Kepler argued that the planets revolve around the sun in elliptical orbits (thus contradicting the perfect, circular universe hitherto envisioned). Studied the planets, their moons, and comets with a telescope. Discovered some "new stars" in the heavens and published works significantly discrediting the older cosmology of PTOLEMY and developing the NEW PHILOSOPHY.

Keroualle (Queroualle), Louise Renee de (1649–1734). Maid of honor to Henrietta, Duchess of Orleans, sister of CHARLES II. She accompanied the Duchess to England in 1670, and Charles admired her greatly. When the Duchess of Orleans died shortly after her return to France, Louise came to England: Charles had a royal yacht meet her at Calais. She was named maid of honor to Queen Catherine. By 1671 she was Charles's primary mistress. In 1672 she had by the King a son, Charles Lennox, Duke of Richmond. Since she was French and Roman Catholic, she was not popular with the English subjects of Charles. In 1673 she was created Duchess of Portsmouth, as well as given other titles. In 1674 Charles gave her considerable yearly income. She used her influence to keep Charles dependent upon France.

Both she and NELL GWYN, another of Charles's mistresses, were at Oxford during the Parliament of 1681 (see the entry on Nell Gwyn for an anecdote involving the two). The Duchess's influence with Charles, the court, and France continued to be strong, despite her lack of public popularity. She was given a lavish apartment at Whitehall, had very expensive tastes, and reaped large sums of money from Charles to satisfy her greed and extravagance. After the death of Charles she became uneasy about her position and lack of popularity: she lived out her life on her French estate.

Marvell comments on the Duchess in several letters, usually remarking on her being granted great income. She is variously referred to as "Madame Querroual," "the Duchess of Portsmouth," and "the Lady Portsmouth."

Kirke, Mary. See CLORA.

Knots. In some contexts, refers to the Gordian knot. Gordius, King of Phrygia, tied the yoke of a wagon to a pole with an intricate, complex knot. An oracle declared that the person who could untie the knot would rule all of Asia. No one could do so, but Alexander the Great, after failing to untie it, simply cut through it with his sword. "Gordian knot" is commonly used to refer to any complex problem.

Marvell, in line 384 of "The First Anniversary of the Government under His Highness the Lord Protector," refers to OLIVER CROMWELL as one who with "his FALCHION all our knots unties."

Know. *Verb*: (1) to recognize or distinguish; (2) to perceive; (3) to be acquainted with.

L

Lacy, John. Dramatist and actor who played the part of Bays in *The Rehearsal* (see DRYDEN, JOHN).

Lambert, Anthony. One of the mayors of Hull to whom Marvell sent letters reporting government matters, since he was a Member of Parliament for the city.

Lame. *Adjective*: (1) crippled in foot or leg; (2) lacking a part, imperfect, defective; (3) metrically defective (of verse).

Languard. A fort at Harwich that was attacked by the Dutch in 1667.

Late. *Adjective*: (1) occurring after the due or customary time; delayed or deferred in time; (2) recent in date, of recent times.

Lately. *Adverb*: (1) after or beyond the usual or proper time; (2) not long since, within recent times, recently.

Latmos (Latmus). Mountain in Asia Minor where CYNTHIA kissed and loved ENDYMION.

Laud, William (1573–1645). Made Dean of Gloucester Cathedral in 1616 by King JAMES I. After the accession of CHARLES I, Laud held the following positions (among others): Bishop of Bath and Wells (1626), Privy Councillor (1627), Bishop of London (1628), Chancellor of the University of Oxford (1629), and Archbishop of Canterbury (1633). Laud enforced strict uniformity, orthodoxy, tradition, and royal authority in matters of the Church of England, criticizing and punishing deviations that favored PURITANISM and CALVINISM, particularly alienating some factions in the House of Commons rapidly gaining strength before and during the English Civil War. Laud was impeached in 1640 and executed by beheading in 1645.

Lauderdale, Duke of. See MAITLAND, JOHN.

Leap. *Verb*: to crack or burst or explode.

Leave. *Verb*: (1) to cease, stop, abandon, forsake an action, habit, or practice; (2) to depart from a place or person; (3) to cause or allow to remain; (4) to bequeath or transmit to heirs at death.

Leslie, John. Bishop of Orkney who built a palace so strong that it withstood the attacks of OLIVER CROMWELL's armies for a long time.

L'Estrange, Sir Roger (1616–1704). A censor of books for the government. He is referred to as the "L." of "B. and L." in *The Rehearsal Transprosed*.

Letany, litany. A form of prayer in which supplications are made with the clergyman leading and the congregation responding.

Lethe. In Greek mythology, the river in Hades that gives forgetfulness of their past to those departed souls that drink of it.

Levellers. A religious sect that felt that the changes preceding the execution of CHARLES I in 1649 had not proceeded far enough and that the Republic was not an absolute democracy with the egalitarianism they wished to see.

Lime-twig. One means of capturing birds in the Renaissance was to smear bird-lime, a sticky substance made from the sap of the holly plant, on branches (lime-twigs) to catch and hold them.

Loadstone (lodestone). Magnet.

Lot(t). In the Bible, nephew of Abraham who was in Sodom when God sent two angels there appearing as men: God had told Abraham that He would not destroy the city if ten righteous men could be found there. Lot greeted the angels as they approached and invited them to stay as guests in his house. That night some men of the city came to Lot's house and told him to bring out his two guests so that they might "know" them sexually. Lot refused, and the men threatened to break down his door. The two angels pulled Lot back into the house and blinded the men. The angels told Lot to gather his family and leave the city, for they planned to destroy it. The angels warned Lot and his family to flee to the mountain from this city in the plain and not to look back. God rained brimstone and fire upon both Sodom and Gomorrah, the cities of the plain, destroying them and their inhabitants. Lot's wife stopped and looked back as they were fleeing and was turned into a pillar of salt. Lot and his two daughters dwelled in a cave in the mountains. The two daughters decided that, since there were no other men that they could have sexual intercourse with and be impregnated by, they would have Lot drink wine and then lie with him in his drunken state. They both did so and became pregnant. The older daughter bore a son named Moab, and the younger had a son named Benammi (or Ammon). See Genesis 18 and 19.

Lovelace, Richard (1618–1657). Attended Charterhouse School and then Gloucester Hall, Oxford. CHARLES I visited Oxford in 1636 and was so impressed by his charm and humility that he ordered that Lovelace immediately be granted the M.A. degree. He served the King in the wars in Scotland in 1639. In 1642 the House of Commons was so offended by his presentation of the Royalist "Kentish Petition" that he was put into the Gatehouse Prison. He served Charles again in 1643–1646. Parliament again imprisoned him (in Peterhouse Prison) in 1648. His estate was confiscated. In 1649 was published his volume of poems titled *Lucasta*. Marvell's commendatory poem "To his Noble Friend Mr. Richard Lovelace, upon his Poems" was published in this volume. After the execution of Charles I and the collapse of the Royalists, Lovelace fell into poverty and lived obscurely until his death.

Lovelace is regarded as one of the Cavalier poets, influenced by both the CLASSICAL and METAPHYSICAL strains. Marvell probably met him in 1637 when Lovelace was in Cambridge for some months.

Loyola, Ignatius. See IGNATIUS OF LOYOLA.

Lucan (Marcus Annaeus Lucanus) [39–65]. Roman poet. Wrote an epic *On the Civil War*. Served Nero but eventually broke with him and joined a conspiracy against him. Was arrested and forced to commit suicide. Despite his narrative and descriptive strengths, Lucan tends toward an overly rhetorical, bombastic style.

Lucasta. See LOVELACE, RICHARD.

Luther, Martin (1483–1546). Initiated the Protestant Reformation in his native Germany, leading to its later spread throughout Europe. Was an Augustinian monk in the Roman Catholic Church. Wanted to raise questions for debate on papal indulgences by nailing his *Theses* on a church door at Wittenberg in 1517. Eventually he was excommunicated, but he refused to recant. He left his monastic order, married, translated the Bible into German, and published the Augsburg Confession that called for a separate church. Luther's writings and arguments emphasize the doctrine of "justification" (salvation) by faith alone for the individual, lessening the importance of salvation through works, sacraments, priests, indulgences, and other means emphasized in the Roman Catholic Church. To an Augustinian monk like Luther, the writings of ST. AUGUSTINE were crucial in their emphasis on the importance of faith to salvation. Luther also disagreed with the Roman Catholic Church's insistence that there are seven true sacraments: Luther instead emphasized the two that are directly sanctioned by Christ, Holy Baptism and Holy Communion. (Compare and contrast the doctrines of CALVIN and Calvinism.)

Luxury. *Noun*: (1) lechery, lust, lasciviousness; (2) indulgence in what is choice or costly.

M

M., J. See MILTON, JOHN.

Machiavelli, Nicolò (1469–1527). Italian statesman, political thinker, and writer. Went on many diplomatic missions on behalf of Florence. After the Medici gained control of Florence in 1512, Machiavelli was dismissed from government service. His most famous and influential work is *The Prince* (1513), an analysis of the way power is gained and maintained by a strong ruler. In the 16th and 17th centuries Machiavelli's work was interpreted as admiration for tyrannical, deceptive, hypocritical cleverness and grabbing of power by any means, and one who was called "Machiavellian" or a "Machiavel" was seen as a most unscrupulous and realistic military and/or political opportunist who believes that the end justifies the means. This kind of opportunist formed many characters in the plays of Shakespeare, Marlowe, and others.

In 1656 when Marvell was in France with OLIVER CROMWELL's ward (WILLIAM DUTTON), he was referred to in a letter by JAMES SCUDAMORE as "a notable English Italo-Machiavellian." This reflects Scudamore's Royalist scorn for Marvell in his role as a tutor serving Cromwell, the man seen as causing the execution of CHARLES I and ruthlessly grabbing power for himself.

Machiavellian. See MACHIAVELLI, NICOLO.

Macrocosm. The "great world" or "large world," as opposed to the "little world" or MICROCOSM. In most contexts the concept refers to the universe, but in others it may refer to the earth or to any large whole or large world in itself (e.g., society or humanity). See MICROCOSM.

Magazine. *Noun*: arsenal.

Magdalen(e). See MARY MAGDALENE.

Maister, Henry. One of the mayors of Hull to whom Marvell sent letters reporting government matters, since he was a Member of Parliament for the city.

Maitland, John, Duke of Lauderdale (1616–1682). From Scotland. He followed Prince Charles (see CHARLES II) to Worcester in 1651 and was taken prisoner. Held until MONCK's entry into London in March 1660. Close advisor to Charles. Given lodgings in Whitehall. Worked to make the King supreme in church and state in Scotland. Generally worked for a policy of toleration in religion and for the King's power to determine religious policy. Regarded as one of the cabal of 1667 (with CLIFFORD, ARLINGTON, BUCKINGHAM, and ASHLEY). Created Duke of Lauderdale in 1672. Charles continued his trust in Lauderdale over the years. The House of Commons several times urged his removal from offices, but Charles refused. Lauderdale was made Earl of Guilford in 1674. His health began to fail in 1680, and he resigned and lost some of his positions toward the end of his life.

Marvell alludes to Lauderdale somewhat in his poetry but more so in his letters. Marvell refers to him at times as Duke of Lauderdale and at other times as Earl of Guilford.

Malmesbury. Town in Wiltshire known for weaving.

Manna. *Noun*: (1) the miraculous food given by God to the Israelites in the wilderness, according to Exodus 16; (2) spiritual nourishment; (3) a TYPE for Christ and/or the bread of Holy Communion representing Christ's body.

Marvell, Andrew (1621–1678). One of the major METAPHYSICAL poets. Born in Yorkshire and educated at Cambridge. From 1650 to 1652 he served as tutor to Mary Fairfax, daughter of THOMAS FAIRFAX, a general for the parliamentary side in the English Civil War. During this time Marvell probably wrote "THE GARDEN" and other major lyric poems. Was appointed Latin secretary to the Council of State. Later he was elected a Member of Parliament from Hull and served as such until his death. Marvell's influence early in the reign of CHARLES II secured JOHN MILTON's release from prison and probably saved him from execution.

Marvell's use of the METAPHYSICAL CONCEIT, his love of paradox, his sometimes shocking images, and his wordplay qualify him as a metaphysical poet much under the influence of JOHN DONNE and GEORGE HERBERT; however, one must note that the CLASSICAL strain and influences from BEN JONSON are also strongly present in much of Marvell's poetry. The combination of influences can be seen in such a poem as his famous "TO HIS COY MISTRESS." Herbert and Marvell are similar to the extent that they both very much fuse the metaphysical and classical styles. (See the section "Marvell's Life" early in this volume, as well as the entries for METAPHYSICAL and CLASSICAL.)

Marvell, Mary. See MARY PALMER. (Marvell's sister who married EDMUND POPPLE was also named Mary.)

Mary Magdalen(e). A follower of Christ who was healed of demons by Christ (Luke 8:2), is commonly regarded as the repentant sinner or harlot who wept and washed Jesus's feet (Luke 7:37), and was once traditionally identified with Mary of Bethina (Bethany) who was the sister of Martha and Lazarus (Luke 10 and John 11, 12). She was later canonized as a saint. Marvell refers to her in "Eyes and Tears."

Match. *Noun*: (1) opponent, (2) equal or counterpart, (3) contest, (4) pairing, (5) wick used to ignite gunpowder.

Maudlin de la Croix. Abbess of Cordova in the sixteenth century who was reputed to be in league with Satan and could levitate.

May, Thomas (1595–1650). Minor poet, dramatist, and translator. Educated at Cambridge. Originally a supporter of CHARLES I and the Royalists, May transferred allegiance to the Parliamentary cause after he was not named poet laureate following the death of his mentor BEN JONSON.

In his satirical "Tom May's Death" Marvell depicts May being expelled from the Elysian Fields by "Ben," who calls May "most servile wit and mercenary pen."

Mayern(e), Theodore Turquet de. Physician to CHARLES I and prospective father-in-law to HENRY HASTINGS.

Mean. *Adjective*: (1) of low degree, rank, or station; (2) inferior, poor in quality; (3) shabby. *Noun*: a condition, quality, disposition, or course of action that is equally removed from two extremes—i.e., a medium or that which is intermediate. *Verb*: (1) to have in mind as a purpose or intention, to purpose or to design; (2) to aim at, to direct one's way to; (3) to signify.

Measure. *Noun*: (1) size or quantity determined by measuring, (2) an estimate or opinion, (3) that by which anything is computed or estimated, (4) an extent or limit not to be exceeded, (5) proportion or symmetry, (6) moderation, (7) meter in poetry or music. *Verb*: (1) to determine the size or quantity of something, (2) to judge the value of something or someone, (3) to appraise by comparison with something else.

Meat. *Noun*: (1) food in general or nourishment or solid food; (2) the edible part of fruits or nuts, the pulp or kernel distinguished from the peel or shell; (3) the flesh of animals as food.

Meet. *Verb*: (1) to find, (2) to come face to face with, (3) to encounter or oppose in battle, (4) to unite or combine, (5) to agree, (6) to experience or undergo. *Adjective*: appropriate, fitting, suitable.

Melchizedek. In Genesis 14:18 he is called "King of Salem" and "the priest of the most high God." See line 3 of Marvell's "Flecknoe, an English Priest at Rome."

Mesheck. See SHADRACK.

Metaphysical. As used in this "Dictionary," "metaphysical" refers to the particular style and content of the poetry of JOHN DONNE and of those poets influenced by and/or similar to him in the 17th century. "Metaphysical" was first applied to the poetry of Donne by the writer JOHN DRYDEN quite late in the century, after all such poetry had been written: he said (in *A Discourse Concerning the Original and Progress of Satire*, 1693) that Donne "affects the metaphysics, not only in his satires, but in his amorous verses, where nature only should reign; and perplexes the minds of the fair sex with nice speculations of philosophy, when he should engage their hearts, and entertain them with the softnesses of love." He thus ridicules Donne and takes him to task for supposedly dwelling on philosophical speculations about the nature of reality and for pretentiously intellectualizing love, when he should be only emotional and romantic. Apparently taking his cue from Dryden, Dr. Samuel Johnson in the 18th century first called Donne and his followers in poetry the "metaphysical poets." Johnson's comments appear in his life of "Cowley" in his series *The Lives of the Poets* (1779). He describes with great hostility many of the characteristics of such poetry. The irony is that he very well describes the style and techniques of metaphysical poetry, but only to denigrate what many in the 17th and 20th centuries praise quite highly! What Johnson considers "bad," many consider "good" in Donne and his followers.

Johnson's label for Donne and his followers has been retained to the present time, and his comments serve as a way to define much of what metaphysical poetry and the metaphysical style indeed are. Johnson says that the metaphysical poets wrote verses with the "modulation . . . so imperfect that they were only to be found to be verses by counting the syllables." This does point to the use of irregular, distorted metrical patterns in some lines and poems, but in good metaphysical poetry such variation functions to convey specific feelings and meanings and thus is not in itself a flaw in poetry but can indeed be a virtue. Donne's contemporary, BEN JONSON, holding much earlier some of the same CLASSICAL assumptions as the later Dr. Johnson, comments to DRUMMOND that "Donne, for not keeping of accent, deserved hanging," thus also disagreeing with such irregular metrics. Similarly Ben Jonson says that "Donne himself, for not being understood, would perish," and Dr. Johnson complains of the metaphysical poets only wanting to "show their learning": it is a demanding, complex, intellectual poetry that is said to be obscure in thought and syntax at times, but it can be quite rewarding, despite the contrary view of its detractors. Ben Jonson also says (in his commonplace book titled *Timber*) that "metaphors far-fet hinder to be understood," and this perhaps anticipates Dr. Johnson's remark that these poets' "conceits were far-fetched": thus, another characteristic of metaphysical poetry is the use of the METAPHYSICAL CONCEIT (see the entry on it for fuller definition and for further comments by Dr. Johnson about it). Dr. Johnson also notes the use of "hyperbole": exaggeration indeed is a characteristic of the works of Donne and his followers. Another characteristic of much metaphysical poetry is implied by a comment of one of Donne's admirers in the 17th century: THOMAS CAREW notes that Donne exiled the "goodly train of gods and goddesses" from noble poetry—i.e., Donne's work, as well as that of some of his followers, does not rely as much on classical allusions, themes, and forms as earlier Elizabethan and CLASSICAL poems do. T.S. Eliot, an admirer of metaphysical poetry in the 20th century, points out its unified "sensibility," the ability to fuse thought and feeling perfectly (see DISSOCIATION OF SENSIBILITY).

Although oversimplified, a working definition of "metaphysical" might be completed by the following characteristics (added to those six characteristics designated above as being extracted from the comments of Jonson, Johnson, Carew, and Eliot): (1) construction of many poems frequently irregular in style and structure—use of irregular divisions, stanzas, and lines; (2) use of the rhythms and pauses of natural speech; (3) use of informal, colloquial, everyday word choice and tone; (4) conveying a sense of unrestrained emotion in many lines and poems; (5) presentation of the poet and/or speaker primarily in a private, personal role writing to or speaking to a select, limited audience or hearer(s); (6) writing many poems in a deliberately anti-PETRARCHAN, anti-PLATONIC, anti-Spenserian vein; (7) use of much paradox, other forms of irony, and wordplay; (8) reliance on argumentative form and content in many poems. (One should compare and contrast these characteristics with those designated as CLASSICAL.)

The "metaphysical poets" embrace a large number of poets, both secular and religious, in the 17th century. Scholars and critics have achieved no absolute agreement about the specific number, particular individuals, and even which are major and which are minor poets. Certainly four major ones are JOHN DONNE, GEORGE HERBERT, ANDREW MARVELL, and HENRY VAUGHAN. Others that might be included as sharing "metaphysical" characteristics, however, are THOMAS CAREW, Henry King, Richard Crashaw, Thomas Traherne, Abraham Cowley, and perhaps other minor writers. In such a classification, however, one should be alert to how much *both* Donne (the "metaphysical") and Jonson (the "classical") influenced Marvell and other younger and later poets after Donne and Jonson: many combine "metaphysical" and "classical" characteristics in their poems.

Metaphysical conceit. One of the characteristics of METAPHYSICAL poetry is the frequent use of the metaphysical conceit, a lengthy, far-fetched, ingenious analogy developed in detail and relating unexpected or remote areas of experience or knowledge. Such a conceit many times is developed over several lines or over several stanzas or even through an entire poem. In a famous essay (actually in his comments on Abraham Cowley in *The Lives of the Poets*) Samuel Johnson, in the 18th century, refers with hostility to the metaphysical poets using a "combination of dissimilar images" and of their "discovery of occult resemblances in things apparently unlike." He also says that in their poetry "the most heterogeneous ideas are yoked by violence together," that they wasted their intelligence on "false conceits," and that their "conceits were far-fetched." All of these remarks describe the metaphysical conceit; however, in the 17th and 20th centuries many poets and critics admire JOHN DONNE, GEORGE HERBERT, ANDREW MARVELL, and other followers of Donne for their employment of such conceits, valuing precisely what Dr. Johnson denigrates (see, for example, DISSOCIATION OF SENSIBILITY for some of T.S. Eliot's praises).

The most famous metaphysical conceit is the "compass" conceit in "A Valediction: Forbidding Mourning" by Donne. Marvell's poetry employs metaphysical conceits that can best be seen as specified and discussed in the individual entries on poems in this "Dictionary." However, a few excellent examples appear in "THE CORONET," "THE DEFINITION OF LOVE," "THE GARDEN," and "ON A DROP OF DEW."

Microcosm. The "little world," as opposed to the "great world" or MACROCOSM. Writers of the Middle Ages and Renaissance usually employ the concept to refer to man (i.e., the individual human), and they depend upon the ideas of ARISTOTLE in this regard. But the word can in some contexts refer to or imply any kind of smaller world in itself that reflects in little the MACROCOSM: e.g., the state as a microcosm of the universe (the King or Queen like God presiding over all, with various ranks and types of people down the scale of being to the lowest, a structure that reflects the NATURAL ORDER or chain of being).

In its most frequent uses the microcosm or little world is believed to contain within it all of the elements and structural principles that are contained in the MACROCOSM that it reflects: for example, the individual human (the microcosm) was believed to have been created with elements and principles corresponding both to the earth (a MACROCOSM) and to the whole universe (a MACROCOSM). Man is composed, in his physical being, of the four ELEMENTs that make up everything on earth. His blood is analogous to the rivers of the earth, and his hair is like grass. Man's passions are like storms on earth (in Shakespeare's *King Lear*, Lear's raging in the storm illustrates the direct correspondence of microcosm and macrocosm). Man's spirit and intellect correspond to God in the universe. As discussed by writers of the time, the correspondences are seemingly endless.

Middleton, Jane. Known as a court beauty during the time of CHARLES II.

Milton, John (1608–1674). Born in London and educated at St. Paul's School. Took his B.A. and M.A. at Christ's College, Cambridge. Began writing some poetry during his years at Cambridge. Following graduation, he lived in the home of his father while reading and studying to prepare for a vocation as a poet or clergyman. He wrote "Lycidas" in 1637. From 1637 to 1639 he travelled on the continent, especially in Italy. He met GALILEO near Florence.

In the 1640's and 1650's Milton became occupied with political, ecclesiastical, and governmental concerns and duties. From his PURITAN sympathies arose his pamphlets against episcopacy and for furthering the Reformation in England. In 1644 was published *Areopagitica*, his prose work defending freedom of the press. After the execution of CHARLES I in 1649, Milton published *The Tenure of Kings and Magistrates*, arguing that free people could depose and punish tyrants. He also attacked Presbyterians as a new threat to freedom. He was made Latin Secretary to the Council of State. By 1651 Milton was blind. He continued to serve in this position with the aid of assistants.

In 1653 he recommended to the Council that Andrew Marvell be appointed his assistant. Instead, Philip Meadows received the post. (Marvell was made Latin Secretary to John Thurloe in 1657.) Just before CHARLES II was restored, Milton published *The Ready and Easy Way to Establish a Free Commonwealth*, a work defending republicanism and arguing against royalism. With the Restoration, Milton was arrested and fined. Marvell and others are credited with intervening on Milton's behalf to save him from execution and to secure his release. *Paradise Lost, Paradise Regained*, and *Samson Agonistes* were published in the years after his release and before his death of gout in 1674. He was buried in St. Giles Church, Cripplegate.

With the second edition of *Paradise Lost* in 1674 was prefixed Marvell's "ON MR. MILTON'S *PARADISE LOST*." In addition, Marvell defended Milton in *The Rehearsal Transprosed* (Part 2), referring to him by the initials "J. M." Marvell also wrote a letter to Milton in June, 1654.

Mine(s). *Noun*: (1) place(s), excavation(s) in the earth from which metals and minerals are taken; (2) abundant source(s) of something; (3) mineral(s) or ore(s).

Miscellaneous Poems. Folio volume published in 1681, three years after Marvell's death, containing the poems generally recognized as Marvell's best, most popular, and most famous. The volume was printed under rather strange circumstances because it was published by Marvell's former landlady and housekeeper, who claimed to be Marvell's widow. She asserted that she had been secretly married to him, a claim unsupported by evidence. The actual situation and motive seem to be tied to a scheme to aid some bankrupts that had been helped by Marvell: see MARY PALMER. The note "To the Reader" in the volume is signed "Mary Marvell," the name that Mary Palmer assumed. She says the following in the note to the reader: "These are to certify every ingenious reader, that all these poems, as also the other things in this book contained, are printed according to the exact copies of my late dear husband, under his own handwriting, being found since his death among his other papers, witness my hand this 15th day of October, 1680."

Although Mary Palmer's immediate motives are questionable, posterity does owe her great thanks for preserving and putting forth the works that have now established Marvell as a major poet. Discounting a few minor variations in some individual copies of the 1681 volume, there are 39 poems in the book. In this "Dictionary" about one-half of these poems are given separate entries: those so entered are the ones that are most frequently found in anthologies and/or deemed to be Marvell's best, most representative, and most famous. The content of all poems of *Miscellaneous Poems*, however, has been examined for significant elements to make up other entries.

Certain poems seem to fall into logical groupings, either designed by Marvell or interpreted this way by scholars and critics. For example, "THE MOWER AGAINST GARDENS," "DAMON THE MOWER," "THE MOWER TO THE GLOWWORMS," and "THE MOWER'S SONG" make up a conscious sequence formulated by Marvell in which Damon's character and experiences are traced and developed. Critics traditionally refer to these as the "Mower Poems." Other poems relate to these by their treatments of nature and various themes. Critics also commonly speak of the "Cromwell Poems": these specifically concern OLIVER CROMWELL and are "An Horatian Ode upon Cromwell's Return from Ireland," "The First Anniversary of the Government under His Highness The Lord Protector, 1655" and "A Poem upon the Death of His Late Highness the Lord Protector." These are not found placed together or in sequence in the volume itself, but they do make up a legitimate group for critical purposes. Another common critical grouping is that of "A DIALOGUE BETWEEN THE RESOLVED SOUL AND CREATED PLEASURE" and "A DIALOGUE BETWEEN THE SOUL AND BODY": critics refer to the "Dialogue Poems." These, in fact, connect to other poems through their Christian themes and concerns with nature, creation, and the dichotomy in human nature. Other important threads through Marvell's work may be seen by the reader of all of the poems entered in this "Dictionary."

Mistress. *Noun*: (1) a woman who employs, cares for, has authority over others; (2) a woman who is loved and courted by a man—i.e., a sweetheart or a lady love; (3) a concubine or a woman used by a man for sexual pleasure in addition to or in place of a wife; (4) as a title or prefix, a term of respect; (5) a title of courtesy for a married woman; (6) a title of courtesy for an unmarried woman or girl.

Mistress Mopsa. Daughter of Miso in Sir Philip Sidney's *Arcadia*. Tells silly, trivial stories.

Monck, George (1608–1670). Duke of Albemarle. Soldier and officer from 1627 through the civil war, including a stint in Ireland. Loyal to CHARLES I. Taken prisoner by Parliamentary forces in 1644, charged with high treason, and committed to the Tower for two years. Was released to serve Parliamentary government in Ireland as a military officer. When OLIVER CROMWELL invaded Scotland in 1650, he took Monck with him. When Cromwell returned to England in 1651, he left Monck as commander-in-chief in Scotland. Monck returned to England in 1652. He was appointed one of the three generals of the fleet. Took command of the army in Scotland again in 1654. Directed the government of Scotland and became respected and popular. Cromwell retained confidence in Monck and his loyalty to the English government. After the death of Cromwell, Monck became dissatisfied that officers under his command were being removed and changed by commissioners. EDWARD HYDE was informed by others that Monck would be the best means to bring about the restoration of CHARLES II. Charles wrote a letter to Monck appealing to him for help and for the good of the country. He also had Monck approached by both Monck's brother and cousin. After further conflicts with elements of Parliament and the Army, Monck decided for restoring the Stuarts. He advised Charles to go to Breda and to offer a general pardon and indemnity. Charles issued this declaration. He also sent Monck a commission as captain-general, with letters for Parliament. Monck presented the letters on May 1, 1660, and the Restoration was voted on that day.

Charles landed at Dover on May 25. Monck met him with expressions of devotion. Charles embraced and kissed him. The next day, at Canterbury, Monck was knighted, invested with the order of the Garter, and made master of the horse. In July he was granted several titles of nobility, including Duke of Albemarle. He was given a pension and an estate in Essex. He continued to serve the government, especially in the conduct of the navy during the Dutch wars. He was called back to London to help with restoring order after the Great Fire, but he was dispatched again to the war when the Dutch fleet appeared in the Thames. His orders were not executed well by those under him, and the Dutch were able to burn eight ships and to capture the *Royal Charles*, Monck's old flagship. Monck retired permanently in 1668. He died on January 3, 1670, and the King announced that he would bear the cost of a funeral and a monument. However, the funeral was delayed greatly: Marvell wrote in a letter of March 21, 1670, "It is almost three months, and he yet lies in the dark unburied, and no talk of him." The funeral finally was carried out in Westminster Abbey on April 30, 1670. Charles never erected the promised monument, but Monck's son's will was carried out when one was put up in 1720.

Monck's wife was Anne. She became Duchess of Albemarle with the granting of the title of Duke to Monck. She was a strict Presbyterian and was reputed to be plain, a poor housekeeper, and rather greedy. She died shortly after her husband (on January 29, 1670).

Marvell refers to Monck several times in "The Last Instructions to a Painter." He also refers to him numerous times in his letters, usually as "my Lord General" or "the General." Monck also is praised by Marvell in "The Character of Holland" and referred to in "The Loyal Scot."

Monk, George. See MONCK, GEORGE.

Monmouth, Duke of. James Scott. See CHARLES II.

Montagu(e), Richard (1577–1641). Stated as his goal to defend the Church of England from attacks by both Roman Catholics and PURITANs. Wrote controversial tracts. Made Bishop of Norwich in 1638.

Mother Midnight. Proverbial phrase usually meaning a midwife, but it also could refer to a prostitute.

Motley. *Adjective*: (1) of many colors, (2) varied or varying, (3) changeable.

Mottly. See MOTLEY.

Move. *Verb*: (1) to change the position of something or someone; (2) to remove or shift; (3) to stir or disturb; (4) to put or keep in motion; (5) to excite, to stimulate, to stir up emotion or passion or anger; (6) to provoke some action or reaction; (7) to urge, exhort, incite, appeal, or propose.

"Mower Against Gardens, The." One of the works in *MISCELLANEOUS POEMS*. This is the first in the sequence of poems referred to as the "Mower Poems" (also see "DAMON THE MOWER," "THE MOWER TO THE GLOWWORMS," and "THE MOWER'S SONG").

The speaker of the poem is Damon the Mower (we learn his name in the second poem of the series). He is a pastoral figure, using his scythe to cut the fields. He is thus here associated with "nature" and the values of the natural world, in contrast to art, especially in the form of what he sees as artificial and as human perversions of nature.

His focus on human sin is evident from the first couplet, in his condemnation of "man" as "luxurious," meaning "lecherous" or "lustful" (see LUXURY, first meaning). The mower pictures man as causing the fall of both nature and the world, after he himself succumbed to temptation in the Garden of Eden. Now man promotes his own "vice" by seducing the world, causing nature to fall away from its original innocence and purity in the same way as man himself. In line 3 the mower accuses humanity of tempting the flowers and plants away from the pure state in nature (humans "allure" them). In other words, man creates his own artificial, botanical gardens, into which he brings God-created plants and changes them from their natural state. He experiments with plants, uses grafting and budding, and generally develops new types of plants and new colors for them. So, the specific "garden" that this mower is against is a man-created botanical garden in which man plays God (echoing his own fall in the Garden of Eden). Man causes the fall of nature, then, in his own private and perverse Garden of Eden. He creates by this means elements that are unnatural and violations of nature. This is reinforced in lines 5–6 by the image of the man-made garden as "square": this is a shape not occurring naturally and generally associated in the Renaissance with the artificial and unnatural (see also "A DIALOGUE BETWEEN THE SOUL AND BODY" where the Body complains of "architects" who "square and hew" the green trees). Also, this man-made garden, enclosed within walls, is like the fallen world after Adam's fall: enclosed within it is a "dead and standing pool of air," forced to stagnate between walls, rather than to freely and freshly rejuvenate by breezes in open nature. This echoes the fact that Adam ("man") introduced death for all humanity with his own fall in the Garden. Here in his garden man is still projecting this death onto all of nature.

Lines 7–10 further develop the means by which man changes plants through concocting compost and fertilizer. The double blossom resulting from this care appropriately reflects the "double" mind of man himself, the mower sarcastically says. Man's hypocritical, deceptive nature is thus condemned. The comment that the "nutriment did change the kind" conveys the mower's feeling that man toys with the very principles and nature of life.

Lines 11–14 pick up the motif of sexual imagery begun in the first three lines. Man's giving new smells to the roses and new colors to flowers, including the white tulip, is presented as man's teaching plants to be like tempting, seductive women, who put on "perfumes" and "paint" various colors on themselves with cosmetics in order to be sexually attractive. The lechery and vice of man mentioned in the first couplet are seen here in the form of man imposing these characteristics on natural entities such as flowers. Man's corruption is reflected in the fallen, corrupted plants that he now creates.

Lines 15–26 develop the sexual imagery even further and more forcefully: the mower suggests that man is also out to prostitute nature, to be a pimp, a panderer, in order to profit from his own whores, his fallen women, his plants. These ulterior motives now suggest more clearly why the mower refers earlier to man's "double" mind, his deceptiveness and hypocrisy. The first example of man's greed, added to his lust already delineated, is that of selling for exorbitant prices such new varieties as the multicolored tulip (with its "onion root," its bulb). Significantly, one was sold for an amount of money equivalent to the worth of a whole meadow: this places in stark contrast the value of man-perverted nature (the new tulip) and the value of unspoiled nature (the meadow). The mower, obviously, is astounded at warped human values that would prefer the perverted over the pure in nature. Marvell here is thinking of some actual sales of such tulip bulbs in Holland in the 1630's, when amazing sums were paid. The many-colored four o'clock (called the Marvel of Peru) was sought after even at the great expense and time to make voyages to America, to the West Indies where it grew. This is another example, to the mower, of rampant human greed that would go so far as to sell nature. But as bad as this reflection on human nature is, even worse is what the mower complains about next. He calls man "that sovereign thing and proud," reinforcing previous implications of humanity perpetuating its Adamic nature of pride and of appropriating God's nature. Man arranges unnatural unions between plants (in his role as pimp), resulting in "forbidden mixtures" and illegitimate offspring—i.e., plants that do not know their parents: they are "uncertain and adulterate fruit" of these illegitimate, adulterous unions of plants. The mower thus presents the techniques of budding and grafting in scathing terms that further develop the sexual motif established at the beginning of the poem. The plants and, more importantly, "man" are pictured more decadently as the poem progresses.

Lines 27–30 picture the garden as a "SERAGLIO," essentially a harem (with wives and concubines). This continues the motif of plants as objects of sexual pleasure, and the comment that there are also "eunuchs" in this garden makes sexless varieties of plants equivalent to the eunuchs (castrated men) entrusted by the ruler to oversee his harem. Man again goes against nature with his employment of asexual propagation of cherries and other fruits.

Lines 31–40 conclude the poem with a summation of the general attitudes already stated and implied by the mower. All the elements of man's artificial gardens (such as fountains and grottos) are "enforced," unnatural forcings and perversions of natural reality. Humanity has forgotten about the "sweet fields," unspoiled and innocent nature (the realm of the mower). "Nature" as found in the "sweet fields" retains its Edenic nature: in a sense, the plants in their natural state correspond to man before the fall. But humans have divorced themselves from nature by perpetuating their fall. The "fauns and fairies" exemplify the fertility and vitality still present in the natural world, as opposed to man's feeble attempts to create images of them in stone statues in their own artificial gardens. But statues even of mythological nature gods can never approach the excellence of the "Gods themselves" that the mower feels dwell inherently in innocent nature in the realm inhabited by him and all natural creatures ("with us"). To the Renaissance Christian, of course, the "Gods" would suggest the Christian God as the creator of and dweller in nature. And we remember that, in Eden, God conversed familiarly with Adam before his fall. In the background is the important assumption that nature is God-created and that to violate that nature is a rebellion against God (see NATURAL ORDER).

As it turns out, the poem is "against gardens" of a very specific type created out of man's own fallen, sinful nature, and, ironically, the poem is even more "against man," and its condemnations are spiritual, moral, and ethical ones. At this point in the series of four "Mower Poems," the mower, Damon, is removed from and feels superior to "man" presented in this poem. He asserts, by implication, his own harmony with nature in his own innocent and unfallen state. The changes occurring in Damon's state in the other three poems, however, become quite interesting and important in grasping Marvell's attitudes, ones perhaps transcending Damon's own.

"Mower to the Glowworms, The." One of the works in *MISCELLANEOUS POEMS*. This is the third in the sequence of poems referred to as the "Mower Poems" (also see "THE MOWER AGAINST GARDENS," "DAMON THE MOWER," and "THE MOWER'S SONG").

In the previous poem of the sequence the mower's name is revealed to be Damon (see "DAMON THE MOWER"). His passion for Juliana, his own pride, and his divorce from innocent nature are also pictured. In this third poem Damon addresses elements of nature from which he now increasingly feels isolated.

The first stanza addresses the "living lamps" (i.e., the glowworms). They are part of harmonious, interdependent natural order within innocent nature itself. They provide light even in darkness for such night creatures as the bird, the "nightingale." The nightingale is pictured (in a METAPHYSICAL CONCEIT) as an artist-scholar, being able to sit up late, study, meditate, and sing unequalled songs of sorrowful beauty, all because of the light provided by the glowworms. Possibly in the background here is the comment by PLINY that "the young nightingales study and meditate how to sing," as translated by PHILEMON HOLLAND and which Marvell probably read. This interdependent order and natural harmony are the facets of existence now forfeited by Damon. He was once a part of this order. The choice of the "nightingale" is important in that it alludes to the myth of PHILOMELA. The reference to "her" suggests Philomela's plaintive, beautiful songs. Marvell also puns on "matchless," since, in Marvell's time, it not only meant unequalled, but also could mean mateless, being without a sexual mate: this double meaning was present even in medieval lyrics such as the one praising the Virgin Mary that begins, "I sing of a maiden," in which she is praised as being both matchless and mateless through a pun on the Middle English word *makelees*. The song of the deserted, sorrowful bird would indeed have special meaning for the lonely mower, alienated from nature and not paired with Juliana.

Stanza 2 addresses the "country comets," another image for the glowworms. Marvell evokes the traditional association of comets as portents of disasters or dire events, such as foreshadowing war or the death of a ruler. But he evokes this sense only to specify that these "comets" in the natural realm are not sinister in the usual way. The glowworms only shine to predict the fall of the grass as it is harvested for hay. Again Marvell seems to be relying on PLINY who says that the glowworms "never appear before hay is ripe, upon the ground, nor yet after it is cut down." So, they appear when it is mature and just before it is cut, thereby foreshadowing its "fall." This fall of the grass in the world of the fields is normal and not threatening, then. It is innocent and harmonious for the dwellers in that world. But a quite serious undercurrent is present here, nevertheless, in light of the mower's own removal of himself from that harmony in nature. In the previous poem in this sequence of Mower Poems, the Biblical "all flesh is grass" is emphatic and important (see "DAMON THE MOWER"). This innocent "fall" of the grass in unfallen nature is not so innocent in its reflection of Damon's own fallen world and fallen flesh. These comets do portend death for Damon as man, reflecting the coming consequences of mortality tied to man's "fall."

Stanza 3 addresses the glowworms literally, as opposed to the metaphorical addresses as "lamps" and "comets" in the preceding stanzas. Their light is "OFFICIOUS" in its kind service to one such as the mower when he literally loses his way in the countryside at night. But certainly more important is the implication that this mower is "wandering" off the path of his original innocence because he has allowed himself to "stray" after the "foolish fires" of passion, not after the literal will-o'-the-wisps. The "night" he is engulfed in is that of disorder and sin that have come as a result of his straying after Juliana, the holder of the "foolish fires." Damon has fallen, just as Adam. The glowworms cannot help him to find his way out of this darkness, and he is no longer a participant in the unhampered harmony of the natural world.

His own recognition of being beyond the glowworms' help (or that of the ordering power of innocent nature) now is made explicit in stanza 4. Their "lights" are "vain" in the face of his having fallen to Juliana and emotion, away from the "lights" of reason. His own "mind" is now "displaced," literally out of its proper place. He has caused his own loss of his "home," the innocent world of unfallen nature and humanity. He has been expelled from his Eden, just as Adam was. The mower, of course, reflects us: the human condition since the fall is mirrored in Damon's fall. In addition, the last two lines of the poem seem to echo Proverbs 27:8 ("As a bird that wandereth from her nest, so is a man that wandereth from his place").

This poem illustrates well the fusion of the METAPHYSICAL with the CLASSICAL. The metaphysical conceits and wordplay are couched in stanzas that epitomize classical symmetry and polish. The first three stanzas begin with parallel phrases ("Ye living lamps," "Ye country comets," "Ye glowworms"). This sets up a pattern of expectation that the final stanza also will begin with such a phrase, but Marvell deliberately violates the parallel. His technique is a good example of form mirroring content, since the first three stanzas all concentrate on the glowworms and their manifestations of ordered, purposeful nature. However, the fourth stanza concentrates on the disordered, alienated mower. So, the order of the first three stanzas suggests the order associated with unfallen nature, as symbolized by the glowworms depicted in each of these stanzas. The breaking of that order in the fourth stanza suggests the breaking of order by and within the mower (and within fallen humanity).

See my "Selected Bibliography: Mower Poems" for a perceptive explication by Christopher Wortham, one that highlights the implications of wordplay, the Philomela myth, and some of the Biblical and Christian echoes in the poem.

"Mower's Song, The." One of the works in *MISCELLANEOUS POEMS*. This is the fourth (and final) in the sequence of poems referred to as the "Mower Poems" (also see "THE MOWER AGAINST GARDENS," "DAMON THE MOWER," and "THE MOWER TO THE GLOWWORMS").

The beginning of this poem is integrally linked to the end of the preceding one ("THE MOWER TO THE GLOWWORMS") by Damon's reference to his "mind," now fallen, "displaced." He now recognizes explicitly that he himself has fallen away from nature, its innocence, and its promise of life. He acknowledges that his mind was once an exact reflection of all nature outside of himself: his mind as a "SURVEY" depicts it as a written description of nature outside of it. The mind could once see its own "hopes" reflected in the mirror, the "GLASS," of the "greenness" externally in nature. Damon was once a participant in and in harmony with innocent nature, but he sees clearly now that this is no longer true. He is like fallen Adam after the entrance of Eve and passion in the Garden of Eden: "Juliana," of course, is the Eve figure here and in the whole sequence of "Mower" poems. The refrain in the first stanza makes it explicit that just as Damon cuts the grass and makes it fall and die, so does Juliana do the same to his mind and self.

The second stanza depicts even more intensely Damon's recognition of his present divorce from nature: he does with "sorrow pine" (withers away toward death), while "these" (the "meadows" of the first stanza) live and thrive in fertility and luxuriance. The mower is not in harmony with, and is hardly now even a part of, innocent and vibrant nature. Just as Adam fell to pride and passion and introduced death for humanity, so has Damon.

In the third and fourth stanzas we see Damon's (i.e., humanity's) new warped and perverse nature in its fallen state, far unlike external nature of which it was once a part. He illogically calls the meadows "unthankful" for destroying the "fellowship" with him, when, of course, it is Damon himself who has destroyed that fellowship. Nature seems joyous while Damon has fallen and is "trodden" upon. A psychological interpretation might be that Damon is projecting his anger at Juliana onto nature. But more deeply and symbolically, Damon is mankind, angry that the sympathy between himself and nature has been destroyed. He should accept responsibility for his own fall but does not want to. In fact, he self-righteously blames the meadows for lacking compassion and vows "revenge" on nature. He will destroy the flowers and grass of the meadows, make them "fall." Thus, he will reestablish harmony on a lower, fallen plane. The connotations of "ruin" and "fall" in line 22 make explicit the idea that it is actually Adam's, man's fall being reenacted in these poems. Adam's fall affected all of nature, and now Damon vows the same action to cause nature's fall. Ironically, at this point we realize that Damon is quite close to the very men he criticized in "THE MOWER AGAINST GARDENS," since he now is the one attempting to destroy nature itself.

In the final stanza he addresses the meadows as his former "companions," saying that now the grass of the meadows will be the "heraldry" on his tomb. So, the grass is compared to coats of arms and inscribed genealogy on the mower's tomb. His tomb, of course, is the earth itself. He was once living like the thriving grass but is now dead like the cut grass. This emphasis on the mower's inevitable death and burial climaxes the image of his pining away in the second stanza. His own fallen nature is inscribed on this grave. Marvell also cleverly links the end of this poem (the end of the sequence) with the cutting and falling of the grass in both "DAMON THE MOWER" and "THE MOWER TO THE GLOWWORMS" because the image again recalls the Biblical "all flesh is grass." So, the genealogy, in one sense, is from dust and earth to grass to flesh to the mower to humanity to the earth and dust again.

As the culmination of the sequence of four "mower" poems, this one allows us to see the progression through them. From the mower in harmony with nature in the first one, we finally see the loss of his original innocent identity and eventual alienation from nature. His experience parallels Adam's, and thus all of humanity's, in forfeiting innocence through free will in choosing pride and passion. And his lot becomes one of sorrow and mortality.

Mr. B. See BAXTER, RICHARD.

Muse. *Noun*: (1) in Greek mythology, one of the nine goddesses who inspired learning and arts [including poetry and music] who frequently are called on [invoked] by a writer or artist for such inspiration; (2) loosely, a poet's inspiration or talent or particular style.

Music of the spheres. See SPHERE.

"My Lord General." A phrase used by Marvell to refer to GEORGE MONCK.

"My Lord Treasurer." A phrase from Marvell's "The King's Speech" that refers to THOMAS OSBORNE, Earl of Danby.

Myrmidons. In mythology, a warlike race created from ants. Served Achilles. Used in Marvell's time to refer to hired ruffians.

N

Naked Truth, The. See MR. SMIRKE.

Narcissus. In mythology, son of the river god Cephisis and the Naiad Liriope. Echo, a nymph, fell in love with him. But earlier, because of a wrong done to Hera by Echo, Hera had punished Echo with a curse: Echo could not begin a conversation and could only repeat the last words of a speaker. So, Echo could not speak to arouse a response in Narcissus. She grieved for her unreturned love and wasted away to nothing. All that was left was her voice that could only repeat the last words of a speaker. Narcissus remained unresponsive to anyone, wrapped in his own pride and self-love. One day he stopped to drink in a still pool and saw his own reflection. He fell in love with the face he saw there, and then he pined for his unrequited love. Finally he was changed into the flower that bears his name.

Natural order. The common concept of the Middle Ages and Renaissance that God created a perfect, ordered universe in which everything is placed in a particular position with an assigned function or purpose. As long as each entity's position and function are maintained, the universe operates smoothly and harmoniously. But if this God-given order, rank, or hierarchy is disrupted, chaos results and is destructive to each entity and to the whole universe. For example, God is at the top of order in the universe, followed by the ranks of angels, humans, animals, plants, and inanimate things. All elements in the cosmos (SPHERE, plant, sun, moon, etc.) have their specific places and functions that must be adhered to so that natural order is maintained.

The concept was easily extended to any MICROCOSM that reflects this MACROCOSM of the universe. For example, in each nation the proper king or queen is like God in the universe, and all subordinate ranks of people have their proper places and functions, being superior to some and inferior to others; therefore, political and social rebellion against proper authority could be viewed as rebellion against and sin against God, since God seemingly ordained natural order to be followed in every realm. The same reflection of natural order can be seen in the hierarchical structure of the church, family, and any group of humans. Indeed, within man as a MICROCOSM his own constituent elements ideally must adhere to natural order (e.g., controlled by his Godlike soul and reason, rather than the rebellious passions and senses), or chaos within the world or universe of himself will result.

Nelthorpe, Edward. See MARY PALMER.

Neo-Platonic. See PLATONIC.

Nestle. *Verb*: (1) to make a nest, (2) to settle in a nest or comfortable place.

Nettleton, Robert. See ST. GILES-IN-THE-FIELDS CHURCH.

New philosophy. The new science (or cosmology or astronomy) encompassing the theory of COPERNICUS that the earth is not the center of the universe (as the conception of PTOLEMY argued) but that the earth (as well as the rest of the solar system) revolves around the sun. The discoveries of KEPLER, GALILEO, and others verified and extended the arguments of Copernicus and became a part of the "new philosophy." This new science questioned the existence of the layers of ELEMENTs surrounding the earth, as envisioned in the Ptolemaic universe: particularly questioned was the element of fire (asserted as nonexistent especially by Kepler). These astronomers argued for the existence of worlds other than earth in the universe, a proposal that (along with the contentions that earth is not the center and that the universe and solar system are not in perfect circles) raised disturbing questions about whether humanity and earth were indeed formed and placed by God as central in his perfect, harmonious creation. What formerly had been assumed to be a perfect and unchanging universe was now being challenged in many ways.

Nonconformist. In a general sense, refers to one who does not conform to the doctrine or discipline of an established church. More specifically, refers to one who adheres to the doctrine of the Church of England but who refuses to conform to its discipline and practice, especially regarding certain ceremonies. After passage of the Act of Uniformity in 1662 and the ejection from their church livings of members who refused to conform, the term was applied to one who was separated from the Church of England. Also see CONVENTICLES ACT and DISSENTER.

Nun Appleton. See THOMAS FAIRFAX and "UPON APPLETON HOUSE."

Nymph. *Noun*: (1) in mythology, a semi-divine creature inhabiting fountains, rivers, or trees; (2) in Renaissance poetry, simply a beautiful girl or young woman. See also DAPHNE, SYRINX, "THE GARDEN," and "THE NYMPH COMPLAINING FOR THE DEATH OF HER FAWN."

"Nymph Complaining for the Death of Her Fawn, The." One of the works in *MISCELLANEOUS POEMS*. This is a poem conducive to interpretation on many levels. It has been looked at by critics as being everything from only a playful fantasy to a literal story of lost love to a profound and complex allegory on a historical or political or religious level or on all of these levels at once. The speaker throughout is the NYMPH, who speaks in simple, almost childish monosyllables and statements. She bemoans the death of her pet FAWN.

A simple psychological interpretation might examine why the nymph loves the fawn so much, in terms of her relationship to Sylvio, the hunter who gave her the fawn. She perhaps transferred the love she had for Sylvio to the fawn, after the "unconstant Sylvio" deserted her. He was unfaithful ("counterfeit" in line 26 and "beguiled" in line 33). A warning sign about the flippant and fickle Sylvio was missed by the naive nymph (but perceived by the mature reader) when Sylvio is quoted (line 32) as saying that he "Hath taught a fawn to hunt his dear," punning on "dear" as "deer," and it turns out that the nymph meant no more to him than an animal he hunted. Ironically, the wild fawn grew "tame," while Sylvio grew "wild" and left the nymph (line 34). Sylvio had no feeling for the nymph's "smart," here (line 35) meaning "pain." She bitterly says that Sylvio left her "his fawn, but took his heart" (line 36): the nymph is bitterly punning on "heart" as "hart," meaning a male deer. So, after her disappointment in human love, the nymph turns to the fawn for fulfillment in love.

But one might also examine the poem on a more significant level by seeing a possible parallel between the nymph and the fawn. The fawn's experience may reflect the nymph's: the nymph was deceived and symbolically killed by Sylvio, parallel to the actual killing of the fawn by the "wanton troopers" (line 1), the "ungentle men" (line 3). The parallel phrasing "ungentle men" and "unconstant Sylvio" further enforces this implication. Another parallel between the nymph and the fawn is that Sylvio's capturing of and then giving away the fawn foreshadows his own capturing of the nymph with his deceitful vows of love and then giving her up. The nymph attributes guilt to both the troopers and Sylvio. In lines 18–24 she refers to the "guilty hands" of the troopers that can never be cleansed of their sin. The blood imagery in this same passage is the stain of guilt and sin that is contrasted to recurring images of whiteness (for example, in lines 55–62, 73, 81, 90,

120): whiteness is possessed by both the nymph and the fawn and clearly is associated with innocence and purity.

The contrast between innocence and experience, in fact, is another level of meaning found in the poem. The nymph and the fawn both exemplify innocence subjected to experience, especially to destructive and violent experience from the world of men. Since the fawn and nymph are both associated with the natural world, they are proper figures of innocence (and thus are connected with ideas developed in poems such as "THE MOWER AGAINST GARDENS," "DAMON THE MOWER," "THE MOWER TO THE GLOWWORMS," "THE MOWER'S SONG," "THE GARDEN," and others by Marvell). Both Sylvio and the troopers, the hunter and soldiers, are destroyers of nature and innocence. The fawn can be taken, then, as the epitome or principle or essence of innocence, and the nymph partakes of this innocence: one notes that the nymph says that the fawn is whiter than she is (lines 60–61), and she obviously loves the fawn more than anything else. So, the nymph gains knowledge and experience of harsh types in this world (from "false and cruel men" [line 54]), but this gain comes with loss of innocence (symbolized by the death of the fawn). On this level Marvell's poem operates as almost an allegory of every person's progression through life. Not only that, Marvell here, as in many other poems, suggests that this is analogous to the fall in Eden, to the Adam experience. Lines 71–74 refer to the nymph's "garden" with elements of white (innocence and purity) and red (passion, sin, guilt), as in the Garden of Eden. The fawn among the lilies in the spring suggests the equivalent early period in Adam's residence in the Garden and reflects the nymph's own early innocent state.

On the historical, political, and religious levels, many elements of the poem are quite suggestive. The first line, in fact, strongly implies the presence of such levels in the use of "wanton troopers": *troopers* was first used in English in 1640 to designate the soldiers of the Scottish Covenanting Army that invaded England that year to support Presbyterianism. But very soon after that the word was commonly applied to the soldiers of the Parliamentary army in the English civil war: see CHARLES I and CROMWELL, OLIVER. In this kind of reading, the fawn can be perceived as the English Church or as the older order or past way of life in England, doomed to be killed by the revolution in both church and state. The nymph might be taken as England itself, seeing its past way of life being destroyed. A new order that values more violence and ruthlessness is taking over. These symbolic levels can be pursued further to see the fawn, in fact, as CHARLES I. Lines 18–19 might suggest the scene of the beheading of Charles, with the emphasis on the spilling of the "warm life-blood" of the fawn by the "guilty hands" of the "troopers." In fact, there seems to be an interesting parallel to this image in lines 55–56 of "An Horatian Ode upon Cromwell's Return from Ireland": as the scene of the execution of Charles is described, Marvell says, "While round the armed bands / Did clap their bloody hands." This explicit statement in the "Ode" seems strongly to enforce the symbolic reading of the fawn's death in the present poem. In addition, in the "Ode" Charles, in placing his head on the chopping block, is described as calmly bowing his head down "as upon a bed." This seems similar to the nymph's description of the fawn's death in lines 93–94: "O help! O help! I see it faint / And die as calmly as a saint." Charles, then, died a kind of Christlike death and was the symbol of the old order and the old England. Perhaps the fawn's death reflects Charles's and the death of all that he symbolized, with the nymph as England seeing Charles and all he represented taken away. Some critics also argue that the fawn can be taken as Christ and the nymph as the Church, enforced by other Biblical echoes found in the poem, especially from *The Song of Solomon*, in the fawn feeding among the lilies. The poem is indeed a complex one that may function on multiple levels.

O

O., J. See OWEN, JOHN.

Oat(e). *Noun*: oaten straw, pastoral flute.

Officious. *Adjective*: (1) attentive, eager to please; (2) kind; (3) dutiful.

"On a Drop of Dew." One of the works in *MISCELLANEOUS POEMS*. In the 1681 publication a Latin version of this poem (titled "*Ros*," meaning "dew") is included with the English one. The poem depends upon the detailed analogy developed that compares the soul to a drop of dew. This METAPHYSICAL CONCEIT gives evidence of Marvell as a METAPHYSICAL poet. On the other hand, the very careful structure and organization (the first eighteen lines delineating the physical characteristics of the dewdrop in the rose, the next eighteen lines applying this relationship to the soul in the body, and the last four lines concluding the poem with a Biblical analogy) attest to the CLASSICAL affinities of Marvell. This poem can be compared to both "A DIALOGUE BETWEEN THE RESOLVED SOUL AND CREATED PLEASURE" and "A DIALOGUE BETWEEN THE SOUL AND BODY" in that all three poems to an extent concern the conflict between the soul with its spiritual, heavenly values and the body with its physical, worldly values. This poem operates through extended analogy and symbolism, as opposed to the dialogue or debate form of the other two.

In general, the poem's conceit compares the soul to a drop of dew, with detailed points of comparisons and implications. For example, the soul dwells in the body as the dewdrop in the rose, but the dew is not part of the rose any more than the soul is part of the body. The soul attempts to maintain its separate identity just as Marvell pictures the dewdrop doing.

Lines 1–8 focus on the "ORIENT" dew (sparkling, pearl-like, and from the east, the realm of light and sun). The dewdrop does not care for its worldly dwelling place, its "mansion," the rose. It still is pulled toward the sky, its origin, and it remains a globe, refusing to diffuse itself into the rose. As a reflecting drop, it "FRAMES" as best it can, its "native element," the sky, the heavens. It makes itself a mirror in this earthly realm, reflecting the sky above it.

Lines 9–18 note how the drop barely touches the rose, maintaining its separateness from the earthly, the physical, as much as possible. It seems to mourn, even to weep (it is its "own tear"), for the realm it came from, a "SPHERE" of the heavens. The dewdrop illustrates the quivering movement of a drop of water, attesting to Marvell's acute observation of natural phenomena. But Marvell makes this movement suggest fearful trembling, the drop being fearful of becoming impure if it loses its unique separateness, diffuses into the rose, and becomes tainted, impure. It has this state of brief pain on the earth until the "sun" evaporates the dew and it is returned to its heavenly origin.

Lines 19–36 make the extended analogy explicit with ingenious details. The soul is like the dewdrop in the rose: it exists within the "human flower." The soul also remembers its divine, heavenly origin and the realm of "light": the soul avoids the "sweet leaves" and "blossoms green," symbols of attractive worldly elements. Just as the dewdrop remains pure and maintains its unique world of itself in circular, globular form, so does the soul have "pure" and "circling" thoughts while in this world: it reflects the divine realm ("greater heaven") within itself ("heaven less"). It is a MICROCOSM reflecting the MACROCOSM of its origin, just as the dewdrop "frames as it can its native element." So, lines 6–8 are developed and extended to the nature of the soul in lines 23–26. The fact that Marvell develops the rose as a symbol of the body and of the earthly realm in general suggests that he recognizes the beauty and attractiveness of humanity and of natural things of this world. But the soul is seen as of a superior realm and of divine purity. The dewdrop reflects light, and so does the soul. Line 24 pictures the soul "recollecting its own light": this comment reveals to us a touch of the Christian Platonism that Marvell is assuming and employing in this poem. "Recollecting" alludes to the PLATONIC belief in reminiscence or recollection: the soul was thought to recapture knowledge that it had previously known in a former state of existence. Lines 27–32 picture the soul deliberately "excluding" the worldly and, instead, "receiving in the day," avoiding the darkness of the earthly. This is why line 31 designates the worldly as the "dark beneath" and the heavenly as "bright above." The soul touches the body by being linked to it, but it is in the world and not of the world. Marvell makes this portion of the poem (lines 27–32) develop and extend symbolically the comments on the dewdrop earlier in lines 9–14. In lines 33–36 are reflected the implications of lines 15–18: the soul anticipates its eventual ascent back to its divine origin in a way similar to the dewdrop being evaporated out of this earthly realm. Implied here also is an analogy between the literal sun in the sky that evaporates the dew and the Son, Christ, the light of the world, who allows the pure soul to be recalled to its heavenly origin. This seems enforced by the fact that Marvell says in line 17 that the "warm sun" will "pity its [the dewdrop's] pain": this certainly suggests that Christ is the warm Son who shows compassion for the human and allows the pure soul with spiritual integrity in this world an "easy" ascent to heaven.

The Biblical and Christian import is driven home in the concluding four lines, the two couplets punctuating the poem. Marvell alludes to Exodus 16:4–21, which pictures the Israelites with Moses in the wilderness receiving manna after the dew had appeared and evaporated in the morning. Moses told them that this manna "is the bread which the Lord hath given you to eat." Manna commonly was taken as a TYPE of both Christ and of the bread of Holy Communion representing the body of Christ. The passage from Exodus states that "when the sun waxed hot, it [the manna] melted." So, both the dew and the manna distilled from it were dissolved and taken up by the sun. Marvell's final statement reflects this: the soul, like the dew and manna, runs "into the glories of th' almighty sun." But clearly the literal sun of the Old Testament passage becomes much more in relation to the soul: it is the "almighty" Son, with his "glories," to whom the pure soul runs.

"On Mr. Milton's *Paradise Lost*." One of the works in *MISCELLANEOUS POEMS*. It was written for and first published in the second edition of *Paradise Lost* (1674) by JOHN MILTON.

In lines 1–10 Marvell says that he at first had misgivings about Milton's ability to encompass such sacred, vast, and infinite topics in one poem ("In slender Book his vast Design unfold"). Lines 11–16, however, show him won over to Milton's undertaking, but still fearing for its ultimate success in explaining such wide fields of thought. By lines 21–30, though, Marvell is "convinced" of Milton's success in not missing "one thought" that is appropriate and in omitting all "improper" elements.

In lines 17–22 and 45–48 Marvell attacks JOHN DRYDEN, who did not adhere to Milton's use of blank verse for the poem when Dryden adapted Milton's poem in an operatic version called *The State of Innocence and the Fall of Man*. He used rhymed couplets. So, Dryden is the "less skillful hand" who changes the poem into scenes for a play. And it is Dryden who uses "tinkling rhyme" which Marvell pictures as "bells" on a "Pack-Horse": Dryden is like a pack-horse that has to be kept awake by rhyme while trudging along in his labored composition. Dryden is the "Town-Bays." (See the entry on Dryden in this "Dictionary" for more on the antagonistic relationship between Marvell and Dryden.) Marvell goes on to say (lines 49–50) that poets such as Dryden use rhymes as ornaments to create interest in their feeble verses. This ornamentation is like BUSHY POINTS used ordinarily only for fashionably fastening hose: such poets use rhyme to hold up their verse like people ordinarily use fasteners to hold up hose.

Lines 41–44 compare Milton to TIRESIAS: Marvell says that God gave Milton the gift of prophesying, in compensation for his loss of sight, just as ZEUS did for Tiresias.

Lines 51–54 conclude the poem in a witty way. Marvell notes that he also is following the "mode," or fashion, of using rhyme, even in this poem that criticizes its use. So, instead of using the word "praise" to end a line, he has to use the word "commend" (so that it will rhyme with the preceding "offend"). He turns this view of himself, then, as being a lesser poet that is dependent on rhyme, into a compliment for Milton whose "sublime" theme is superbly conveyed by the appropriate verse form that needs not the crutch called "rhyme."

Opposition. See "THE DEFINITION OF LOVE."

Order, idea of. See NATURAL ORDER.

Orient. *Adjective*: (1) associated with the east, (2) pearl-like, (3) sparkling, (4) precious.

Ormus. Ormuz, or Hormuz, an island in the Persian Gulf. It had a famous diamond market and was a center for trade in pearls and other jewels. Known generally as a commercial center of great wealth.

Osborne, Thomas, Earl of Danby (1631–1712). Inherited family estates in Yorkshire upon his father's death in 1647. After the Restoration GEORGE VILLIERS, Duke of Buckingham, brought him to court. Elected Member of Parliament from York in 1665. Aided Buckingham and his friends in their attack on EDWARD HYDE, Earl of Clarendon. Following Buckingham's recommendation in 1668, the post of Treasurership of the Navy was conferred by CHARLES II jointly on Osborne and Thomas Lyttelton. Later Osborne was made sole Treasurer of the Navy. In June 1673, he was made Lord High Treasurer of England and chief minister of Charles. In 1674 he became Earl of Danby. He was a staunch Royalist but also a zealous Protestant who wanted no conciliatory relations with Roman Catholicism. In 1674 Danby ended the Dutch war. In 1677 he supported the wedding between Mary, daughter of the Duke of York (see JAMES II), and William of Orange. Danby did not sanction the bribes Charles II received from Louis XIV as the price for maintaining peace, but he had no choice but to serve the King's wishes in the matter, if he wanted to retain his powerful position. Danby's increasing unpopularity in the eyes of both the public and Parliament led to his resignation of his office of Lord Treasurer in 1679. But Parliament was not satisfied by this action and passed a bill of attainder against Danby. He came back to London, surrendered, and was sent to the Tower, where he remained for almost five years. Under JAMES II the impeachment was annulled, and Danby again sat in the House of Lords. Later he supported William and Mary and was well rewarded by them. He remained active in government until his death at the age of 81.

Marvell refers to Danby in his satirical "The King's Speech," a prose piece of 1675. In the King's voice Danby is referred to as "my Lord Treasurer." Also see CHARING CROSS.

"Our mother of England." Phrase used by Marvell in *Mr. Smirke; or, the Divine in Mode* to refer to the Church of England. See SMIRKE, MR.

Ovid (43 B.C.–A.D. 18). Roman poet whose Latin name is Publius Ovidius Naso and who sometimes is referred to as "Naso." Studied rhetoric, travelled, and eventually decided to be a poet. His most famous and influential works are *Amores*, *Ars amatoria*, and *Metamorphoses*. Ovid is regarded as an entertaining storyteller and writer of amorous and erotic verse. Marvell was influenced by Ovid, as evidenced in characters, tales, and allusions appearing in his own work.

Owen, John (1616–1683). Vice-Chancellor of Oxford under OLIVER CROMWELL. Attended Queen's College, Oxford, taking B.A. and M.A. degrees. PURITAN clergyman. Attended Cromwell as chaplain in Ireland. Appointed as preacher to the Council of State in 1650. Given many offices at Oxford by Cromwell. Served as a preacher during the Restoration. Wrote many prose treatises. Marvell refers to him as "J. O." in *The Rehearsal Transprosed*, defending him from criticism by SAMUEL PARKER.

Oxenbridge, Jane. See DUTTON, WILLIAM.

Oxenbridge, John (1608–1674). See DUTTON, WILLIAM.

P

Page. *Noun*: a boy employed as a servant or attendant.

Palmer, Barbara. See VILLIERS, BARBARA.

Palmer, Mary. Marvell's landlady and housekeeper. In 1677 Marvell sheltered Richard Thompson and Edward Nelthorpe (both of whom Marvell knew through Yorkshire, family, and marital connections) from harsh bankruptcy laws by keeping them in a home rented in the name of Mary Palmer on Great Russell Street. Marvell's *MISCELLANEOUS POEMS* was published in 1681 (three years after Marvell's death), and "To the Reader" is signed by "Mary Marvell," supposedly the wife of Andrew Marvell. This woman actually is Mary Palmer. She was part of an elaborate scheme thought up by the bankrupts concealed by Marvell: they wanted to be able to claim and protect five hundred pounds that had been deposited with a goldsmith (in Marvell's name) by Nelthorpe. (See *MISCELLANEOUS POEMS* for further details.)

Palmer, Roger. Earl of Castlemaine, a Roman Catholic. Husband of BARBARA VILLIERS, who left her husband to become a mistress of CHARLES II. After Barbara left him, Palmer went to the Levant in 1664 with the Venetian admiral Andrea Conaro: Marvell refers to Palmer as "Pilgrim Palmer" in "The Last Instructions to a Painter."

Pan. Greek god of shepherds, flocks, forests, wild life, and fertility. Part man and part goat. Lecherous and playful. He pursued the nymph SYRINX who was transformed into a reed.
   Marvell refers to Pan as the mythological figure (e.g., in "THE GARDEN"). But he also alludes to him as a symbol of Christ, a traditional symbolic use in Renaissance pastoral poetry (e.g., in "Clorinda and Damon").

Panique, Panic. *Adjective*: referring to Pan, the god of Nature, and suggesting something natural or permeating nature.

Paracelsus (1493–1541). Physician whose full name was Philippus Aureolus Theophrastus Bombast von Hohenheim. Marvell was aware of and influenced by some of his ideas and terms concerning ALCHEMY and medicine. Paracelsus attempted to discredit GALEN and the

HUMORS. He saw God as the ultimate alchemist who derived the creation out of chemical processes. Paracelsus also popularized the terms MICROCOSM and MACROCOSM.

In medical treatment, Paracelsus and the chemics (or chemiques) disagreed with the methods of Galen and the GALENISTS. Instead of correcting imbalances of HUMORS with foods of opposite qualities, the chemics tried to purge from the body the essence of the disease by using an antagonistic medicine.

Parker, Samuel (1640–1688). Archdeacon of Canterbury. Took B.A. at Wadham College, Oxford, in 1659 and M.A. at Trinity College in 1663. He cast aside his PURITAN upbringing and became a stalwart of the Church of England. In 1667 became chaplain to Archbishop SHELDON, and in 1670 was made Archdeacon of Canterbury. Wrote much on ecclesiastical and political matters, including attacks on the Puritans and DISSENTERs. Among his books are *A Discourse of Ecclesiastical Policy* (1670), *A Defense and Continuation of the Ecclesiastical Policy* (1671), and *A Preface Showing What Grounds There Are for Fears and Jealousies of Popery*. The *Preface* was prefixed to Bishop JOHN BRAMHALL's *Vindication* in 1672, and this *Preface* by Parker led to Marvell's writing of *The Rehearsal Transprosed*, in which he attacks and satirizes Parker's own attacks on freedom of conscience and his doctrine of intolerance exhibited in his works. Marvell refers to him as "Mr. Bay(e)s" (see BAYS, MR.).

Parnassus. Mountain in Greece that was sacred to the Muses, Apollo, and Dionysius.

Pasiphae. In mythology, wife of Minos, King of Crete. She fell in love with a bull and bore the Minotaur from their sexual union. Minos had Daedalus place the Minotaur in a labyrinth.

Pastoral. A pastoral work of literature strictly is one in which the major characters are shepherds (in Latin "pastor" means "shepherd"). The form, introduced by Theocritus, later accrued from Vergil and others certain conventional elements and ideals that were continued in the Renaissance. The work usually presents the country or non-urban life as ideal, natural, innocent, simple, and peaceful. The corruptions and vices of the city and court are imagined as lacking in the pastoral setting, many times referred to as a "garden" or like the Garden of Eden or Paradise. Shepherds usually are natural musicians playing on their "pipes" or "reeds," like wooden flutes. Many of Marvell's poems use and/or rely upon pastoral elements.

A Marvell Dictionary   P   *131*

Patrick, Simon (1626–1707). Bishop of Ely. Took B.A. and M.A. at Cambridge. Presented the rectory of St. Paul's, Covent Garden, in 1662. Took D.D. degree in 1666. Became a royal chaplain in 1671. Went to Ely in 1691. Wrote numerous ecclesiastical works, including "A Friendly Debate between a Conformist and a Nonconformist" (1669), in which he defended the FIVE MILE ACT.

Paul's. See ST. PAUL'S CATHEDRAL.

Pease, Anne. Mother of Marvell. Died in 1638.

Pelican, The Sad. In line 6 of "Flecknoe, an English Priest at Rome" Marvell pictures The Sad Pelican inn as the lodging place of Flecknoe. He calls it a "subject divine," since the pelican was taken as a symbol of Christ: the pelican was believed to feed its offspring with its own flesh and blood, as Christ sacrificed his own body at the Crucifixion.

Pencil. *Noun*: paintbrush.

Pepys, Samuel (1633–1703). Took B.A. and M.A. degrees at Cambridge. Married in 1655. In 1660 he became secretary to Sir Edward Montague, who took command of the fleet that brought CHARLES II to England. Later that year Pepys became clerk of the acts of the navy and sat on the navy board. In succeeding years he accumulated other positions, but his major work was in the navy office. He worked diligently and reformed abuses. During the Dutch War he supplied the fleet. During the official defense of the navy before Parliament in 1668, Pepys made a speech that many praised as excellent. Proposed impeachments were dropped as a result of the effectiveness of his speech.

Pepys enjoyed the favor and confidence of the Duke of York (see JAMES II) and was recognized as the most important naval official. Pepys kept a diary from 1660 to 1669, quitting his writing of it only from a fear of failing eyesight (a fear that proved unwarranted). In 1672 he was appointed Secretary of the Admiralty. He eventually retired to live primarily at Clapham until his death. His *Diary* was left with his library at Magdalene College, Cambridge.

Marvell refers to Pepys in his letters, especially to Pepys's reporting of the state of the Navy and its supplies.

Pestilence. *Noun*: plague.

Petrarch. See PETRARCHAN.

Petrarchan. Francesco Petrarca (1304–1374), better known as Petrarch, was an Italian poet most famous for his lyrics concerning his love for Laura, either a real or imagined lady. According to Petrarch, she was indeed a real lady who was married. By his account he met her in 1327, and she died in 1348. His lyrics portray his love for her, doomed to lack physical response and fulfillment. Among these lyrics those in the sonnet form give Petrarch his lasting fame and influence.

As an adjective "Petrarchan" can be found in reference to the particular sonnet form that Petrarch used (also called the "Italian") that was introduced into English by Sir Thomas Wyatt, eventually being employed and adapted by later Renaissance poets.

"Petrarchan," however, also refers to the content of these sonnets, particularly to the assumptions about love, women, and the relationship between men and women. The "Petrarchan love convention" is a particular set of literary assumptions, descriptions, and techniques that stem from Petrarch's sonnets to Laura that were continued and developed further by poets up to Marvell's time (especially by Sir Philip Sidney and EDMUND SPENSER). In a poem (or poems) employing this convention, the speaker typically is a man talking to or about the extremely beautiful woman he wishes to win as his love. This "Petrarchan lady" is beautiful, but she also is proud and disdainful. Usually she cruelly rejects the man's overtures to her. The man is her humble subject and worshipper in a kind of idealized and spiritualized love-religion, with the lady as a goddess (or, at least, presented as if on a pedestal above the lowly man). The lady ordinarily is blonde (the ideal) and is described with stereotypical characteristics and comparisons such as cheeks like roses, lips like cherries, teeth like pearls, eyes like suns or stars or crystals, breath like perfume, and hair like fine golden wire. With her goddesslike power, she has the ability to grant the man mercy ("pity") and life (by accepting him) or suffering and death (by rejecting him). She typically will not respond to the man, and this plunges the man into despondency and disillusionment. Despite his tears (like rain) and sighs (like winds), she cruelly rejects him: his passion causes him to "burn" with desire, but her rejection causes him to "freeze." The man sometimes must turn to other concerns and activities (going to war, reading philosophy, writing poetry, etc.) to purge him of his grief and to occupy his mind after this great disappointment in love. Many times the poet will use a "Petrarchan conceit," a lengthy, detailed analogy comparing the love or the lady or the man to something else (e.g., the love relationship to a journey at sea or a declaration of love to a military campaign). Cupid, with his "darts" (arrows), at times is portrayed as helping the lady to tempt, capture, tantalize, and torture her victims.

Marvell writes with full knowledge of the Petrarchan love convention when he alludes to and plays with its elements in some of his own poems.

Pett, Peter (1610–1670). Superintendent of the dockyard at Chatham.

Phaeton (Phaethon). Foolish son of the sun god Phoebus (or Helios). He drove his father's chariot (the chariot of the sun) one day, but he could not guide the horses and almost burned up heaven and earth. ZEUS killed him. He was the brother of the HELIADES, the daughters of Helios.

Phancy. See FANCY.

Phantastik, phantastick. See FANTASTIC.

Philippus Aureolus Theophrastus Bombast von Hohenheim. See PARACELSUS.

Philomela, Philomel, Philomena. In Greek mythology, the daughter of King Pandion of Athens. Sister of Procne, who married Tereus, King of Thrace. Tereus raped Philomela and cut out her tongue so that she could never tell about it. But she wove a tapestry picturing her rape and sent it to Procne. The sisters plotted their revenge on Tereus. They killed his son, cooked the body, and served it as food to Tereus. After they revealed the truth, he took a knife and chased the two sisters. During the pursuit the gods changed all three into birds—Tereus into a hawk, Procne into a nightingale, and Philomela into a swallow. OVID does not specify what birds the sisters became, and other Roman versions confuse the tale by making Philomela the nightingale and Procne the swallow. This latter version is the one traditionally followed in English literature, and Philomela is regarded as the nightingale. The song of the nightingale is seen as plaintively sorrowful, but lovely. See "THE MOWER TO THE GLOWWORMS" for this association.

Philosophy. *Noun*: (1) the love of wisdom; (2) advanced knowledge and study of natural, moral, political, and metaphysical matters; (3) science [natural philosophy]. Also see NEW PHILOSOPHY.

Phlegm. See HUMOR. The dominance of phlegm over the other three humors was believed to cause a person to lack energy and to be lazy, slothful.

Phlegmatic(k). See HUMOR.

Physic, phisick, physicke. *Noun*: (1) medical science, medicine; (2) the medical profession; (3) medical treatment. *Adjective*: medical or medicinal.

Picture. *Noun*: (1) the art of painting, (2) portrait, (3) miniature portrait, (4) mental image or impression of something or someone.

"Picture of Little T. C. in a Prospect of Flowers, The." One of the works in *MISCELLANEOUS POEMS*. With some assurance, "T. C." has been identified as THEOPHILA CORNEWALL, a young girl born in 1644. So, the poet himself, Marvell himself, might be taken as the speaker, if approached from the biographical point of view that he is writing the poem to honor a particular family of his own time that he knows. Of course, Marvell expands the poem into universal and timeless dimensions.

The poem is a "PICTURE" of the little girl painted verbally by Marvell as he sees her in a "prospect," a visible scene, with flowers in the background or painted around the human subject. But the term "PROSPECT" in the title is quite well chosen and has multiple meanings in the poem. The term itself can indicate a picture or sketch. It also can mean simply a visible scene or landscape. But it can indicate a mental survey and an inspection or examination. Marvell's poem becomes all of these. But another important meaning of "prospect" is a mental looking forward, a consideration or regard to something future. Marvell's poem ultimately becomes this kind of "prospect," considering the future of this young girl, in terms of the future of flowers. I would, in fact, suggest that Marvell's picture of T. C. "in a prospect of flowers" is deliberately ambiguous in a most significant way: T. C. is seen "in" a prospect of flowers, with flowers surrounding her, but she also is "in" a prospect of flowers because she is within them, she *is* one of the flowers. In fact, she is the most important flower in the "prospect," and she is the one whose "prospect," whose future status, is uppermost. Her future is projected as if she were a flower herself.

Stanza 1 refers to T. C. as a "NYMPH," primarily meaning a young girl, but a touch of mythological creature also is relevant. She dwells in a life of "simplicity," uncomplicated by the complexity of later maturation and adulthood. She is extremely young, just beginning her "golden days" of youth. She is at one with innocent, unspoiled nature, literally lying in the "green grass." Green is Marvell's favorite color, used frequently in his poems to connote things natural, unspoiled, innocent, fecund, and full of life and imagination. It is, in fact, as if this little girl is in her unfallen state, paralleling Adam in the Garden before his fall. Adam began life with golden days in the greenness of Eden: Marvell seems to suggest that this girl's early life repeats the early history of humanity. Her "FAIR aspect," her beautiful appearance, is powerful enough in itself to tame the inferior beauty of wild nature. The suggestion of her Adamic nature is strongly enforced by Marvell's echo in line 6 of Genesis 2:19–20, in which Adam is pictured as naming the animals and birds, "and whatsoever Adam called every living creature, that was the name thereof." The young girl similarly names the flowers. In her play among the flowers, she imposes her own order and wishes on nature, exemplified by her conversations with the roses to tell them what colors and smells are best in them. Marvell's "only with the roses plays" seems deliberately ambiguous. Does she choose to play only with the roses, her favorites, and not other flowers? Or does she only trifle with them, not handling them more seriously and closely because of the thorns? This ambiguity takes on added importance in stanza 4.

In stanza 2 the girl is called a "darling of the gods," a likely play on the little girl's name, since "Theophila" means "dear to the gods." Marvell then begins a military METAPHYSICAL CONCEIT that extends over two stanzas, with a view of her in the future in a battle with both Cupid ("wanton Love") and men. Her "chaster laws," her insistence on virtuous chastity in the face of the lustful God of Love and the passion of men, will put her at odds with them. She will break Cupid's weapon (his "bow") and tear the flags ("ensigns") of his passionate army. Her severe "command" will triumph. Since her future "prospect" is thus, any man, in the face of such power, would do well to appease her, to make his peace with her.

Marvell, or the speaker of the poem, in stanza 3 follows his own advice and vows to "compound" (come to terms) with her, since the case is as he has described it in the previous stanza. He will make his peace with her "in time," before it is too late. He will "parley" (discuss) with her eyes in order to arrive at terms of peace before she becomes a mature woman who can wound him with her eyes. She will be able to kill with attraction and rejection, like the PETRARCHAN lady. Marvell is continuing the military conceit, of course, and cleverly puns on the word "glancing" in "glancing wheels": suggested are the wheels of a chariot which this goddesslike woman will be driving, dealing blows to men's hearts by hitting them with the wheels. But these "glancing wheels" will literally be the *glances* from her round and powerful eyes. The speaker, by his peace with her, has removed himself from the fray. He will observe her victories occurring in the hot sun and in the heat of men's passions as he himself lies in the cool shade of a contemplative retreat into nature. (It is interesting to compare some facets of "THE GARDEN" here.) But certainly a secondary suggestion here is that the speaker, a mature adult now, might literally be dead and "laid" in his grave when this little girl reaches the apex of her feminine power.

After projecting into the future in the previous two stanzas, Marvell returns to the present in stanza 4 with "Meantime." He says that every "verdant thing" (every green element in nature) is charmed, fascinated by the superior beauty of this little being among them. The speaker tells her to "Reform the errors of the spring": in a sense, she is asked to attempt to impose order and perfection into this world, an attempt that ultimately must be frustrated and impossible to achieve. She may very admirably and naively *think* now, as a child, that she can effect such changes and improvements as giving tulips a sweet smell to correspond to their great beauty to sight, an improvement that nature itself has not made so far. In this world she will find that all things do *not* possess all good characteristics possible to be wished in them. She also may *think* that she can remove thorns from roses, but in the real and fallen world—and especially in the world of her mature adulthood—she will find that pleasure and pain are not easily separated, any more than the petals and thorns of roses. This wish for the rose reminds us of her playing with them in stanza 1 and the ambiguity there. To "disarm" the rose might also suggest a wish to remove the pain of passion in sexual love, to restore love to innocent chastity, as she has been depicted as imposing on men in her future life (stanzas 2 and 3). But the climactic reformation that the speaker clearly relates as an ideal that the girl can never effect is to prolong the age of the violet: clearly, the violet is an image of mortality, of the shortness of life, and of the certainty of change and death for anything in this fallen world, however beautiful and innocent. In the fallen world outside of T. C.'s present Eden, the lack of such ideals of perfection and immortality will be even more apparent. In fact, T. C. will discover human weakness to change this state of the world. Ironically, the older and wiser speaker seems to bring into question now the probability that T. C. will indeed be able to impose her ideal of virtuous chastity on mankind. Marvell deflates our own naive optimism temporarily experienced as we admired the picture of the powerful goddess in stanzas 2 and 3. But she is human, and how likely is it that she will be able to impose chastity, restraint, and lack of procreation on fallen men? Not very. As optimistic as is human striving to impose order, ideals, perfection, and completeness into earthly existence, such a view is ultimately a childlike illusion. And, sadly, T. C. will not be able to bring about this Utopia any more than we have been able to. We admire the attempt, but we recognize that "simplicity" is doomed in the face of life's complexity.

In the final stanza the view of T. C. as not only a part of the "prospect," the scene, of flowers, since she is one herself, but also as a vision of both her own and the human's "prospect," the future result of being only a flower, is explicit. She is a growing "young beauty of the woods" herself, just as a flower growing in the woods. But the harsh voice of reality impinges with the warning that she should only pick the mature flowers and not the "buds," the potential flowers. Otherwise, FLORA, the goddess of flowers, might avenge T. C.'s crime of killing her infants by prematurely bringing about the death of little T. C., herself at the present time only a human bud. If she were to die so young, it would be the death of her future "prospect" with all its hopes of striving for order, ideals, and perfection, whether or not they are possible to achieve. So, Marvell does imply, despite life's sorrows, that there are *hopes* in human attempts both to continue life and to improve it, and these hopes are symbolized by T. C., in all of her sad sweetness.

Pierce, William (1580–1670). Bishop of Bath and Wells.

Pillars, Seth's. See SETH.

Planisphere. See "THE DEFINITION OF LOVE."

Plato (about 427–about 347 B.C.). Greek philosopher. Influenced by Socrates. Established a school (the Academy) in Athens about 387 B.C. and taught there until he died. His most famous and influential works are the dialogues, including the *Symposium*, the *Republic*, the *Timaeus*, and the *Laws*. For some of his and his followers' basic ideas, see PLATONIC.

Platonic, Platonique. In its strict use, referring to the beliefs of PLATO, but, more generally and loosely, to the beliefs and later developments of his philosophy as pursued by followers such as Plotinus (3rd century A.D.) and Dionysius the Areopagite (the philosophy of these followers is more properly called "Neo-Platonic"). Most writers of Marvell's time generally do not make sharp distinctions between the doctrines of Plato himself and those of the Neo-Platonists. (Generally throughout this "Dictionary" the term "Platonic" is used in senses that embrace concepts from both Platonism and Neo-Platonism.)

Plato argues that each physical entity in this world is a mere shadow or imitation of the original or real Idea (or Form) of that kind or class of creature that exists in an external and unchanging realm beyond time and physical space. Since the soul knew these Ideas in its previous state of existence, human reason tries to recollect them. The ultimate Idea is the Idea of the Good. The greatest wisdom of man, as well as the greatest goal for man, is contemplation of and striving toward this Good. The soul and intellect, therefore, are valued as real, while the body and senses are comparatively unreal. From the value placed on the soul, it follows that true beauty is spiritual and that true love is spiritual. Union of spirits, then, is "Platonic love" and is a reality beyond mere physical union of lovers. A lover is severely limited if he or she contemplates only the beauty of a single individual when one should ascend to beauty of the many in physical bodies and then higher to intellectual beauty and then higher to the beauty of the Idea.

    Neo-Platonism suffuses Plato's thought with mystical and/or Christian concepts, effecting a reconciliation of philosophies. Plotinus developed the precise argument that the "Absolute" or "One" (source of all beauty, truth, and goodness) generates everything material and spiritual in the world. Since God is easily identified as the "One," Plotinus's arguments fostered development of more specifically Christian Neo-Platonism by AUGUSTINE, medieval Christian philosophers, and such Renaissance Christian humanists as Castiglione. They saw God at the top of that stair of love ascended by one's soul through the help of reason. The beauty of the body gives only an external hint of the beauty and goodness of the soul within, and that soul in turn reflects its divine origin. In ideal love conventions (expressed most memorably for the writers of the Renaissance in Sir Thomas Hoby's translation of Castiglione's *The Courtier*) the ideal courtier (or lover) resists the temptations of the senses and physical attraction through passion by asserting his reason to overcome passion. His angelic and Godlike reason leads him up the ladder of love to a sense of spiritual beauty in the one woman, in all women, over everything beautiful in the world, and ultimately to a ravishment with heavenly beauty as the soul ascends the ladder into a union with God. See also HIERARCHY, THE HEAVENLY.

    Marvell alludes in "The First Anniversary of the Government under His Highness the Lord Protector" (line 17) to "Platonic years." This phrase refers to the belief (originating in Plato's *Timaeus*) that an estimated period of 26,000 to 36,000 solar years is a Platonic year, the time necessary to complete a cycle by the heavenly bodies, at which time they would return to their original positions and a new cycle would begin. Also see "ON A DROP OF DEW" in which Marvell uses the Platonic doctrine of recollection (or reminiscence) in combination with Christian assumptions about the soul.

Player. *Noun*: an actor or actress.

Pleasure. *Noun*: (1) enjoyment, delight; (2) sensuous, physical enjoyment; (3) sensual, sexual enjoyment; (4) the source of or object that gives enjoyment; (5) wish or will.

Pliny [the Elder] (23–79). Roman historian, encyclopedist, biographer, soldier, and advisor to the Emperors Vespasian and Titus. His reputation rests on his surviving *Natural History*, a compendium that ranges over various fields of ancient science. When Mt. Vesuvius erupted in 79, he went there to help citizens in danger and to observe the event closely. He was killed by smoke at the base of the volcano.

Marvell probably read *Natural History* in the English translation by PHILEMON HOLLAND. See, for example, "THE MOWER TO THE GLOWWORMS."

Pluto. In Greek mythology, god of the underworld, of Hades. He also is called "Hades."

"Poor man's book." Reference in one of Marvell's letters to Herbert Croft, author of *The Naked Truth*. See SMIRKE, MR.

Popple, Edmund. Marvell's brother-in-law, married to his sister Mary. Sheriff in Hull. Acted as Marvell's banker and handled his business affairs. Father of WILLIAM POPPLE. Some of Marvell's letters are written to him.

Popple, William (1638–1708). See EDMUND POPPLE and ST. GILES-IN-THE-FIELDS CHURCH.

Porridge. Term used by DISSENTERs for the Church of England service.

Portsmouth, Duchess of. See KEROUALLE, LOUISE RENEE DE.

Possess. *Verb*: (1) to reside in or occupy; (2) to hold as property, to own; (3) to have [as an attribute or quality]; (4) to seize or take; (5) [of a demon or spirit] to occupy, dominate, and control a body or other entity; (6) to have another person sexually, to have sexual intercourse with.

Pothecare. See APOTHECARY.

Poultney, Sir William. One of the original owners of land granted to Clarendon (see HYDE, EDWARD) in 1664.

Powder. *Noun*: gunpowder.

Practice, practise. *Verb*: (1) to do or perform an action, (2) to do or perform habitually or constantly, (3) to perform repeatedly in order to study or to acquire skill or proficiency in something, (4) to scheme or plot or plan.

Prefer. *Verb*: (1) to advance in status or promote; (2) to offer, present, recommend; (3) to hold one thing or person before others in esteem, to like better.

Prepare. *Verb*: (1) to make ready, set in order, equip; (2) to make ready mentally or spiritually; (3) to study for a lesson or speech or sermon, etc.; (4) to make ready for a journey; (5) to go.

Prerogative. *Noun*: (1) an exclusive right or privilege, (2) precedence or superiority.

Preston's Field. OLIVER CROMWELL defeated the Scots near Preston on August 17, 1648.

Pretend. *Verb*: (1) to profess or claim by right; (2) to declare falsely in order to deceive; (3) to aspire.

Prevent. *Verb*: (1) to anticipate or prepare for; (2) to arrive before, to precede, to outrun; (3) to outdo or surpass; (4) to forestall by precautionary measures; (5) to cut off or preclude someone or something from an action; (6) to stop or hinder; (7) to frustrate or defeat.

Prideaux, John (1578–1650). Bishop of Worcester.

Prime Mover. See FIRST MOVER.

Primrose, James. See WITTY, ROBERT.

Primum Mobile. See FIRST MOVER.

Profane. *Adjective*: (1) secular, common, civil, not sacred; (2) unholy, desecrating something that is holy or sacred; (3) irreverent, blasphemous, impious.

Proserpine. In mythology, wife of PLUTO (or Hades or Dis) and Queen of Hades. Daughter of Demeter, the goddess of grain. Also known as Proserpina or Persephone. She was gathering posies in the vale of Enna and pulled on a beautiful flower. As she did, a hole opened in the ground from which Hades (Pluto) appeared and carried her into his underworld kingdom. While Demeter grieved for her daughter, no crops grew. Later an agreement was made by Hades with Demeter that Proserpine could remain on earth with Demeter for two thirds of the year and with Hades for one third.

Prospect. *Noun*: (1) a visible scene or landscape; (2) a picture or sketch; (3) a mental survey; (4) an inspection or examination; (5) a mental looking forward, a consideration or regard to something future.

Prove. *Verb*: (1) to test or try, (2) to find out or learn, (3) to experience, (4) to establish something as true, (5) to show the existence or reality or validity of something.

Ptolemaic. Referring to Ptolemy and/or his concept of the universe. See PTOLEMY.

Ptolemy (Claudius Ptolemaeus). Greek astronomer, mathematician, and geographer in Alexandria, Egypt, during the 2nd century. Formulated (by building on earlier observations) the basic concept of the universe generally known as the "Ptolemaic" view, although many of its ideas were, in the Middle Ages, fused with some from ARISTOTLE. Ptolemy argued that the universe is geocentric—i.e., earth is its center. He argued that the earth itself does not move. The other created entities (moon, sun, planets, and stars) revolve around the earth in concentric, solid, transparent SPHEREs. The FIRST MOVER is the outermost sphere that gives the first motion to all of the spheres and maintains their harmony, resulting in the MUSIC OF THE SPHERES. His view of the universe was accepted from his own century without serious question until the early 16th century when COPERNICUS proposed the heliocentric view. Ptolemy's ideas were increasingly challenged and discredited by other scientists of the NEW PHILOSOPHY. Terms, ideas, and metaphors from the Ptolemaic astronomy are numerous in Marvell's works.

Pure. *Adjective*: (1) not mixed or adulterated with anything else; (2) unsullied, uncorrupted, clean; (3) visually clear, transparent; (4) perfect; (5) genuine, real; (6) free from moral defilement, untainted by evil; (7) chaste, sexually undefiled.

Puritan. *Noun*: (1) a type of Protestant beginning during Queen Elizabeth's reign who wished to "purify" the Church of England by further ridding it of what were regarded as corrupt practices and forms of worship remaining from the Roman Catholic Church, such as some of the hierarchical organization, ceremonies, emphasis on beautiful forms of worship, clerical vestments, etc.; (2) later loosely applied to one who separated from the Church of England for worship [but see NONCONFORMIST]; (3) one who is, or wishes to be seen as, extremely precise and scrupulous in morality, religion, and manners, etc.

Puritanism. The doctrines and practices of the Puritans. See PURITAN.

Q

Quaint. *Adjective*: (1) fastidious; (2) old-fashioned; (3) odd, idiosyncratic; (4) ingenious; (5) elaborate; (6) beautiful or fine or dainty.

Queroualle. See KEROUALLE.

Quetch. *Verb*: to utter a sound.

Quick. *Adjective*: (1) characterized by the presence of life, alive; (2) vivid, lifelike; (3) live, burning [coal]; (4) lively, sprightly; (5) rapid.

R

Rational Soul. See TRIPARTITE SOUL.

Ravish. *Verb*: (1) to seize and carry off with violence, (2) to rape [sexually violate] a woman, (3) to carry away from earth, (4) to carry away [mystically] in spirit and not in body, (5) to fill with ecstasy or delight.

Receipt. *Noun*: (1) a place for the reception of people or things, (2) a chamber, (3) accommodation or provided space.

Remora. *Noun*: a sucking fish believed to be able to stop ships by attaching itself to them.

Remove. *Noun*: the act of changing one's place, departure to another place. *Verb*: (1) to move from out of an occupied place; (2) to withdraw from a place, to go away; (3) to transfer a cause or person for trial from one court of law to another; (4) to dismiss; (5) to dispose of; (6) to take away from.

Repair. *Verb*: (1) to go [to a place], (2) to restore to a sound condition, (3) to furnish or provide with, (4) to replace decayed or damaged parts, (5) to renew or restore by making up for previous decay or loss.

Rest. *Verb*: (1) to take repose by lying down; (2) to take repose by refraining from activity or effort; (3) to take repose by sleeping; (4) to lie in death or the grave; (5) to remain or stay; (6) to stop or cease at a certain point; (7) to be at peace or to have quiet of mind; (8) to be supported by something; (9) to rely upon, trust to, or depend upon something or someone; (10) to remain confident or hopeful; (11) to remain to be done; (12) to reside in or exist in.

Richardson, Christopher. One of the mayors of Hull to whom Marvell sent letters reporting government matters, since he was a Member of Parliament for the city.

Rise. *Verb*: (1) to get up from sitting, lying, resting, sleeping; (2) to recover from sin, from a spiritual fall; (3) to come back from death or the grave, to experience resurrection; (4) to take up arms for battle;

(5) to move above the earth's horizon [said of the sun and other heavenly bodies]; (6) to ascend; (7) to be elated with joy or hope; (8) to appear, spring up, come into existence.

Rivetus, Andreus, Junior. See MR. SMIRKE.

Rochester, Earl of. See WILMOT, JOHN.

Rochet. *Noun*: a clerical vestment made of linen.

Rogers, John. One of the mayors of Hull to whom Marvell sent letters reporting government matters, since he was a Member of Parliament for the city.

Roscius, Quintus (about 134–62 B.C.). Roman actor and friend of CICERO.

Ruyter, Michel Adriaans-Zoon de (1607–1676). Dutch naval officer who served under Admiral Tromp in the first Dutch War (1652–1654). After Tromp's death he became Vice-Admiral of Holland. He had chief command in the second Dutch War (1665–1667). Won some significant victories over the English in 1666. In 1667 he led an expedition up the Thames River, destroying Upnor Castle and burning many English ships. In the third Dutch War (1672–1678) he defeated an English and French fleet at Sole Bay. Wounded in battle and died in 1676.

Marvell wrote "The Last Instructions to a Painter" soon after Ruyter's incursion into the Thames in June 1667. The poem attacks the conduct of the war under Clarendon (see HYDE, EDWARD), and Ruyter is mentioned several times in the poem. Also, his burning of the *Royal Oak* commanded by DOUGLAS is the basis of Marvell's praise of Douglas in "The Loyal Scot."

S

Sable. The color black in heraldry.

Sad. *Adjective*: (1) serious, somber; (2) sorrowful, mournful; (3) steadfast.

Sad Pelican, The. See PELICAN, THE SAD.

St. Augustine. See AUGUSTINE, SAINT.

St. Giles-in-the-Fields Church. The church in London where Marvell is buried beneath the floor in an unmarked grave. There is a memorial tablet that was placed in the church in 1764 by his grand-nephew Robert Nettleton. Apparently the epitaph on it was written in the late seventeenth century by Marvell's favorite nephew, William Popple, one to whom Marvell wrote many of his letters.

St. Paul's Cathedral. Cathedral in London. The building in the early seventeenth century was the fourth one to be built on the site that originally had held a Roman temple dedicated to Diana. This fourth Cathedral was built in the late eleventh century and existed until destroyed by the Great Fire in 1666: it was much larger than the fifth (and present) Cathedral built by Christopher Wren. The older Cathedral burned down when Clarendon House (see HYDE, EDWARD) was almost finished. The stones that had earlier been intended to repair the Cathedral (a plan that had been abandoned) were purchased by Clarendon to build his own house.

Sam(p)son. Son of Manoah of the Danites who was so strong that he killed a lion with his hands. Married a Philistine woman who betrayed Sampson: she talked him into revealing the solution to a riddle he had posed to the Philistines about the lion's carcass with honey in it, and she then told it to her people. After his father-in-law kept Sampson from his wife and gave her to another man, Sampson tied firebrands on the tails of three hundred foxes and let them run through the Philistines' fields of grain, thus burning their crops and vineyards. The Philistines later tried to hold Sampson bound in cords, but he burst them and then killed one thousand of them with the jawbone of an ass. Eventually he loved a woman named Delilah who, for silver offered her by the Philistines, finally had Sampson tell her that the secret of his strength lay in his uncut hair. She took the money from the Philistines and had Sampson shaved while he slept. When he awoke, his strength was gone. The Philistines took him, blinded him, and put him in prison in Gaza. His hair grew while he was imprisoned; therefore, when thousands of Philistines gathered and brought Sampson there in order to mock him, he was able to push apart the two pillars his hands were touching and to destroy the building, the Philistines, and himself. Marvell alludes to this incident in "ON MR. MILTON'S *PARADISE LOST*." See Judges 13–16.

Sanbenitas. *Noun*: black garment that impenitents had to wear when executed by the Inquisition.

Sconce, sconse. *Noun*: a fort or earthwork defense.

Scotch forts. Forts built by OLIVER CROMWELL in Scotland at Ayr, Leith, Perth, and Inverness.

Scott, James, Duke of Monmouth. See CHARLES II.

Scudamore, James (1624–1668). Royalist who refers (in a letter) to Marvell in France in 1656 as the "governor" of WILLIAM DUTTON. He also calls Marvell "a notable English Italo-Machiavellian."

Scutcheon. *Noun*: a shield or shield-shaped surface painted with a coat of arms.

Seal. *Noun*: (1) a design pressed into a piece of wax attached to a letter or other document to attest to its authenticity; (2) a piece of wax bearing the impression of a design or other symbol of authentication on a document; (3) a symbol of a covenant or confirmation, especially in a theological context; (4) the impression of a signet ring on something to claim ownership or to authenticate; (5) an impressed mark as a sign on anything; (6) a piece of wax that holds something closed; (7) a sign or symbol of a high office.

Security. *Noun*: (1) condition of being protected from danger; (2) confidence and freedom from doubt or care; (3) something which makes secure.

Seize. *Verb*: (1) to take hold of, to grasp; (2) [in legal use] to take possession of (property).

Sensibility. See DISSOCIATION OF SENSIBILITY.

Sensible Soul. See TRIPARTITE SOUL.

Sensitive Soul. See TRIPARTITE SOUL.

Sequestration. *Noun*: confiscation of property.

Seraglio. *Noun*: (1) an enclosure, (2) portion of a Mohammedan dwelling or palace reserved for wives and concubines of the ruler—i.e., a harem.

Seth. Third son of Adam and Eve. Eve said that God sent her this son to replace Abel who had been killed by Cain. See Genesis 4:25–26 and 5:3–7.
   In "The Loyal Scot" (line 153) Marvell follows Josephus's comment that Seth's descendants began the study of astronomy and the order of the heavenly bodies and were said to have preserved their discoveries by inscribing them on two pillars (one brick and the other stone). Marvell, however, also here alludes to Seth Ward, Bishop of Salisbury, a persecutor of DISSENTERs.

Severall, sev'rall, several. *Adjective*: (1) separate, distinct; (2) distinctive, particular; (3) various, diverse.

Shadow. *Noun*: (1) darkness caused by a body intercepting the light of the sun or other luminous element, (2) a symbol or prefiguration.

Shadrack. Shadrach, Meshach, and Abednego, the three Jewish men who did not worship the golden image constructed by Nebuchadnezzar, were cast into the fiery furnace as punishment, and were miraculously preserved untouched and unharmed by an angel of God. See Daniel 3.

Shaftesbury, Earl of. See COOPER, ANTHONY ASHLEY.

Sharp. *Adjective*: (1) having a keen cutting edge or fine point; (2) intellectually discerning, perceptive, clever.

Sheldon, Gilbert (1598–1677). Archbishop of Canterbury. Ordained in 1622. Served in various positions as chaplain, vicar, and rector. In 1626 he was elected warden of All Souls' College. Attended CHARLES I from time to time during the civil war. Communicated frequently with EDWARD HYDE and other royalist leaders. At the Restoration of CHARLES II he was made Dean of the Chapel Royal. Elected Bishop of London. Made Archbishop of Canterbury in 1663.

Marvell refers to him sarcastically in "The Last Instructions to a Painter" as "Grave Primate Sheldon." He also refers to him and to the Sheldonian Theater that Sheldon funded at Oxford: in "The Loyal Scot" Marvell ascribes to Sheldon and his followers an "all but masquerade" religion (line 167) and then says, "The conscious prelate therefore did not err, / When for a church he built a theatre" (lines 168–69). Sheldon also employed SAMUEL PARKER as his chaplain: Marvell's *The Rehearsal Transprosed* has Parker as the butt of the satire, and Marvell also alludes in it to Sheldon as the patron of Parker. Sheldon had the reputation of being lascivious: PEPYS calls him a "wencher."

Sheppey Isle. Island at the mouth of the Thames River.

Shires, William. One of the mayors of Hull to whom Marvell sent letters reporting government matters, since he was a Member of Parliament for the city.

Shole, shoal. *Noun*: (1) a large number of persons thronging together or classed together, (2) a crowd.

Shrowd, shroud. *Noun*: (1) protection or temporary shelter; (2) winding sheet for a corpse, a death shroud.

Sibthorpianism. Opinions of Robert Sibthorpe, anti-PURITAN and absolutist vicar of Brackley in the 1620's.

Sibyl. *Noun*: the Cumean Sibyl, a legendary prophetess who aided Aeneas and who sold three books of prophecy to Tarquinius Superbus. She recorded her predictions on dead leaves. Other women of antiquity also were prophetesses at various locations and were called Sibyls, but this particular one apparently is alluded to by Marvell in "UPON APPLETON HOUSE" (line 577).

Sidney, Henry (1641–1704). Groom of the Bedchamber to the Duke of York and Master of the Horse to the Duchess of York. James, because of jealousy, dismissed him. See JAMES II.

Silly, sillie. *Adjective*: (1) happy, lucky; (2) innocent, naive, harmless; (3) pitiable, helpless, defenseless; (4) insignificant, poor; (5) foolish, simple.

Simpson, John. One of the FIFTH MONARCHY men who preached sedition against OLIVER CROMWELL and was imprisoned in 1654.

Sirens. In mythology, sea nymphs who, with enchanting singing, lured sailors to their death on the rocks. CIRCE warned Odysseus of them, so he closed the ears of his sailors with wax and had himself tied to the mast of the ship. When they failed with Odysseus, the sirens killed themselves. They were also referred to as "mermaids."

Smirke, Mr. In Marvell's prose pamphlet *Mr. Smirke; or, the Divine in Mode*, he alludes to a minor character (Mr. Smirke, chaplain to Lady Biggot) in a play titled *The Man of Mode* by George Etherege. In doing so, Marvell is satirically comparing Francis Turner, author of the pamphlet *Animadversions Upon a Late Pamphlet Intituled The Naked Truth*, to this character. Marvell's pamphlet is an answer to Turner's and is a defense of Herbert Croft's *The Naked Truth*. Croft was Bishop of Hereford and wrote on behalf of reconciliation and moderate reform in the church. Turner's pamphlet ridiculed this moderation, and Marvell defends it. Marvell says in his own work that "all sober men cannot but give their assent and consent to it [i.e., to *The Naked Truth*]." Marvell published his pamphlet under the pseudonym "Andreus Rivetus, Junior" in 1676.

Snuff. *Noun*: wick of a candle or portion of the wick that is already burned and blackened and must be removed to again light the candle effectively.

Soul, Feminine. The soul is referred to as feminine in Castiglione's *The Courtier* and in countless other writers of the Renaissance.

Soul(s), Tripartite or Three. See TRIPARTITE SOUL.

Span. *Noun*: (1) distance from the tip of the thumb to the tip of the little finger or from the tip of the thumb to the tip of the forefinger of a fully extended hand: this distance averaging nine inches was used as a measure of length; (2) a very small space or length; (3) a short space of time, frequently referring to the short time of a human's life.

Speed. *Verb*: (1) to succeed or prosper; (2) to attain one's purpose or desire; (3) to make progress; (4) to hasten; (5) to make haste.

Spell. *Verb*: (1) to read letter by letter; (2) to discover by close study or observation; (3) to decipher, comprehend, understand; (4) to contemplate, consider.

Spenser, Edmund (1552?–1599). English poet. Educated at Cambridge. Served in the Earl of Leicester's household in 1579.

Wrote *The Shepherd's Calendar*. Appointed secretary to Lord Grey of Wilton in 1580, serving him in Ireland. Spenser lived in Ireland until very near the end of his life. After he was forced to flee Ireland following an insurrection in 1598, he died the following year in London in near poverty. Robert Devereux, Earl of Essex, paid for his funeral. He was buried in Westminster Abbey, and Lady Anne Clifford erected a monument for him there about twenty years later.

Spenser's masterpiece is *The Faerie Queene*, dedicated to Queen Elizabeth, and portraying her as Gloriana, on one of the many allegorical levels in the long epic poem. Spenser also wrote *Four Hymns*, specifically reflecting the heavy influence from PLATONIC thought on Spenser. Among several other works, also important are his PETRARCHAN sonnet sequence entitled *Amoretti* that concerns his courtship of Elizabeth Boyle and his *Epithalamion* that depicts their marriage. Christian Platonism suffuses all of Spenser's major works.

In "Tom May's Death" Marvell pictures Spenser's (and Chaucer's) "dust" rising from their graves in Westminster Abbey, rising "against thee [May]" and expelling May from a burial place next to them.

Sphere(s). *Noun*: (1) one of the solid, transparent globes in which all of the known planets, the sun, the moon, and the stars are placed, according to the system envisioned largely by PTOLEMY. These Ptolemaic spheres were thought to number either 9, 10, or 11. Some contended that angels or INTELLIGENCEs managed each separate sphere. It was believed that, as the spheres revolved, they created a perfect music known as the music of the spheres. Adam and Eve could hear the music before their fall, but no human after the fall can hear it—i.e., no being stained with sin can hear the music of the spheres. (See also HIERARCHY, THE HEAVENLY); (2) the circular, visible outer limit of space; (3) heaven; (4) domain in which one lives and acts; (5) a round body or ball.

Stay. *Verb*: (1) to stop or halt or stand still; (2) to cease carrying out some activity; (3) to remain in a place, rather than leaving; (4) to remain unmoving in position or unchanging in condition; (5) to tarry, linger, delay; (6) to reside in a place for a time; (7) to wait, to be inactive; (8) to detain or hold back or stop someone or something; (9) to support, sustain, hold up, comfort. *Noun*: (1) a delay; (2) a stop or pause; (3) a cessation; (4) a support.

Stephen's Alley. Street in Westminster where THOMAS MAY lived (see "Tom May's Death"). Known for its many taverns.

Stew(s), stew(es). *Noun*: brothel(s), house(s) of prostitution. So called because of their development from some heated public bathhouses.

Still. *Adverb*: ever or always or continually. *Adjective*: motionless or silent. *Verb*: to quiet or to calm.

Stock(s). *Noun*: (1) trunk of a tree or stem of a plant; (2) a fund, a sum of money; (3) a store, accumulated supply or wealth; (4) [put into the] stocks: instrument of punishment and public ridicule made of a wooden frame with holes into which the ankles (and sometimes the wrists) could be locked.

Stocks-Market. See VINER, SIR ROBERT.

Store. *Noun*: (1) sufficient or abundant supply; (2) a person's accumulated goods or money; (3) a treasure; (4) a stock of anything laid up for future use.

Straight. *Adjective*: (1) not crooked; (2) direct, undeviating; (3) honest, proper. *Adverb*: (1) immediately, without delay; (2) in a direct course, by the shortest way.

Stuart. Family ruling England for most of the seventeenth century. See JAMES I, CHARLES I, CHARLES II, and JAMES II.

Stuart, Charles. See CHARLES I and CHARLES II.

Stuart, James. See JAMES I and JAMES II.

Stupid. *Adjective*: (1) stupefied or stunned, (2) lacking consciousness or thought or feeling.

Sublunary. *Adjective*: below the moon—referring to the realm of the created universe below the SPHERE of the moon, according to the PTOLEMAIC concept of the universe; this area includes the earth and the layers of the other three ELEMENTs (water, air, and fire). Anything in the sublunary realm is associated with the worldly, earthly, and physical, and is subject to time, change, decay, and death.

Subtil, subtile, subtill, subtle, suttle. *Adjective*: (1) impalpable, fine, or delicate; (2) involving discrimination or fine points, abstruse, difficult; (3) clever or sly.

Sudden, suddain. *Adjective*: (1) happening without warning, (2) hasty or rash, (3) prompt or immediate, (4) brief or momentary.

Survey. *Noun*: a written description embodying the result of an examination or inspection of something, such as of a tract of land.

Sylvio. The fickle hunter in "THE NYMPH COMPLAINING FOR THE DEATH OF HER FAWN" who gives the FAWN to the NYMPH and then deceives and leaves her.

Syrinx. In Greek mythology, a NYMPH loved by PAN and, when pursued by him, was transformed into a reed by other nymphs.

T

T. C. See CORNEWALL, THEOPHILA.

Taper. *Noun*: a candle.

Tenarif(e). The high volcanic peak on the island of Tenarife in the Canary Islands (or the island itself).

Tereus. See PHILOMELA.

Thessalian Tempe. The vale of Tempe in Thessaly, regarded as a kind of paradise in ancient times.

Things indifferent. See INDIFFERENT THINGS.

Thompson, Richard. See PALMER, MARY.

Thorndike, Herbert (1598–1672). Clergyman in the Church of England. Holder of fellowship at Trinity College, Cambridge, and writer of various tracts.

Three Books of God. See BOOKS OF GOD.

Three Souls. See TRIPARTITE SOUL.

Thurloe, John (1616–1668). Studied law. In January 1645, he was appointed one of the secretaries to the commissioners of Parliament. In 1652 he was made Secretary to the Council of State. Was known for the very effective spy system he conducted under CROMWELL. After the Restoration of CHARLES II, Thurloe resided in Oxfordshire and at his chambers at Lincoln's Inn. The government still drew on his great knowledge of foreign affairs, even when he was no longer officially in the government.

Marvell was made Latin Secretary to Thurloe in 1657. In this capacity he wrote some of the official correspondence and received and attended some of the foreign envoys in England.

Thwaites, Isabella. Ancestor of THOMAS FAIRFAX. Her marriage to William Fairfax in 1518 resulted in children who were granted Nun

Appleton at the dissolution of the monasteries and nunneries in 1542. See "UPON APPLETON HOUSE."

Tippet. *Noun*: a band of silk worn around the neck by clergymen.

Tiresias. In mythology, the greatest of all prophets. Son of Chariclo, a nymph. He was born a man but became a woman when he happened upon two snakes copulating and then killed the female. Seven years later he came upon another two snakes copulating: he killed the male and became a man again. ZEUS and Hera were arguing one time about whether the male or female received greater enjoyment from sexual intercourse. They called upon Tiresias to settle the argument. Tiresias said that the woman's enjoyment is greater. This angered Hera, who had argued that the man's was. She struck Tiresias blind. Zeus then granted him infallible skill as a prophet.

In "ON MR. MILTON'S *PARADISE LOST*," Marvell compliments Milton by comparing him to Tiresias.

Tiring room. The dressing room of a theater—i.e., (at)tiring.

"To His Coy Mistress." One of the works in *MISCELLANEOUS POEMS*. Marvell's most famous poem and one of his best. It also is one of the greatest, if not *the* greatest, of *carpe diem* poems, those employing the theme of "seize the day," to urge one to live fully while time and life are available in the face of coming age and death. This CLASSICAL theme was renewed especially in the 17th century with particularly influential examples in poems by JONSON and Herrick. The classical theme and some typical classical stylistics, such as octosyllabic couplets, are combined with some quite METAPHYSICAL characteristics, showing also the influence of DONNE on Marvell. It is on the surface a seduction poem, but the intensity of its concerns with time, age, and death makes it far more. Numerous critics have noted that the poem is structured in three verse paragraphs according to a logical, argumentative form, much like a syllogism. It has, in a sense, the first premise in the first verse paragraph, the second premise in the second paragraph, and the conclusion ("Now therefore . . .") in the third.

In the first verse paragraph the speaker allows his wit and imagination to hold forth. He poses the assumption in lines 1–2 that *if* he and the lady he is addressing ("coy" in the title implies the sense of her being modest and reserved, and "MISTRESS" is used in the sense of a lady love or sweetheart who is being courted) had infinite space ("world") and time, then her "coyness," her reluctant modesty, would not be a crime. Of course, lingering in the background here is the fact that they (and no humans) have infinite space and time. In fact, these are two primary limitations imposed on all mortal life, So, the implied feeling on the part of the speaker is that her coyness *is* a crime, although he overtly disregards the fact at this point for the sake of his argument. The speaker addresses her as "Lady," a very polite, formal, courtly tone, typical of some of the poems of JONSON and some of his followers. He imagines how they could live and proceed in their courtship if they had endless world and time. In lines 3–4 he says that they could very leisurely proceed by sitting down and thinking about what to do, without being rushed. Marvell here effectively uses stress variations to convey their slowing down: at least six of the eight syllables in line 3 are heavily stressed and slow the reader's pace, and the last three syllables of line 4 have heavy stresses. In addition, Marvell uses sounds that further slow the reading: five of the words in lines 3–4 begin with *w*, the sound in English that takes longest time to form and pronounce, and the last four syllables of line 4 have words with *o*, also adding length in pronunciation and effectively dragging out the line. The slow-moving lines convey the leisurely pace at which their courtship could be carried on. She could be on one side of the world, in India by the Ganges River, while he could be on the other side of the world, in England on the banks of the Humber River (lines 5–7): the choice of the Humber is a witty self-reference by Marvell, since he came from the city of Hull, in Yorkshire, on the Humber. His primary point is that, *if* they had infinite world and time, their courtship would not be impeded, because eventually they would get together at some future point in time and space. Also (lines 7–10), with their being immortal and possessing infinite time, he would be able to love her before the Old Testament flood, and she could play the PETRARCHAN lady and reject him up to the time that the Jews were believed eventually to be converted to Christianity, before the end of the world and the Last Judgment. In other words, he could court her from the beginning to near the end of all earthly time, confident in the fact that she would eventually yield to him after such a lengthy and elaborate courtship. Their love could linger eons before its eventual fulfillment, then, if time were not a limiting factor. His "vegetable love" would grow slowly but to great vastness (lines 11–12). Marvell seems to be alluding here to the concept of the TRIPARTITE SOUL, in which the vegetative (or "vegetable") soul is common to plants, animals, and humans and is responsible for reproduction, nourishment, and growth. In lines 13–18 the speaker imagines, with great hyperbole, how centuries and eras could be spent adoring and praising each part of the woman. Again, he is confident that finally ("the last age") she will respond, will "show" her "heart." In the final couplet of this first verse paragraph, the speaker again uses the courtly address "Lady" and compliments her highly: he tells her that she "deserves this state"—i.e., her great beauty and value make her worthy of the dignified, ceremonious, and lavish treatment and praise that he would like to provide her over thousands of years, as he has just outlined. And he says that he would not like "to love at lower rate"—i.e., he would like to be able to love her at this slow "rate," slow pace, but obviously he also means "lower rate" to convey the sense that she is of high worth, not to be rated any lower in quality than this lavish treatment would imply that she deserves.

The second verse paragraph shifts to harsh reality, after all of the playful imagining in the first one. Not only is there no infinite "world" and "time" available for this man and woman, but, in fact, there is precious little space and time available for them (or for any human). With the word "But" in line 21, everything turns toward utter seriousness and to the fearful reality of short time and coming death. The speaker personifies Time as the driver of a chariot with wings, and, therefore, Time is a rapid pursuer that the speaker feels is pushing him from behind. And he sees in front of both himself and the lady "vast eternity" like an endless desert, nothingness beyond physical death. This is a frightening image used by the speaker to urge the lady to "seize the day," to love and live fully while life and time are still available to them. He follows this image with a series of others in lines 25–32. The great physical beauty she now has will exist no more in the grave. And in her burial "vault" there will be no "echoing song" of love from the man for this lady to hear. Life, beauty, music, and love are placed in violent contrast to death, decay, silence, and nothingness. Marvell possibly is playing here on "echoing" to suggest the story of the nymph Echo and NARCISSUS, establishing a parallel between himself and Echo, with the lady here being rather like Narcissus. [See my fuller and more specific arguments on this in my "Marvell's 'To His Coy Mistress' and Sandys's Translation of Ovid's *Metamorphoses*," cited in the "Selected Bibliography."] Metaphysical grimness and grotesqueness appear in his assertion that "worms" of the grave will violate her chastity, her virginity, that she has preserved in life. So, the man implies that this woman is being ridiculous in not yielding her virginity to him during life, in light of what will happen to it in the grave. Lines 29–30 ("And your quaint honor turn to dust, / And into ashes all my lust") play on the burial service's committal of the body to the earth ("ashes to ashes, dust to dust"): Marvell makes it lust to ashes and honor to dust. He also seems to be punning and using other wordplay in these lines. "QUAINT" suggests both fastidious and old-fashioned, if not odd, but there also seems to be a play on the Middle English *queynte*, specifically meaning the female genitals. In addition, "honor" in the Renaissance meant not only chastity or purity but also was used in some contexts to mean the vagina. The speaker concludes this grim verse paragraph with a witty, playful, ironic understatement (lines 31-32): he really *knows* that there is no embracing in the private chamber of the grave, but he wants the lady also truly to know it and to act accordingly on this knowledge right now.

The third verse paragraph draws the conclusion to his *carpe diem* argument and indicates what the lady's actions should be. The first two lines of this conclusion (lines 33-34) contain, however, the most famous and highly debated textual crux in Marvell's poetry. The 1681 *MISCELLANEOUS POEMS* has "morning glew" ending line 34. Many editors and scholars have argued that "glew" should be changed to "lew" or "dew" or other words. However, George deF. Lord (see "Works" in the "Selected Bibliography") argues that the 1681 first printing of "glew" should be retained, since it probably is a northern dialectical version of *glow*, with which the Yorkshireman Andrew Marvell would have been familiar. So, it is likely that Marvell is comparing the "hue" of the lady's youthful skin to the glowing of the sky at dawn. I feel that this editorial argument is further supported by a passage from OVID, as translated by George Sandys, in which Echo's skin is described as glowing ("she forth-with glows"). Other phrases in this same passage from Ovid seem in the background when Marvell refers to "instant fires" in line 36. [For fuller and more specific arguments, see my essay (cited earlier) listed in the "Selected Bibliography."] So, the speaker urges the lady in her youthful prime of beauty and vitality to join him and "let us sport us while we may." The *carpe diem* insistence is strong in the phrase "while we may," because they will not always be able to make love, since the grim future of the grave lies in wait. In lines 38-40 the man compares himself and the lady to "amorous birds of prey" who will "our time devour." In other words, he poses the possibility to her that they can live and love so fully and actively that they will use, will eat up, time. So, they will control time (or, at least, seem to do so). At any rate, they will not allow themselves to "languish in his [Time's] slow-chapped power." They will not inertly let Time's slow-moving, steady, powerful, unstopping jaws just grind them away. In lines 41-44 the speaker urges her to join him in rolling up all of their "strength" [his masculine strength] and their "sweetness" [her feminine sweetness] into one unified being, into a "ball." They then will powerfully and rapidly roll through the "iron gates of life." Being rolled into a "ball" certainly suggests their sexual union literally. But this activity of using time and life expands the sexual image into one of the couple powerfully forging a way through life itself, with all of its mortal obstacles ("gates of life"). Marvell also here plays against the more common phrase "gates of death." These lovers will contend with both life and death through vital activity. They will live so fully that time will not seem to affect them. In fact, the final couplet of the poem implies that they will live so fully that they will seem to be ahead of time, with his "winged chariot." The speaker acknowledges that they will not, in fact, be able to stop the sun, the symbol of time. Here Marvell obviously is alluding to an incident involving ZEUS: he did make the sun stand still in order to have a longer night in which to make love to Alcmena. But, he says, "we will make him [the sun, but also Time] run." The sun, or Time, will have to run to keep up with these active lovers. So, they will not allow themselves to become slaves of time, because they will "seize the day" and seem to control it, make it do their bidding.

Toback. Tobacco.

Toy. *Noun*: a trifle, a trivial thing.

Trace. *Verb*: (1) to follow the footprints of or to pursue, (2) to determine the course of something.

Transubstantiation. *Noun*: in theological usage, this is the miraculous change of the bread and wine of the Eucharist (or Holy Communion) into the body and blood of Christ, a belief primarily associated with Roman Catholicism. It is the source of much debate among Protestant factions regarding the extent to which the body and blood are really present or only symbolically so in the bread and wine.

Travel. *Verb*: (1) to afflict or trouble, (2) to labor or work hard, (3) to journey.

Tree. The noun has some special Biblical and Christian senses: (1) the Tree of Knowledge (of good and evil) in Eden, the fruit from which Adam and Eve were forbidden to eat (also referred to as the "forbidden tree," "fruitful tree," and "Adam's tree") [see Genesis 2 and 3]; (2) the Tree of Life in Eden that held immortality for humanity [see Genesis 2 and Revelation 22]; (3) the cross on which Christ was crucified, Christ's cross (one of the three "trees") on Calvary or Golgotha (the hill near Jerusalem where Christ was crucified). Also referred to as "Christ's tree." An old Christian belief held that Christ's cross was made of the wood from the Tree of Knowledge and that Christ was crucified on the very site on which the Tree of Knowledge grew in Eden. Also, the Tree of Life has been interpreted as a symbolic foreshadowing of Christ and his granting of immortality again to humanity through his "tree"; (4) "David's tree" refers to that mentioned in one of the Psalms (attributed to David): "And he shall be like a tree planted by the rivers of water, that bringeth forth his fruit in his season; his leaf also shall not wither; and whatsoever he doeth shall prosper" (Psalms 1:3).

Tree, Forbidden. See TREE.

Tree of Knowledge. See TREE.

Trencher. *Noun*: a plate on which food is served, frequently ornamented with moral sayings, lessons.

Trepan. *Verb*: to entrap or ensnare.

Trick-track. A variety of backgammon.

Trinity College. The college at Cambridge University attended by Marvell. He matriculated here as sizar in 1633 and took his Bachelor of Arts degree in 1639. Marvell contributed some verses to a Cambridge volume of 1637 that honored the birth of the fifth child of the King and Queen. After taking his Bachelor of Arts degree, Marvell continued to live at Cambridge during 1640, apparently planning to proceed to the Master of Arts. But after his father died in early 1641, Marvell left Cambridge.

Tripartite Soul. A concept inherited from Scholastic Philosophy and ARISTOTLE that was still alluded to in Marvell's time. The "soul" many times was assumed actually to consist of three souls or three parts of the soul. The vegetative (or vegetable) soul is possessed by plants, animals, and humans, and it is responsible for growth and reproduction. The sensitive (or sensible) soul is possessed by animals and humans, and it is responsible for the functioning of the five senses. The rational (or intellectual) soul is possessed by humans, and it is responsible for reason, understanding, and free will. This third soul distinguishes humans from plants and animals, places humanity just below the angels and God in the hierarchy of creatures (see NATURAL ORDER), and makes humans potentially angelic and godlike.

Triplet, Thomas (1603–1670). Prebendary of Westminster.

Tripp, John. One of the mayors of Hull to whom Marvell sent letters reporting government matters, since he was a Member of Parliament for the city.

True. *Adjective*: (1) steadfast, loyal, faithful; (2) consistent with fact, agreeing with reality; (3) exact, accurate, correct; (4) proper, legitimate; (5) real, genuine, not imaginary.

Try. *Verb*: (1) to separate, choose, select; (2) to search by examination; (3) to determine; (4) to examine and determine judicially; (5) to test or prove the strength or goodness or truth of something; (6) to experience or undergo; (7) to attempt to do or perform.

Tulipant. *Noun*: turban.

Tullie. See CICERO.

Tully. See CICERO.

Turner, [Sir] Edward (1617–1676). Speaker of the House of Commons, 1661–1673.

Turner, Francis. See MR. SMIRKE.

Turtles. Turtledoves (symbolic of paired, faithful lovers).

Tuttle-field. Tothill Fields in Westminster. Used to drill troops.

Two Books of God. See BOOKS OF GOD.

Tyburn. A famous site of public executions in London from 1388 to 1783. A permanent gallows for hanging was constructed here in 1571.

Type. *Noun*: (1) a symbol or emblem; (2) a person, object, or event of the Old Testament that prefigures or foreshadows a person, thing, or event of the New Testament.

U

"Upon Appleton House." One of the works in *MISCELLANEOUS POEMS*. A country house poem, following in the tradition of JONSON's "To Penshurst." The poem is made up of 97 stanzas with 8 lines in each stanza (776 lines in the poem): octosyllabic couplets are employed throughout.

When THOMAS FAIRFAX retired from his military and governmental positions in 1650, he went to his country estates in Yorkshire, one of which was Nun Appleton. The house at this time possibly was still the one built from the ruins of the original Cistercian nunnery, acquired by the Fairfax family at the dissolution of the monasteries and nunneries in 1542. The house, then, in 1650 might have been small and humble, in contrast to later rebuildings on the site. Marvell moved to Nun Appleton in 1650 or 1651 to become the tutor of Fairfax's daughter Mary (Maria). He served in this capacity during 1651 and 1652 and probably wrote the poem during this period. Most scholars believe that Marvell lived on this estate before the new house was built. But others contend that the new house had, in fact, already been built before Marvell came. No definitive evidence has yet been discovered to solve this problem.

A general structure or progression for the poem may be discerned. Stanzas 1–10 describe the house itself. Stanzas 11–35 present the history of the house as a nunnery. Stanzas 36–46 describe the flower gardens. Stanzas 47–60 focus on the meadows. Stanzas 61–81 treat the woods. Stanzas 62–97 compliment Mary Fairfax, the heart of the estate, and the restored order around her.

The description of the Fairfax house as "sober" satirizes the pompous grandeur of other large homes built with high columns. Stanza 2 notes that all creatures have dwellings appropriate to ("equal") them and asks why "man" should build such "unproportioned" dwellings (such as those lavish, showy ones that are unlike Nun Appleton) for himself. Marvell satirically and critically relates proud men who build such dwellings to those proud men who built the Tower of BABEL (stanza 3). Such unnecessary size in a home causes both the owners and the winds blowing through it to lose themselves in its vastness. It is ridiculous for a "wanton mote of dust" (i.e., man himself) to surround himself with marble. In stanza 4 Marvell contrasts all of this proud showiness to Nun Appleton and its owners. He says that this home came from a "more sober age and mind," thus echoing the "sober frame" of line 1. Men literally stoop to enter small doors, symbolic of the humility in this household. This earthly humility prepares this family for entering ultimately "heaven's gate." Stanzas 5 and 6 say that future visitors will wonder how Thomas Fairfax and Ann Vere (his wife) were able to live in such a small dwelling. The speaker emphasizes that it is humility that allows the greater to be contained in less. He implies that mathematicians can waste time trying to square the circle, to make a circle contain the same area as a square. But the true mathematics, the "holy mathematics," is in a true man of humility, one who exemplifies human perfection (symbolized by the square) superimposed with divine perfection (symbolized by the circle). Stanza 9 praises Fairfax's generosity to the poor waiting outside his door, as well as his hospitality to friends who adorn his home with their presence. Stanza 10 alludes to other Fairfax estates with more space but asserts that Nun Appleton is the ideal of Nature.

In the stanzas concerned with the history of the house (11–35) Isabella Thwaites is discussed. She had as her guardian the Prioress of Nun Appleton, Lady Anna Langton. She was wooed by William Fairfax of Streeton (an ancestor of Thomas Fairfax). To prevent Isabella's marriage to William, the Prioress shut her up. But an appeal to higher authority was made, she was released by force, and the marriage occurred in 1518. The house eventually was surrendered to the sons of this union at the dissolution in 1542. Marvell presents William Fairfax as a heroic figure rescuing Isabella from the subtle sexual enticements of the nuns and from their false religion.

Stanza 36 refers to the "hero" who retired here to peace. Most critics think that this refers to Sir Thomas Fairfax, son of William and Isabella, although others see it as an allusion to the Lord Fairfax of Marvell's time. This hero projected his military interests into the design of his garden, shaping it as a fort. Stanzas 37 and 38 continue the military analogy with the bee beating drums and with each flower displaying silken banners, drying the "pan" of its musket lock which holds the priming, and filling powder flasks. Stanza 38 does refer to Lord Fairfax of Marvell's time as the "governor" of this fort-garden. The flowers pay tribute to him and his wife ("governess"). But Marvell cleverly says that the flowers do not pay tribute to Mary (the "virgin nymph") because they mistake her as a flower herself! Stanzas 39–43 continue the military analogy at length, with praise of England as the garden of the world inserted in stanza 41: the speaker deplores the wasting of this garden with war. Stanzas 44–46 concentrate on praising Fairfax who might have restored England's garden and had it flourish as well as his own. But it "pleased him and God" to prefer his five flower forts to the five seaports on the southern coast of England ("Cinque Ports") over which he had jurisdiction as Warden. Stanza 46 refers to Cawood Castle, about two miles southeast of Nun Appleton, which was the seat of the Archbishop of York until he fled from it in 1642.

Stanzas 47–60 turn to the meadows of the estate. Here Marvell presents the meadows and the people and actions in them as if they were not only summarizing human history in Old Testament terms but also summarizing recent English history as a repetition of that in the Old Testament. Stanza 47 alludes to the report made by spies sent to Canaan in Numbers 13:33 ("And there we saw the giants, the sons of Anak, which come of the giants: and we were in our own sight as grasshoppers, and so we were in their sight"). In stanza 49 the mowers in the meadows appear to be walking through the sea of green as the "Israelites" walked through the Red Sea. These perhaps symbolize the Parliamentary forces in the civil war, those who hope to bring a new promised land to England. One of the mowers unknowingly kills with his blade the innocent rail (stanza 50), detesting his own bloody stroke. This seems to refer to the execution of King CHARLES I: Fairfax had opposed this execution. Stanza 53 comments that the "mower now commands the field": the parliamentary forces now rule. In stanzas 56–57 a "levelled space" is described from which "Levellers take pattern at." This refers to the political movement of the time, opposed by both Fairfax and OLIVER CROMWELL, which wanted equality in rank, wealth, and parliamentary representation. Stanzas 59–60 describe how waters from Denton, an estate on higher ground than Nun Appleton, flood the meadow. This seems to be a version of the Old Testament flood, a fact supported in stanza 61 with references to the "Flood" and to the "ark." Perhaps the parallel in England is the climax of the civil war and/or the political revolution in the state.

Stanzas 61–81 turn to the woods, with the speaker taking "sanctuary" there from the "Flood." The wood is a "green" ark, giving him salvation. The speaker finds welcome retreat from the active life of turmoil in contemplative, regenerative passivity in nature. "Green," of course, is Marvell's favorite word, with connotations of innocence, purity, vitality, creativity, etc. (See his other poems such as "THE GARDEN" and the four "MOWER" poems.) The examination of active and passive existences also recurs in Marvell's work. Stanza 63 pictures the forest, the wood, as a fifth element, distinguished from the traditional four ELEMENTs of which everything mortal is composed. The forest seems to be a quintessence (see ALCHEMY), pure and of the substance composing heavenly bodies. In stanza 64 the forest becomes at once a nature temple and a church, with trees like columns and with "winged choirs." The nightingale, dove, and other birds populate the woods, and the speaker also finds the "hewel," the green woodpecker, who "mines" through and fells the "tallest oak" which had a "traitor-worm" in it (stanzas 68–70). This description might also hint at the

A Marvell Dictionary U 165

execution of Charles I in the aftermath of the war. In stanza 71 the speaker sees himself as a part of nature (the human shape as "inverted tree"). He imagines in stanza 73 reading a "mosaic" in nature, in "Nature's mystic book." In stanza 76 he sees himself in retreat and safe from "the world." In stanza 77 he imagines being bound and embraced by vines but also sees himself as being crucified ("briars nail me through"). In stanza 78 a fusion of Moses parting the sea and Christ providing the path through the woods of this world occurs. Stanza 79 returns to the river flowing through the meadows: it now seems to be the "only snake" (Eden without Satan?). The speaker finds his ease (salvation?) stretched out on the river's bank in stanzas 80–81: regeneration seems to have come from both nature and the large truths of Christian history. In a way, then, one could say that in this section, after the violence of the preceding one, the speaker symbolically experiences the two major BOOKS OF GOD, the Bible and Nature, within the church-temple of the woods and recovers his emotional and spiritual greenness, resurrected into a restored harmony with life itself in this little Edenic microcosm of the Fairfax estate.

Stanzas 82–97 focus on the entrance of Maria Fairfax and her role in the innocence and order of the estate. In stanzas 83–86 she is the innocent, pre-fallen, Adamic creature of this Eden and the one to whom all of Nature pays respect and admiration. Stanza 87 credits her with being the source of the gardens' beauty, the woods' straightness, the meadow's sweetness, and the river's purity. She is repaid by these elements of the estate in that the meadows give her a carpet upon which to walk, the gardens give her flowers for a crown, the river provides her a mirror, and the woods give her a screen to surround her and bestow privacy (stanza 88). Stanzas 90–94 praise Maria's virtue, resistance of temptations, strict nurturing by her parents, knowledge, and choice in marriage. Stanzas 95–96 contrast inferior worldly reputed paradises ("THESSALIAN TEMPE's Seat," "ARANJUEZ," "BEL-RETIRO," and the "IDALIAN GROVE") to the Appleton estate, the Edenic home of Maria. Appleton is the "lesser world," the MICROCOSM, but, paradoxically, it now surpasses the world outside, the MACROCOSM, in perfection, innocence, order. It retains the essence of Paradise itself and thus is "Paradise's only map," not to be found elsewhere on earth.

The final stanza (97) looks at a scene suggesting the fallen world just outside this Edenic one. It is a world of disorder, with boats on men's heads and darkness descending. The speaker and Maria retreat into their own ordered world.

Use. *Verb*: (1) to follow as a custom, (2) to be usual or customary, (3) to carry on an occupation or profession or function, (4) to spend time in a certain way, (5) to put into practice or carry into action, (6) to employ something for a certain purpose, (7) to make use of land by working or tilling or occupying, (8) to take or partake of as food or drink, (9) to do a thing customarily or by habit. *Noun*: (1) act of employing a thing for any purpose; (2) spending; (3) habit or custom; (4) distinctive ritual, liturgy, service, or worship in a particular church or ecclesiastical division.

V

Vade. *Verb*: to decay, pass away, die.

Vain. *Adjective*: (1) having no value, worth, or significance; (2) having no effect or power, futile, fruitless, useless; (3) empty; (4) foolish, silly, thoughtless; (5) proud, displaying personal vanity. Marvell primarily uses the word in the senses of 1 through 4, but possibly suggests sense 5 in a few puns.

Vandal. *Noun*: one of a Germanic tribe that overran the Roman Empire in its latter stages, destroying many marks of its civilization, art, culture, and history. The word variously connotes anyone or anything barbaric, rude, uncivilized, lacking culture or taste, ignorant, passionate, violent, or destructive. Usually associated with GOTH.

Vaughan, Henry (1621–1695). One of the major METAPHYSICAL poets. Born in Wales. After apparently studying law for a time in London, he returned to Wales where he eventually settled into a medical practice. His early works are secular and reflect more the influence of JONSON and the CLASSICAL strain in both subject matter and style. But about 1648–50 illness, war, death, and a reading of the poetry of GEORGE HERBERT led to a spiritual transformation in Vaughan. Thereafter he wrote the religious poetry on which his poetic reputation rests. The influences of both DONNE and Herbert are quite apparent in Vaughan, and generally METAPHYSICAL CONCEITs, colloquialisms, wordplay, and paradox dominate his work, although some of the classical style remains. Like Herbert and Marvell, then, he is primarily metaphysical, but not exclusively. The quality of his poetry varies from poem to poem and line to line, and he is generally regarded as ranking fourth in the line of quality behind Donne, Herbert, and Marvell, as far as the major metaphysicals are concerned. Influences from ALCHEMY and mysticism combine with Christianity in Vaughan to create some unique spiritual beliefs and poems. His major book of poetry is *Silex Scintillans* (1650, expanded in 1655), and two of his best and most famous poems are "The Retreat" and "The World." Vaughan acknowledges his poetic debt to Herbert. He chose to emphasize, ultimately, Christian poetry over secular. He uses many of Herbert's titles for titles of his own poems, and he employs many of Herbert's lines or close versions of them in his own poems. Other echoes of Herbert in words, phrases, images, and style permeate Vaughan's work.

Vegetable Soul. See TRIPARTITE SOUL.

Vegetative Soul. See TRIPARTITE SOUL.

Venus. In mythology, Roman name for the Greek goddess of love, Aphrodite. Known also as the goddess of beauty. Married to Vulcan (god of fire) but was unfaithful to him in having many lovers, resulting in many children by her. One of her sons was Cupid, god of love. Although primarily symbolic of physical beauty, love, and passion, she also is seen in some contexts as the principle of fertility and generative love.

Vera. Ann(e) Vere, wife of THOMAS FAIRFAX.

Vere, Ann(e). See THOMAS FAIRFAX.

Vertue. See VIRTUE.

Verulam. See BACON, FRANCIS.

Villiers, Barbara (1641–1709). Daughter of William Villiers. Married Roger Palmer in 1659. Palmer was shortly after made Earl of Castlemaine, so Barbara became Countess of Castlemaine. The interest of CHARLES II in her as a sexual intimate and mistress apparently began early in 1660. The King had Queen Catherine, despite the Queen's strong opposition, accept Lady Castlemaine as one of the ladies of her bedchamber. Barbara was assigned lodgings at Whitehall. In late 1663 she converted to Roman Catholicism. Rumors of her having other lovers at the time did not prevent the King from spending about four evenings a week at her lodgings. She had several children by the King, and in 1666 was given luxurious rooms at Hampton Court. She had gained influence in court that no one could ignore at this point.

In 1667 she was suspected of having an affair with HENRY JERMYN, and this caused a quarrel with the King. Charles apologized to her for his own doubts. She and her followers had a large share in bringing down Clarendon [see EDWARD HYDE]. In 1668 she retaliated for King Charles's attraction to the actress NELL GWYN by having an affair of her own with the actor Charles Hart. The King gave her more property and money in 1669 and made her Duchess of Cleveland in 1670. She had great income but lived lavishly and spent large sums. She took new lovers frequently.

By 1674 her influence dwindled in the face of being supplanted by Charles's mistress the Duchess of Portsmouth (see KEROUALLE,

A Marvell Dictionary V 169

LOUISE RENEE DE). She lived for a time in France and returned to England shortly before the death of Charles II.

Marvell especially satirizes her lasciviousness and alludes to the Henry Jermyn affair in "The Last Instructions to a Painter," lines 79–104. Marvell also refers to her in his letters: in one of August 9, 1671, he refers to her many sources of income and says, "All promotions, spiritual and temporal, pass under her cognizance."

Villiers, Francis (1629–1648). Second son of the first Duke of Buckingham and brother to the second Duke (see VILLIERS, GEORGE). Killed in a Royalist uprising near Kingston-on-Thames in 1648. Marvell memorializes him in "An Elegy upon the Death of My Lord Francis Villiers."

Villiers, George, Duke of Buckingham (1628–1687). Brother to FRANCIS VILLIERS. CHARLES I raised the young George Villiers with his own children. Served the King in the civil war. He escaped to Holland in 1648, and his estates were confiscated in 1651. Policy disagreements estranged Villiers from Prince Charles (see CHARLES II) in 1654. In the summer of 1657 Buckingham was tired of exile and of trying to regain the favor of Charles. He returned to England with the plan of marrying Mary Fairfax, daughter of THOMAS FAIRFAX. He hoped to use Fairfax's influence to secure OLIVER CROMWELL's pardon and regain some of his property. Mary was on the verge of marrying the Earl of Chesterfield but broke it off in favor of Buckingham. Buckingham married her in Yorkshire on September 15, 1657. Cromwell and his Council suspected this to be a part of a Presbyterian plot and, in October, ordered Buckingham's arrest. But he hid himself away to avoid capture. Eventually Cromwell's leniency allowed Buckingham to live at York House in honorable confinement. But Buckingham could not restrain himself and was arrested and sent to the Tower in 1658 when he violated his confinement. After Cromwell's death he was released (in 1659) by Parliament on his word of honor and on Fairfax's security.

With the Restoration of Charles, Buckingham became a gentleman of the King's bedchamber and was made a member of the Privy Council. His confiscated estates were restored to him, and their income made him extremely wealthy. Buckingham was opposed mightily to Clarendon (see HYDE, EDWARD), and he plotted for his overthrow. Through boisterous opposition to the Crown's policies, Buckingham alienated Charles, who had him accused of treasonable practices. In February of 1667 his arrest was ordered, and he was ejected from the Privy Council and other offices. He hid for awhile but then gave himself up in June and was sent to the Tower. After the fall of

Clarendon in August, however, Buckingham was restored to the Privy Council and his other positions in September 1667.

Buckingham was involved in sexual intrigue with the Countess of Shrewsbury and was challenged to a duel in 1668 by her husband, who was mortally wounded as a result. Buckingham continued living openly with the Countess.

Buckingham pursued policies of toleration in religion. He also was at odds with James, Duke of York (see JAMES II). Buckingham was one of the members of the cabal (with Lauderdale [see MAITLAND, JOHN], CLIFFORD, ARLINGTON, and ASHLEY). Generally supported by Lauderdale and Ashley, Buckingham was in conflict with Arlington. But Arlington ultimately had the upper hand in political and foreign matters, and Buckingham had so alienated Charles by 1674 that he was removed from offices, as Parliament requested.

At this point Buckingham reformed his way of life. He attended church with his wife, paid debts, and argued forcefully for relief of DISSENTERs. Buckingham was a friend of NELL GWYN and others of "the merry gang," as Marvell referred to them in his letters. With the accession of James, Buckingham retired to Yorkshire. After his death in April 1687, he was buried in Westminster Abbey.

Buckingham wrote some poetry and plays, including *The Rehearsal*. In this play Buckingham had DRYDEN represented by the character "Bayes." Taking his cue from Buckingham, Marvell wrote his prose work *The Rehearsal Transprosed*, in which he made Samuel Parker, Archdeacon of Canterbury, into the "Bayes" of his own work. Marvell alludes to Buckingham, to his arrest, and to his opposition to Clarendon in both "Clarendon's Housewarming" and "The Last Instructions to a Painter." Many references to Buckingham are also made in Marvell's letters.

Viner, Sir Robert (1631–1688). London goldsmith and financier. Knighted in 1665 and given baronetcy in 1666. Elected Lord Mayor of London in 1674. Enjoyed a close relationship with CHARLES II, who attended Viner's mayoralty feast. Viner set up an equestrian statue in honor of the King in Stocks Market. He bought it on the continent, and it originally represented Sobieski, King of Poland, trampling a Turk beneath his horse's hooves. But Viner transformed it into Charles trampling OLIVER CROMWELL. Ludicrously, the Turk's turban remained on Cromwell's head. It was displayed to the public on May 29, 1672, the anniversary of Charles's birth and of his Restoration.

Viner was known as Charles's goldsmith and principal banker. He thrived in these roles until the government closed the Exchequer in a move to save embarrassment at extravagances by the government, which now would not repay the loans or interest from their bankers. Viner was put out of business and forced into bankruptcy.

Marvell writes of Viner in "Upon Sir Robert Viner's Setting Up of the King's Statue in Wool-Church Market" (also known as "The Statue in Stocks-Market"). He alludes to Viner also in "Upon His Majesty's Being Made Free of the City" and in "A Dialogue between Two Horses."

Virtue. *Noun*: (1) conformity of life and conduct with principles of morality; (2) physical strength, force, or energy; (3) courage, valor; (4) particular power, efficacy, or good quality inherent in such things as plants, medicines, or precious stones.

W

Waller, Edmund (1606–1687). Poet and Member of Parliament. Educated at Eton and at King's College, Cambridge. Left without a degree. Studied law at Lincoln's Inn. Served in Parliament and argued for religious toleration and against bishops prior to the civil war. But he switched sides to support CHARLES I during the war. In 1643 he was fined and banished for trying to seize London for the King. He lived in Paris several years. In 1651 he secured OLIVER CROMWELL's permission to return to England. After CHARLES II was restored, Waller was returned to Parliament and again had royal favor. Waller's poetry was written in heroic couplets, and he was praised highly for his style by DRYDEN and others. His poetry is largely of the CLASSICAL line.

Waller wrote "Instructions to a Painter" (1665) in praise of the Duke of York (see JAMES II) and commenting on the Dutch wars. This fostered several other poems in this "advice-to-a-painter" genre. There were anonymously published "Second Advice," "Third Advice," "Fourth Advice," and "Fifth Advice" in 1666 and 1667. Marvell then wrote his "The Last Instructions to a Painter" in 1667. In it he refers to "Old Waller, trumpet-general."

Want. *Verb*: to lack or be without. *Noun*: (1) deficiency, shortage, or lack of something; (2) poverty or destitution.

Ward, Seth. See SETH.

Waste. *Verb*: (1) to devastate or ruin; (2) to use up, diminish; (3) to employ uselessly; (4) to expend needlessly or to squander; (5) to spend or to pass unprofitably or idly.

Water. *Noun*: (1) one of the four ELEMENTs; (2) the liquid of which oceans, seas, lakes, ponds, and rivers are made; (3) liquid that falls as rain; (4) drink that sustains life; (5) in some contexts, liquid for washing, cleansing; (6) in some contexts, water of baptism that cleanses the spirit; (7) in some contexts, a reference to tears.

Whifflers. *Noun*: triflers.

Wilmot, John, Earl of Rochester (1647–1680). Attended Oxford, went on a European tour, and returned to the court of CHARLES II in 1664. Fought in naval wars against the Dutch. Married Elizabeth Malet, by whom he had four children. But he spent much time in London with several mistresses and a number of profligate friends. Wrote poetry, largely satirical, blunt, and witty.
     Marvell refers to Rochester several times in his letters. In one to EDWARD HARLEY he refers to Rochester and others as the "merry gang." Rochester himself admired Marvell's *The Rehearsal Transprosed*.

Wilson, Richard. One of the mayors of Hull to whom Marvell sent letters reporting government matters, since he was a Member of Parliament for the city.

Winestead-in-Holderness. Marvell's birthplace in Yorkshire.

Wink(e). *Verb*: to close the eyes.

Wit. *Noun*: (1) intelligence or understanding; (2) cleverness or mental quickness; (3) talent for brilliant and amusing statement; (4) quality of speech and writing that aptly associates thoughts, usually in a surprising or unexpected way.

Wittal. See WITTOL.

Wittol. *Noun*: a man who is aware of and does not object to his wife's adultery.

Witty, Robert. Physician at HULL and previously usher at Hull Grammar School in 1632–42. He translated a Latin work by James Primrose (who also was a physician in Hull) and published it in 1651 as *Popular Errors*, a work concerning errors and misconceptions about medicine. Marvell wrote an English poem titled "To His Worthy Friend Dr. Witty upon his Translation of the *Popular Errors*" which was published as a commendatory poem in this volume. He also contributed a shorter Latin poem.

Wood, Sir Henry (1597–1671). Served as Clerk of the Spicery to CHARLES I and as Clerk Comptroller of the Board of Green Cloth, a position which entailed maintaining order in the palace and examining accounts.

Wool-church Market. See VINER, SIR ROBERT.

Worm. *Noun*: (1) maggot [especially the "worm" of the grave]; (2) segmented earthworm; (3) larva or grub or caterpillar that destroys vegetation.

Y

Yield, yeild. *Verb*: (1) to give in, submit, surrender; (2) to grant or concede; (3) to produce or give forth.

York, Duchess of. See JAMES II.

York, Duke of. See JAMES II.

Z

Zephyr. *Noun*: the west wind.

Zeus. In Greek mythology, son of Cronus and Rhea. The most powerful of the Greek gods. Ruled heaven, earth, gods, and humanity. Married seven times and had many extramarital affairs and children. Transformed himself into various forms (e.g., shower of gold, satyr, swan, bull) to satisfy his lust with such loves as Leda and Europa. Also see AESCULAPIUS. In Roman mythology, Zeus is called Jove or Jupiter, the names preferred by Marvell.

Zodiack, zodiac. *Noun*: (1) a circle in the celestial sphere in which the movements of the sun, moon, and planets were assumed to occur: the circle is divided into twelve parts or "signs"; (2) figuratively used to refer to a set of twelve.

Zone, the. *Noun*: the Torrid Zone, the area of high temperature on the earth's surface around the equator between the tropics of Cancer and Capricorn.

SELECTED BIBLIOGRAPHY

I. WORKS [All of Marvell's works are listed by editor.]

A. Poetry

Donno, Elizabeth Story, ed. *Andrew Marvell: The Complete Poems.*
    London and Harmondsworth, England: Penguin Books, 1972.
Lord, George deF., ed. *Andrew Marvell: Complete Poetry.* New York:
    Random House, 1968.
Lord, George deF., ed. *Poems on Affairs of State: Augustan Satirical
    Verse, 1660–1714*, volume 1. New Haven and London: Yale
    University Press, 1963. [Contains Marvell's satirical poems]
MacDonald, Hugh, ed. *The Poems of Andrew Marvell.* Cambridge,
    Massachusetts: Harvard University Press, 1952.
McQueen, William A., and Kiffin A. Rockwell, eds. *The Latin Poetry
    of Andrew Marvell.* Chapel Hill, North Carolina: The
    University of North Carolina Studies in Comparative Literature
    and The University of North Carolina Press, 1964. [Marvell's
    Latin verse, with translations on facing pages]

B. Prose

Smith, D.I.B., ed. *The Rehearsal Transpros'd* and *The Rehearsal
    Transpros'd: The Second Part.* Oxford: Clarendon Press, 1971.

C. Poetry and Prose

Grosart, Alexander B., ed. *The Complete Works in Verse and Prose of Andrew Marvell*. London: Robson, 1872–75. 4 vols.
Kermode, Frank, and Keith Walker, eds. *Andrew Marvell*. Oxford: Oxford University Press, 1990.
Margoliouth, H.M., ed. *The Poems and Letters of Andrew Marvell*. 3rd ed. Revised by Pierre Legouis with the collaboration of E.E. Duncan-Jones. Oxford: Clarendon Press, 1971. 2 vols. [The standard edition]
Wilcher, Robert, ed. *Andrew Marvell: Selected Poetry and Prose*. London and New York: Methuen, 1986.

II. BIBLIOGRAPHIES, CONCORDANCES, AND OTHER RESEARCH TOOLS

Collins, Dan S. *Andrew Marvell: A Reference Guide*. Boston: G.K. Hall & Co., 1981. [Annotated guide to comments, articles, essays, and books on Marvell from 1641 to 1980]
Dees, Jerome S. "Recent Studies in Andrew Marvell (1973–1990)." *English Literary Renaissance* 22 (1992): 273–95.
Guffey, George R. *A Concordance to the English Poems of Andrew Marvell*. Chapel Hill: University of North Carolina Press, 1974.
Szanto, Gillian. "Recent Studies in Marvell." *English Literary Renaissance* 5 (1975): 273–86. [Covers selected works on Marvell from about 1945 to 1972]

III. LIFE

Burdon, Pauline. "Marvell and his Kindred: The Family Network in the Later Years: I. The Alureds." *Notes and Queries* 31 (1984): 379–85.
Burdon, Pauline. "Marvell and His Kindred: The Family Network in the Later Years: II. Nelthorpes, Thompsons, and Popples." *Notes and Queries* 32 (1985): 172–80.
Burdon, Pauline. "The Second Mrs. Marvell." *Notes and Queries* 29 (1982): 33–44.
Hill, Christopher. "Milton and Marvell." In *Approaches to Marvell: The York Tercentenary Lectures*, edited by C.A. Patrides, 1–30. London: Routledge and Kegan Paul, 1978. [Notes the aids given by the writers to each other, their common friends, their political ties, their literary links, and their philosophical similarities]

Hunt, John Dixon. *Andrew Marvell: His Life and Writings.* London: Elek Books, 1978.
Kelliher, Hilton. *Andrew Marvell: Poet and Politician, 1621-78.* London: The British Library, 1978.
Kenyon, John. "Andrew Marvell: Life and Times." In *Andrew Marvell: Essays on the Tercentenary of His Death*, edited by R.L. Brett, 1–35. University of Hull Publications. Oxford: Oxford University Press for the University of Hull, 1979.
Lamont, William. "The Religion of Andrew Marvell: Locating the 'Bloody Horse.' " In *The Political Identity of Andrew Marvell*, edited by Conal Condren and A.D. Cousins, 135–56. Aldershot, England: Scolar Press, Gower Publishing, 1990. [Argues that Marvell is "in a very clearly defined wing of Protestant nonconformity"]
Legouis, Pierre. *Andrew Marvell: Poet, Puritan, Patriot.* Oxford: Clarendon Press, 1965. [Abridgement in English of 1928 French original]
Margoliouth, H.M. "Andrew Marvell: Some Biographical Points." *Modern Language Review* 17 (1922): 351–61.
Smith, Donal. "The Political Beliefs of Andrew Marvell." *University of Toronto Quarterly* 36 (1966–67): 55–67.
Tupper, Fred S. "Mary Palmer, Alias Mrs. Andrew Marvell." *PMLA* 53 (1938): 367–92.

IV. REPUTATION AND INFLUENCE

Brant, Robert L. "Hawthorne and Marvell." *American Literature* 30 (1958–59): 366. [Argues that Hawthorne alludes to Marvell's "The Unfortunate Lover" in the last line of *The Scarlet Letter* and that the echo provides aesthetic distance and a "redeeming light"]
Brittin, Norman A. "Emerson and the Metaphysical Poets." *American Literature* 8 (1936–37): 1–21. [Discusses Emerson's references to Marvell and influences from him in Emerson's own poetry, including his tetrameter couplets and use of the adjective "green"]
Comley, Nancy R. "Marvell, Tennyson, and 'The Islet': An Inversion of Pastoral." *Victorian Poetry* 16 (1978): 270–74. [Contends that Tennyson's "The Islet" is a parody of Marvell's "A Dialogue between Thyrsis and Dorinda"]
Davidson, Peter. "An Early Echo of Poems by Marvell." *Notes and Queries* 33 (1986): 41. [Argues that Daniel Scargill in an epitaph of 1680/1 echoes "A Dialogue between Thyrsis and Dorinda" and "To His Coy Mistress"]

Donno, Elizabeth Story, ed. *Andrew Marvell: The Critical Heritage*. London: Routledge and Kegan Paul, 1978. [Presents allusions to and criticisms of Marvell from 1673 to 1923]

Donno, Elizabeth Story. "The Unhoopable Marvell." In *Tercentenary Essays in Honor of Andrew Marvell*, edited by Kenneth Friedenreich, 21–45. Hamden, Connecticut: Archon, 1977. [Traces some fluctuations in Marvell's poetic reputation and possible reasons and also notes how his originality makes Marvell not easily classifiable]

Ehrenpreis, Irvin. "Four of Swift's Sources." *Modern Language Notes* 70 (1955): 95–100. [Notes that one of Swift's sources is Marvell's *The Rehearsal Transprosed*]

Eliot, Thomas Stearns. "Andrew Marvell." *[London] Times Literary Supplement*, 31 March 1921, pp. 201–202.

Hammond, Paul. "Dryden's Use of Marvell's *Horatian Ode* in *Absalom and Achitophel*." *Notes and Queries* 35 (1988): 173–74. [Notes several verbal echoes and parallels, as well as similar sentiment]

Herendeen, Warren. "Andrew Marvell and Christina Rossetti." *Seventeenth-Century News* 30 (1972–73): 8–9. [Argues that several lines in Rossetti's "Goblin Market" seem to echo Marvell's "Bermudas" and "The Garden"]

Millgate, Michael. "Melville and Marvell: A Note on *Billy Budd*." *English Studies* 49 (1968): 47–50. [Argues that several lines of "Upon Appleton House" suggested elements of Melville's story, including the name of the Captain and the name of Billy Budd]

Wilding, Michael, ed. *Marvell: Modern Judgements*. London: Macmillan and Co., 1969. [The "Introduction" provides a useful survey of Marvell's early reputation through the 19th century.]

Wilding, Michael. "Marvell's Reputation for Patriotism and Probity." *Notes and Queries* 17 (1970): 252–54. [Points out several comments on Marvell in the 18th and 19th centuries that focus on his patriotism and political integrity, rather than on his poetry]

V. CRITICAL STUDIES

A. Background

Bush, Douglas. *Mythology and the Renaissance Tradition in English Poetry*. Revised ed. New York: Norton, 1963.

Eliot, Thomas Stearns. "The Metaphysical Poets." *[London] Times Literary Supplement*, October 20, 1921, pp. 669–70. [A famous and influential essay, reprinted frequently in collections of essays and in anthologies. Marvell is only briefly mentioned in this piece, but see Eliot's comments on him in the (March 31, 1921) item cited in this bibliography under "Reputation and Influence."]

Hunt, John Dixon. " 'Loose Nature' and the 'Garden Square': The Gardenist Background for Marvell's Poetry." In *Approaches to Marvell: The York Tercentenary Lectures*, edited by C.A. Patrides, 331–51. London: Routledge and Kegan Paul, 1978.

Nicolson, Marjorie Hope. *The Breaking of the Circle: Studies in the Effect of the "New Science" upon Seventeenth-Century Poetry*. Revised ed. New York: Columbia University Press, 1960. [Argues that Marvell held to the older view of the circle as a symbol of infinity and perfection, even in the face of the new astronomy]

Røstvig, Maren-Sofie. *The Happy Man: Studies in the Metamorphoses of a Classical Ideal*. 2nd edition. New York: Humanities Press, 1962. 2 vols. [First published in 1954, but material on Marvell rewritten in the revised (2nd) edition. Discusses "happy man" literature as a genre, notes Marvell's debts to other writers, and examines Marvell's contributions to this type]

Tuve, Rosemond. *Elizabethan and Metaphysical Imagery: Renaissance Poetic and Twentieth-Century Critics*. Chicago: University of Chicago Press, 1947.

B. General: Poetry and Prose

Bradbrook, M.C., and M.G. Lloyd Thomas. *Andrew Marvell*. Cambridge: Cambridge University Press, 1940.

Chernaik, Warren L. *The Poet's Time: Politics and Religion in the Work of Andrew Marvell*. Cambridge: Cambridge University Press, 1983.

Griffin, Patsy. *The Modest Ambition of Andrew Marvell: A Study of Marvell and His Relation to Lovelace, Fairfax, Cromwell, and Milton*. Newark: University of Delaware Press and London: Associated University Presses, 1995.

Hodge, R.I.V. *Foreshortened Time: Andrew Marvell and Seventeenth Century Revolutions*. Cambridge and Ipswich, England: D.S. Brewer; Totowa, New Jersey: Rowman and Littlefield, 1978.

Hyman, Lawrence W. *Andrew Marvell*. Twayne's English Authors. New York: Twayne Publishers, 1964.

Klause, John. *The Unfortunate Fall: Theodicy and the Moral Imagination of Andrew Marvell*. Hamden, Connecticut: Shoe String Press (Archon Books), 1983.

MacCaffrey, Isabel G. "Some Notes on Marvell's Poetry, Suggested by a Reading of His Prose." *Modern Philology* 61 (1963–64): 261–69.
Patterson, Annabel. *Marvell and the Civic Crown*. Princeton, New Jersey: Princeton University Press, 1978.
Press, John. *Andrew Marvell*. Revised ed. London: Longmans, Green & Co., 1966.
Wallace, John M. *Destiny His Choice: The Loyalism of Andrew Marvell*. Cambridge: Cambridge University Press, 1968.
Wilcher, Robert. *Andrew Marvell*. Cambridge: Cambridge University Press, 1985.

C. Poetry

1. Latin Poetry

Bain, Carl E. "The Latin Poetry of Andrew Marvell." *Philological Quarterly* 38 (1959): 436–49.
Stocker, Margarita. "Remodeling Virgil: Marvell's New Astraea." *Studies in Philology* 84 (1987): 159–79. [Examines "A Letter to Dr. Ingelo" in light of Marvell's own aims as a poet and as a "Protestant reformer committed to the ideals of Cromwell's regime in the 1650's"]

2. *Miscellaneous Poems*, 1681: Major Poems and Groups

a. *Bermudas*

Brockbank, Phillip. "The Politics of Paradise: 'Bermudas.' " In *Approaches to Marvell: The York Tercentenary Lectures*, edited by C.A. Patrides, 174–93. London: Routledge and Kegan Paul, 1978. [Surveys historical background of Bermuda and explores its reflection in the poem]
Cummings, R.M. "The Difficulty of Marvell's 'Bermudas.' " *Modern Philology* 67 (1969–70): 331–40. [Argues that the "imagery on which the poem moves summons up more associations than the poem, as it is organized, can contain" and that the "elusive associations that the poem sometimes excites will reveal quite intelligible discrepancies between the point of view of the singers and what they are supposed to be singing about"]

Fizdale, Tay. "Irony in Marvell's 'Bermudas.' " *ELH* 42 (1975): 203–13. [Regards the poem as essentially ironic, with Marvell presenting the Puritans in Bermuda as arrogant, self-focusing, interested in physical riches, and fallen]

Hardman, C.B. "Marvell's 'Bermudas' and Sandys's *Psalms*." *Review of English Studies* 32 (1981): 64–67. [Argues that Marvell was influenced by Sandys's paraphrase of the Psalms and not by those in the Authorized Version. Uses parallel passages from both versions and Marvell's poem as evidence]

Hardman, C.B. "Marvell's Rowers." *Essays in Criticism* 27 (1977): 93–99. [Sees an integral relationship between the rowing and singing, making work pleasurable and praising God, to whom all human activity is indebted and dedicated]

Kawasaki, Toshihiko. "Marvell's 'Bermudas'—A Little World, or a New World?" *ELH* 43 (1976): 38–52. [Sees the history of Bermuda ambivalent in itself and this ambivalence reflected in the poem, with the question of whether the place is "abundantly self-sufficient" or dependent upon God's providential purpose never answered in the poem]

Wilding, Michael. " 'Apples' in Marvell's 'Bermudas.' " *English Language Notes* 6 (1968–69): 254–57. [Discounts the usual explanation of "apples" as pineapples, since they are not from a "tree," in favor of the apples of Eden]

Winterton, J.B. "Some Notes on Marvell's 'Bermudas.' " *Notes and Queries* 15 (1968): 102. [Sees the "apples" as the apples of Eden, the "Pearl" as a reference to the pearl of great price in Matthew 13:46, and the parenthetical "perhaps" as a witty reference to the solid spheres of the old cosmology that would allow easy "rebounding"]

b. *The Coronet*

Clark, James Andrew. " 'The Coronet': Marvell's 'Curious Frame' of Allusion." In *"Bright Shootes of Everlastingnesse": The Seventeenth-Century Religious Lyric*, edited by Claude J. Summers and Ted-Larry Pebworth, 145–61. Columbia: University of Missouri Press, 1987. [Sees the poem as a "texture, a weaving of quotations, echoes, and allusions that stand in default of a work yet to be framed" and notes "Marvell's odd mixture of confidence in and disdain for his own poetic offering"]

Hardy, John Edward. *The Curious Frame: Seven Poems in Text and Context*. Notre Dame, Indiana: University of Notre Dame Press, 1962. [Chapter 3 is "Andrew Marvell's 'The Coronet': The Frame of Curiosity." Sees the speaker as "Man" and contends that language is the "true, central, hidden theme of the poem"]

King, Bruce. "A Reading of Marvell's 'The Coronet.' " *Modern Language Review* 68 (1973): 741–49. [Argues that, upon close examination, the poem is "typically Marvellian" and that it is necessary to recognize Biblical allusions and the significance of traditional Christian symbols to understand it]

c. *The "Cromwell" Poems*

Brooks, Cleanth. "Marvell's 'Horatian Ode.' " *English Institute Essays* (1946): 127–58. [Relying primarily upon a close reading of the poem itself, Brooks sees a "tension between the speaker's admiration for the kingliness which has won Cromwell the power and his awareness that the power can be maintained only by a continual exertion of those talents for kingship—this tension is never relaxed."]

Bush, Douglas. "Marvell's 'Horatian Ode.' " *Sewanee Review* 60 (1952): 363–76. [Sees the poem as an embodiment of the metaphysical and classical modes and argues for looking at the poem as a "historical document," in contrast to the approach used by Cleanth Brooks in his reading of the poem in itself]

Carens, James F. "Andrew Marvell's Cromwell Poems." *Bucknell Review* 7 (1957–58): 41–70.

Coolidge, John S. "Marvell and Horace." *Modern Philology* 63 (1965–66): 111–20. [Argues that in "An Horatian Ode" Marvell assumes Horace's views of men and events and that praise is given to both Charles and Cromwell in the contexts of the demands and virtues of their ages, the old and the new]

Cornelius, David K. "Marvell's 'Horatian Ode.' " *The Explicator* 35 (Spring 1977): 18–19. [Sees the last stanza as crucial in depicting Cromwell as never being able to have divine sanction]

Corns, Thomas. "Marvell's 'Horatian Ode.' " *The Explicator* 35 (Winter 1976): 11–12. [Sees the scene of the execution of Charles as "royal actor" in harmony with the general ambiguity of the poem]

Crane, David. "Marvell and Milton on Cromwell." *Notes and Queries* 33 (1986): 464. [Suggests that the opening lines of Milton's sonnet "To the Lord General Cromwell" are indebted to lines 9–16 of Marvell's "An Horatian Ode"]

Cruttwell, Patrick. "The War's and Fortune's Son." *Essays in Criticism* 2 (1952): 24–37. [Argues that Marvell is like Shakespeare in the ability to see both heroic and deplorable characteristics in a single individual (such as Cromwell)]

Dingley, R.J. " 'Caresbrooks Narrow Case': A Possible Allusion in Marvell." *Notes and Queries* 28 (1981): 49–51.
Donnelly, M.L. " 'And still new stopps to various time apply'd': Marvell, Cromwell, and the Problem of Representation at Midcentury." In *On the Celebrated and Neglected Poems of Andrew Marvell*, edited by Claude J. Summers and Ted-Larry Pebworth, 154–68. Columbia: University of Missouri Press, 1992.
Edwards, Thomas R. *Imagination and Power: A Study of Poetry on Public Themes*. New York: Oxford University Press, 1971. [Pp. 66–82 concern "An Horatian Ode"]
Gerard, Albert S. "Marvell's *An Horatian Ode upon Cromwell's Return from Ireland*, 118." *The Explicator* 20 (1961–62): Item 22. [Explains "Spirits of the shady Night" as "the enemies of Cromwell and his God"—i.e., Royalists, Irish, Scots, and any other oppressors of "all States not free"]
Greene, Thomas M. "The Balance of Power in Marvell's 'Horatian Ode.' " *ELH* 60 (1993): 379–96. [Assumes "Marvell's own bafflement" by the historical events surrounding the "Ode" and that indeed "the fragment of history meditated by the ode is represented not only as inherently mysterious but arcane"]
Gregory, E.R. "Marvell's 'Horatian Ode': A Reconsideration." *Forum* 10 (1972): 11–18. [Argues that praise for Cromwell is ironic and that Marvell at this time felt nostalgic toward monarchy]
Guild, Nicholas. "The Context of Marvell's Allusion to Lucan in 'An Horatian Ode.' " *Papers on Language and Literature* 14 (1978): 406–13.
Guild, Nicholas. "Marvell's 'The First Anniversary of the Government Under O. C.' " *Papers on Language and Literature* 11 (1975): 242–53. [Sees the poem as an argument that Cromwell retain the position of Lord Protector and not accept that of King]
Hayes, Thomas W. "The Dialectic of History in Marvell's *Horatian Ode*." *Clio* 1 (October 1971): 26–36. [Sees a conflict between (1) Justice and Charles I and (2) Fate and Cromwell]
Hirst, Derek. " 'That Sober Liberty': Marvell's Cromwell in 1654." In *The Golden & the Brazen World: Papers in Literature and History, 1650–1800*, edited by John M. Wallace, 17–53. Berkeley and Los Angeles: University of California Press, 1985. [Concerns "The First Anniversary"]
Knights, L.C. *Public Voices: Literature and Politics with Special Reference to the Seventeenth Century*. London: Chatto & Windus, 1971. [Pp. 82–93 concern "An Horatian Ode."]

Larson, Charles. "Marvell's Richard Cromwell: 'He, Vertue Dead, Revives.' " *Mosaic* 19 (Spring 1986): 57–67. [Concerns "A Poem upon the Death of His Late Highness the Lord Protector"]

Lerner, L.D. "Andrew Marvell: 'An Horatian Ode upon Cromwel's Return from Ireland.' " In *Interpretations: Essays on Twelve English Poems*, edited by John Wain, 59–74. London: Routledge and Kegan Paul, 1955. [Contends that Marvell considers Cromwell to be "a force disruptive of nature, which is nonetheless natural: or (if you prefer) disruptive of society but nonetheless the product of inevitable social forces"]

MacLean, Gerald M. *Time's Witness: Historical Representation in English Poetry, 1603–1660*. Madison: University of Wisconsin Press, 1990. [Discusses "The First Anniversary" on pp. 240–55]

McGlamery, Gayla S. "The Rhetoric of Apocalypse and Practical Politics in Marvell's 'The First Anniversary of the Government under O. C.' " *South Atlantic Review* 55 (November 1990): 19–35. [Argues that the poem presents Cromwell as both an "agent of Heaven" and a "healing, revitalizing force within the Commonwealth" who may bring people into political harmony and into conformity with God's will]

Monsarrat, G.D. "Marvell's Use of 'Nor Yet,' With Special Reference to the 'Horatian Ode.' " *English Language Notes* 18 (1980–81): 104–108.

Nevo, Ruth. *The Dial of Virtue: A Study of Poems on Affairs of State in the Seventeenth Century*. Princeton, New Jersey: Princeton University Press, 1963. [Includes studies of "An Horatian Ode" and "The First Anniversary"]

Norbrook, David. "Marvell's 'Horatian Ode' and the Politics of Genre." In *Literature and the English Civil War,* edited by Thomas Healy and Jonathan Sawday, 147–69. Cambridge: Cambridge University Press, 1990. [Argues against reading the poem as "maintaining an equal balance between Charles and Cromwell," in favor of seeing it as one of urgency for seizing the occasion to establish a republic with Cromwell as the moving force]

Orwen, William R. "Marvell's 'Bergamot.' " *Notes and Queries* 2 (1955): 340–41. [Notes that the bergamot is a pear associated with kings and that Marvell's reference to it in "An Horatian Ode" suggests that Cromwell acted as if he planned to become king]

Owen, William R., Jr. "Marvell's Narrow Case." *Notes and Queries* 2 (1955): 201. [Argues that "narrow case" in line 52 of "An Horatian Ode" refers to the narrow casement of Charles's bedroom window at Carisbrooke]

Patterson, Annabel. "Against Polarization: Literature and Politics in Marvell's Cromwell Poems." *English Literary Renaissance* 5 (1975): 251–72.

Proudfoot, L. "Marvell: Sallust and the Horatian Ode." *Notes and Queries* 196 (1951): 434.

Revard, Stella P. "Building the Foundations of a Good Commonwealth: Marvell, Pindar, and the Power of Music." In *"The Muses Common-Weale": Poetry and Politics in the Seventeenth Century*, edited by Claude J. Summers and Ted-Larry Pebworth, 177–90. Columbia: University of Missouri Press, 1988. [Concerns "The First Anniversary"]

Richards, Judith. "Literary Criticism and the Historian: Towards Reconstructing Marvell's Meaning in 'An Horatian Ode.' " *Literature and History* 7 (1981): 25–47.

Selden, Raman. "Historical Thought and Marvell's *Horatian Ode*." *Durham University Journal* 34 (1972–73): 41–53. [Sees the language of the poem as being concerned with antitheses such as the ideal and the actual, the providential and the human, and justice and fate]

Siemon, James Edward. "Art and Argument in Marvell's Horatian Ode Upon Cromwels Return from Ireland." *Neuphilologische Mitteilungen* 73 (1972): 823–35. [Sees in the poem "a pattern balancing fear of Cromwell against respect for him; respect for him against respect for Charles; Charles's virtue against Cromwell's; Charles's decorum against Cromwell's"]

Stapleton, M.L. " 'He Nothing Common Did or Mean': Marvell's Charles I and Horace's *Non Humilis Mulier*." *English Language Notes* (March 1993): 31–40.

Summers, Claude J. "The Frightened Architects of Marvell's 'Horatian Ode.' " *Seventeenth-Century News* 28 (1970): 4. [Identifies the frightened "architects" as Thomas Fairfax and other more moderate Parliamentarians]

Syfret, R.H. "Marvell's 'Horatian Ode.' " *Review of English Studies* 12 (1961): 160–72. [Feels that "in so far as there is a moral or emotional judgement made in the poem, it goes against Cromwell"]

Szilagyi, Stephen. "Credible Praise: Marvell's Dilemma in His Elegy on Oliver Cromwell." *Modern Language Studies* 16 (Summer 1986): 109–21.

Vickers, Brian. "Machiavelli and Marvell's *Horatian Ode*." *Notes and Queries* 36 (1989): 32–38. [Argues for several ways in which Marvell recalled and was influenced by Machiavelli as he wrote "An Horatian Ode"]

Wilding, Michael. "Marvell's 'An Horatian Ode Upon Cromwell's Return from Ireland,' the Levellers, and the Junta." *Modern Language Review* 82 (1987): 1–14. [Argues for reading the poem as an "appeal to support the military junta" and as an "appeal to the poet-intellectuals and other such members of the elite to identify with the Cromwellian army group"]

Williamson, George. *Milton & Others*. Chicago, Illinois: University of Chicago Press, 1965. [Chapter 7 is "Bias in Marvell's *Horatian Ode*."]

Wilson, A.J.N. "Andrew Marvell: 'An Horatian Ode upon Cromwel's Return from Ireland': The Thread of the Poem and Its Use of Classical Allusion." *The Critical Quarterly* 11 (1969): 325–41. [Sees Cromwell portrayed in terms of the Roman concept of Fate]

Wilson, A.J.N. "Andrew Marvell's 'The First Anniversary Under Oliver Cromwell': The Poem and Its Frame of Reference." *Modern Language Review* 69 (1974): 254–73. [Argues for the necessity of paying attention to the politics of the poem to appreciate it fully and sees strong parallels between Cromwell and leaders of Rome]

Worden, Blair. "Andrew Marvell, Oliver Cromwell, and the Horatian Ode." In *Politics of Discourse: The Literature and History of Seventeenth-Century England*, edited by Kevin Sharpe and Steven N. Zwicker, 147–80. Berkeley and Los Angeles: University of California Press, 1987. [Contends that Marvell sees Cromwell more as a force than as a person and as an idea rather than a program and as one who is "inescapable"]

Wortham, Christopher. "Marvell's Cromwell Poems: An Accidental Triptych." In *The Political Identity of Andrew Marvell*, edited by Conal Condren and A.D. Cousins, 16–52. Aldershot, England: Scolar Press, Gower Publishing, 1990. [Argues that the three Cromwell poems "record the process by which Marvell came first to admire Cromwell, with some hesitation and almost grudgingly; then to revere Cromwell as elder statesman; and finally to lament his passing as the end of hope for a new order in England"]

Zwicker, Steven N. "Models of Governance in Marvell's 'The First Anniversary.'" *Criticism* 16 (1974): 1–12. [Sees Marvell associating Cromwell with Old Testament prophets and judges and finally with Christ as savior]

d. The Definition of Love

Crook, Nora C. "Marvell's 'The Definition of Love,' 25–26."
  The Explicator 32 (1973–74): Item 73. [Argues that "loves
  oblique" and "every angle greet" allude to a passage in Horace
  that depicts lovers' assignations in dark corners]
Davison, Dennis. "Marvell's 'The Definition of Love.' " *Review of
  English Studies* 6 (1955): 141–46. [Emphasizes many stock
  images and themes and echoes of other poetry but argues that
  Marvell still did "produce a poem which is essentially original"]
Dorenkamp, Angela G. "Marvell's Geometry of Love." *English
  Language Notes* 9 (1971–72): 111–15. [Focus is upon the
  mathematical meaning of "definition" and its implications of the
  "*limits* of this love within the limitless universe"]
Greenwood, E.B. "Marvell's Impossible Love." *Essays in Criticism* 27
  (1977): 100–109. [Emphasizes the concept of penetration, of two
  bodies occupying precisely the same space at the same time, and
  its impossibility as depicted in the poem. F.W. Bateson adds a
  comment after Greenwood's essay that argues for a probable
  personal situation in Marvell's own life being more significant for
  the poem.]
Hanley, Katherine, CSJ. "Andrew Marvell's 'The Definition of Love.' "
  Concerning Poetry 2 (Fall 1969): 73–74. [Notes the ambiguity of
  the title and the play on three primary meanings of "definition"]
Schmitter, Dean Morgan, and Pierre Legouis. "The Cartography of
  'The Definition of Love.' " *Review of English Studies* 12 (1961):
  49–54. [Morgan argues that the primary imagery is terrestrial,
  and Legouis argues that it is celestial.]
Sokol, B.J. "The *Symposium*, Two Kinds of 'Definition,' and Marvell's
  'The Definition of Love.' " *Notes and Queries* 35 (1988): 169–70.
Toliver, Harold E. "Marvell's 'Definition of Love' and Poetry of Self-
  Exploration." *Bucknell Review* 10 (1961–62): 263–74.
Zwicky, Laurie. "Marvell's 'The Definition of Love.' " *The Explicator*
  22 (1963–64): Item 52. [Argues against the lovers being spatially
  separated, in favor of the idea that it is the "foreordained nature
  of man itself" that prevents their union]

e. The "Dialogue" Poems

Bossy, Michel-André. "Medieval Debates of Body and Soul."
  Comparative Literature 28 (1976): 144–63. [Discusses "A
  Dialogue between the Resolved Soul and Created Pleasure" and
  "A Dialogue between the Soul and Body" in the context of their

medieval predecessors. Notes the features retained by Marvell from the medieval tradition but also comments on his "virtuosity" that changes the tradition. Bossy calls "A Dialogue between the Soul and Body" the "subtlest of all debates between sinful Soul and Body."]

Osmond, Rosalie. "Body and Soul Dialogues in the Seventeenth Century." *English Literary Renaissance* 4 (1974): 364–403. [Discusses "A Dialogue between the Soul and Body" and "A Dialogue between the Resolved Soul and Created Pleasure" as very late manifestations of their genre. Osmond notes the presence of more philosophical than moral debate in the former poem and argues that the latter poem is far removed from the debate tradition, with only a conflict of values and little argument in it.]

Toliver, Harold. "The Strategy of Marvell's Resolve against Created Pleasure." *Studies in English Literature, 1500–1900* 4, (1964): 57–69. [Concerns "A Dialogue between the Resolved Soul and Created Pleasure"]

f. *The Garden*

Carpenter, Margaret Ann. "Marvell's 'Garden.' " *Studies in English Literature, 1500–1900* 10 (1970): 155–69. [Emphasizes the last stanza as the culmination of the poem's ideas]

Cunnar, Eugene R. "Names on Trees, the Hermaphrodite, and 'The Garden.' " In *On the Celebrated and Neglected Poems of Andrew Marvell*, edited by Claude J. Summers and Ted-Larry Pebworth, 121–38. Columbia and London: University of Missouri Press, 1992. [Concentrates on Marvell's anti-Petrarchan stance in the poem]

Empson, William. "Marvell's 'Garden.' " *Scrutiny* 1 (1932–33): 236–40.

Godshalk, William L. "Marvell's 'Garden' and the Theologians." *Studies in Philology* 66 (1969): 639–53. [Relates the poem to seventeenth-century theological ideas and treatises]

Herron, Dale. "Marvell's 'Garden' and the Landscape of Poetry." *Journal of English and Germanic Philology* 73 (1974): 328–37. [Sees the poem's progress in terms of "interlocking stages of withdrawal and return"]

Kermode, Frank. "The Argument of Marvell's 'Garden.' " *Essays in Criticism* 2 (1952): 225–41. [Asserts that the poem is in a tradition that contrasts that of a naturalist paradise]

Klonsky, Milton. "A Guide through the Garden." *Sewanee Review* 58 (1950): 16–35. [A neo-Platonic reading of "The Garden"]
Potter, John M. "Another Porker in the Garden of Epicurus: Marvell's 'Hortus' and 'The Garden.' " *Studies in English Literature, 1500–1900* 11 (1971): 137–51. [Argues for a reading of "The Garden" in the context of the Garden of Epicurus, as portrayed in Horace's poetry, and supports its validity with Marvell's Latin version]
Pritchard, Allan. "Marvell's 'The Garden': A Restoration Poem?" *Studies in English Literature, 1500–1900* 23 (1983): 371–88.
Røstvig, Maren-Sofie. "Andrew Marvell's 'The Garden': A Hermetic Poem." *English Studies* 40 (1959): 65–76.
Serio, John N. "Andrew Marvell's 'The Garden': An Anagogic Reading." *Ohio University Review* 12 (1970): 68–76. [Sees the poem in spiritual, mystical terms, expressing "the final unity between spirit and sense that is necessary to an imaginative vision"]
Siemon, James Edward. "Generic Limits in Marvell's 'Garden.' " *Papers on Language and Literature* 8 (1972): 261–72. [Argues that the poem "explores the possibilities of pastoral as a genre without committing itself to the genre" and that the formal possibilities of the poem "are resolved outside of the limits of Renaissance pastoral"]
Stempel, Daniel. " 'The Garden': Marvell's Cartesian Ecstasy." *Journal of the History of Ideas* 28 (1967): 99–114.
Summers, Joseph H. "Reading Marvell's 'Garden.' " *Centennial Review* 13 (1969): 18–37. [Emphasizes Marvell's humor and exaggeration]
Thomason, T. Katherine. "The Stoic Ground of Marvell's 'Garden.' " *Texas Studies in Literature and Language* 24 (1982): 222–41.

g. The "Mower" Poems

Alpers, Paul. "Convening and Convention in Pastoral Poetry." *New Literary History* 14 (1982–83): 277–304. [A large portion of the essay focuses on "Damon the Mower"]
Anderson, Linda. "The Nature of Marvell's Mower." *Studies in English Literature, 1500–1900* 31 (1991): 131–46. [Examines the immature, childish nature of the mower]
Baldwin, Dean R. "Marvell's 'Mower Poems.' " *The Explicator* 35, no. 3 (1977): 25–26.
Baruch, Elaine Hoffman. "Theme and Counterthemes in 'Damon the Mower.' " *Comparative Literature* 26 (1974): 242–59.

Cinquemani, A.M. "Marvell's 'The Mower Against Gardens,' 9–10."
The Explicator 20 (1961–62): Item 77. [Argues that the "pink" is
a kind of carnation and that "double" refers to the process of
doubling, in which the stamens and carpels are converted into
petals, thus increasing the number of petals. Also argues that the
"nutriment" is fertilizer, which causes the doubling]

Edgecombe, Rodney. "*Pastorale à clef*: A Tentative New View of
Marvell's 'Mower Poems.' " *Durham University Journal* 55
(1994): 209–17. [Interprets Juliana as Charles I and Damon as "an
alternative mode of government"]

Everett, Barbara. "Marvell's 'The Mower's Song.' " *Critical Quarterly*
4 (1962): 219–24.

Godshalk, William Leigh. "Marvell's 'The Mower to the Glo-worms.' "
The Explicator 25 (1966–67): Item 12. [Argues that the poem
contrasts reason and passion, with the glowworms associated with
contentment, creativity, humility, and natural reason]

Kegl, Rosemary. " 'Joyning my Labour to my Pain': The Politics of
Labor in Marvell's Mower Poems." In *Soliciting Interpretation:
Literary Theory and Seventeenth-Century English Poetry*, edited
by Elizabeth D. Harvey and Katharine Eisaman Maus, 89–118.
Chicago: University of Chicago Press, 1990.

Sessions, W.A. "Marvell's Mower: The Wit of Survival." In *The Wit of
Seventeenth-Century Poetry*, edited by Claude J. Summers and
Ted-Larry Pebworth, 183–98. Columbia and London: University
of Missouri Press, 1995.

Wortham, Christopher. "Marvell's 'The Mower to the Glo-worms.' "
The Explicator 49 (1990–91): 142–44. [Comments on the
importance of the fusion of classical and Christian allusions,
including the Philomela myth and an echo of Proverbs]

h. *The Nymph Complaining for the Death of Her Fawn*

Allen, D.C. "Marvell's 'Nymph.' " *ELH* 23 (1956): 93–111. [Contends
that the poem is "about the loss of first love, a loss augmented by
a virginal sense of deprivation and unfulfillment"]

Asp, Carolyn. "Marvell's Nymph: Unravished Bride of Quietness."
Papers on Language and Literature 14 (1978): 394–405.
[Concludes that "the meaning of the poem is essentially negative, a
warning to those who would constrict the vitality of nature and
the potential of art into a limited mirror of the self"]

Coolidge, John S. "The Religious Significance of Marvell's 'The Nymph
Complaining for the Death of Her Faun.' " *Philological Quarterly*
59 (1980): 11–25. [Examines numerous religious echoes and

implications and sees the final representation of the fawn in a statue as living religion become aesthetic sensibility]

Emerson, Everett H. "Andrew Marvell's 'The Nymph Complaining for the Death of Her Faun.'" *Etudes Anglaises* 8 (April-June, 1955): 107–10. [Argues that the poem laments the destruction of the Anglican church by the Parliamentary troopers]

Estrin, Barbara L. "The Nymph and the Revenge of Silence." In *On the Celebrated and Neglected Poems of Andrew Marvell*, edited by Claude J. Summers and Ted-Larry Pebworth, 101–120. Columbia: University of Missouri Press, 1992. [Argues that Marvell's female narrator successfully enacts "deprivational revenge" upon Sylvio and the soldiers]

Foster, Ruel E. "A Tonal Study: Marvell, 'The Nymph Complaining for the Death of Her Faun.'" *University of Kansas City Review* 22 (1955–56): 72–78. [Argues that "a richly simple speech presents obliquely the primitivistic conflict, nature vs. civilization." Also says that Marvell dallies with overtones from myth, folklore, and religion blended into a general tone of stoicism]

Hartman, Geoffrey H. "'The Nymph Complaining for the Death of Her Fawn': A Brief Allegory." *Essays in Criticism* 18 (1968): 113–35. [Examines pagan and Christian elements in the poem and sees it largely as a depiction of history intruding into a pastoral world]

Le Comte, Edward S. "Marvell's 'The Nymph Complaining for the Death of Her Fawn.'" *Modern Philology* 50 (1952–53): 97–101. [Argues against allegorical readings, in favor of reading the poem as a parody of Petrarchan love poetry]

Miner, Earl. "The Death of Innocence in Marvell's 'Nymph Complaining for the Death of Her Faun.'" *Modern Philology* 65 (1967–68): 9–16. [Sees the nymph lamenting the loss of her innocence but also allows for political implications concerning the death of the old order in England]

Sandstroem, Yvonne. "Marvell's 'Nymph Complaining' as Historical Allegory." *Studies in English Literature, 1500–1900* 30 (1990): 93–114. [Uses Spenser's *Daphnaida* to argue that Marvell's poem should be read as political allegory and contends that the fawn symbolizes Charles I]

Sellin, Paul R. "'The Nymph Complaining' as a Stesichorean *Calyca*." In *On the Celebrated and Neglected Poems of Andrew Marvell*, edited by Claude J. Summers and Ted-Larry Pebworth, 86–100. Columbia: University of Missouri Press, 1992.

Spinrad, Phoebe S. "Death, Loss, and Marvell's Nymph." *PMLA* 97 (1982): 50–59. [Sees the poem primarily confronting questions of time, death, loss, and mutability, without finding answers]

Spitzer, Leo. "Marvell's 'Nymph Complaining for the Death of Her Faun': Sources Versus Meaning." *Modern Language Quarterly* 19 (1958): 231–43. [Focuses on the nymph as the protagonist of the poem and on the fawn's fate as a reflection of the nymph's tragedy]

Teunissen, John J., and Evelyn J. Hinz. "What is the Nymph Complaining For?" *ELH* 45 (1978): 410–28. [Argues that the nymph actually is complaining about the death of her child and that the fawn is a projection invented to account for her grief]

Thomason, T. Katharine. "Marvell's Complaint Against His Nymph." *Studies in English Literature, 1500–1900* 18 (1978): 95–105. [Argues that Marvell criticizes the nymph's "extreme expression of the pastoral motive of retreat"]

Williamson, Karina. "Marvell's 'The Nymph Complaining for the Death of Her Fawn': A Reply." *Modern Philology* 51 (1953–54): 268–71. [Replies to the essay by Le Comte on the poem. Argues that the poem indeed may be read allegorically and that the extensive Christian references would not be overlooked by Marvell's contemporaries]

i. *On a Drop of Dew*

Giles, Richard F. "Marvell's 'On a Drop of Dew.' " *The Explicator* 39 (Spring 1981): 14–18. [Concerns various meanings of "recollecting," with emphasis on a Roman Catholic one tied to spiritual recollection by friars in certain monasteries]

Looney, Barbara A. "Marvell's Dewdrop: Two Possibilities for the Soul." *John Donne Journal* 8 (1989): 191–93. [Notes the contrast between the English and Latin versions of the poem. The Latin version contains "no religious references," and the dewdrop becomes "purer" through its earthly sojourn.]

Muldrow, George M. "The Forty Lines of Andrew Marvell's 'On a Drop of Dew.' " *English Language Notes* 23 (March 1986): 23–27. [Emphasizes the numerological importance of forty lines by referring to Augustine's view that forty is a "fit symbol" for "this life of toil, the chief work in which is to exercise self-control, in abstaining from the world's friendship, which never ceases deceitfully caressing us, and scattering profusely around us its bewitching allurements"]

Rosa, Alfred F. "Andrew Marvell's 'On a Drop of Dew': A Reading and Possible Source." *Concerning Poetry* 5 (Spring 1972): 57–59.

Saveson, J.E. "Marvell's 'On a Drop of Dew.' " *Notes and Queries* 5 (July 1958): 289–90. [Emphasizes resolution in the poem through

Christian symbolism, with the manna as the Eucharist and Christ and grace]

j. On Mr. Milton's "Paradise Lost"

Gross, Kenneth. " 'Pardon Me, Mighty Poet': Versions of the Bard in Marvell's 'On Mr. Milton's *Paradise Lost.*' " *Milton Studies* 16 (1982): 77–96. [Says that Marvell speaks to Milton in Milton's own voice, with sympathy and respect, but that Marvell also maintains the integrity of his own poetic mode]

Parker, G.F. "Marvell on Milton: Why the Poem Rhymes Not." *The Cambridge Quarterly* 20:3 (1991): 183–209.

Wittreich, Joseph Anthony, Jr. "Perplexing the Explanation: Marvell's 'On Mr. Milton's *Paradise Lost.*' " In *Approaches to Marvell*, edited by C.A. Patrides, 280–305. London: Routledge and Kegan Paul, 1978. [Sees the poem as "covertly, a self-justifying one"]

k. The Picture of Little T. C. in a Prospect of Flowers

Dyson, A.E., and Julian Lovelock. *Masterful Images: English Poetry from Metaphysicals to Romantics*. London: Macmillan; New York: Barnes and Noble, 1976. [Chapter 3 is "Serpent in Eden: Marvell's 'The Picture of Little T. C. in a Prospect of Flowers.' "]

Lerner, Laurence. *An Introduction to English Poetry*. London: Edward Arnold Publishers, 1975. [Chapter 6 gives a reading of "The Picture of Little T. C. in a Prospect of Flowers," with relationships made to other poems by Marvell and to those of other poets.]

Margoliouth, H.M. "Andrew Marvell: Some Biographical Points." *Modern Language Review* 17 (1922): 351–61. [Identifies "T. C." as Theophila Cornewall, born in 1644]

Simmons, J.L. "Marvell's 'The Picture of Little T. C. in a Prospect of Flowers.' " *The Explicator* 22 (1963–64): Item 62. [Explication of the poem, emphasizing the allusions to Adam and Eden]

l. To His Coy Mistress

Baumann, Michael. "Marvell's 'To His Coy Mistress.' " *The Explicator* 31 (1972–73): Item 72. [Explains "Time's winged chariot" as a reference to the common Renaissance pictorial representation of Time as an aged figure, a destroyer, in triumph]

Belsey, Catherine. "Love and Death in 'To His Coy Mistress.' " In *Post-Structuralist Readings of English Poetry*, edited by Richard Machin and Christopher Norris, 105–21. Cambridge: Cambridge University Press, 1987.

Brody, Jules. "The Resurrection of the Body: A New Reading of Marvell's 'To His Coy Mistress.' " *ELH* 56 (1989): 53–79. [Sees the poem as parodic and ultimately a "worldly celebration of lust"]

Brunner, Larry. " 'Love at Lower Rate': A Christian Reading of 'To His Coy Mistress.' " *Christianity and Literature* 38 (Summer 1989): 25–44.

Buttrey, T.V., and Ruth Smith. "World and Time in Marvell's 'To His Coy Mistress.' " *Anglia* 103 (1985): 401–405.

Christian, Henry A. "Marvell's Mistress' Rubies." *Modern Language Studies* 11 (Winter 1980–81): 33–37. [Examines the associations with rubies in Proverbs]

Clayton, Thomas. " 'Morning Glew' and Other Sweat Leaves in the Folio Text of Andrew Marvell's Major Pre-Restoration Poems." *English Literary Renaissance* 2 (1972): 356–75. [Primarily treats the textual crux in lines 33–34 and argues for "glew" as "glue"]

Crider, Richard. "Marvell's Valid Logic." *College Literature* 12 (1985): 113–21.

Cunningham, J.V. "Logic and Lyric." *Modern Philology* 51 (1953–54): 33–41. [Includes an examination of the syllogistic structure of "To His Coy Mistress"]

D'Avanzo, Mario L. "Marvell's 'To His Coy Mistress.' " *The Explicator* 36, no. 2 (1978): 18–19. [Argues that the "iron gates of life" alludes parodically to Matthew 7:13–14, with the "strait gate" that leads "unto life"]

Fogle, French. "Marvell's 'Tough Reasonableness' and the Coy Mistress." In *Tercentenary Essays in Honor of Andrew Marvell*, edited by Kenneth Friedenreich, 121–39. Hamden, Connecticut: Archon, 1977. [Surveys some twentieth-century critical views of "To His Coy Mistress"]

Gwynn, Frederick L. "Marvell's 'To His Coy Mistress,' 33–46." *The Explicator* 11 (1952–53): Item 49. [Argues for the importance of the Phaethon myth in interpreting images of the sun and time]

Hackett, John. "Logic and Rhetoric in Marvell's 'Coy Mistress.' " In *Tercentenary Essays in Honor of Andrew Marvell*, edited by Kenneth Friedenreich, 140–52. Hamden, Connecticut: Archon, 1977.

Hartwig, Joan. "The Principle of Measure in 'To His Coy Mistress.' " *College English* 25 (1963–64): 572–75. [Discusses the importance of the concept of the three souls]

Heaton, Cherrill P. "Marvell's 'To His Coy Mistress,' 41–42." *The Explicator* 30 (1971–72): Item 48. [Interprets "ball" as the "amorous birds of prey" engaged in sexual intercourse in the air]

Karon, Jeffrey W. "Cohesion as Logic: The Possible Worlds of Marvell's 'To His Coy Mistress.' " *Style* 27 (1993): 91–105. [Contends that "failing to examine the logical links between clauses would prevent our seeing how the poem unfolds within the confines set up in the first two lines"]

Keogh, J.G.. "Marvell's 'To His Coy Mistress,' 41–46." *The Explicator* 28 (1969–70): Item 13. [Emphasizes imagery of warfare, cannon, and cannonball]

King, Bruce. "Irony in Marvell's 'To His Coy Mistress.' " *Southern Review* n. s. 5, (1969): 689–703. [Sees the poem as a satire on libertine verse and as a moral, Christian piece]

Miller, Clarence H. "Sophistry and Truth in 'To His Coy Mistress.' " *College Literature* 2 (1975): 97–104.

Moldenhauer, Joseph J. "The Voices of Seduction in 'To His Coy Mistress': A Rhetorical Analysis." *Texas Studies in Literature and Language* 10 (1968–69): 189–206. [Examines the "persuasive discourse," the persona, and specifics in words and images of the poem, leading to the conclusion that "To His Coy Mistress" is "the unchallenged masterpiece among lyrics of seduction"]

Randall, Dale B.J. "Once More to the G(r)ates: An Old Crux and a New Reading of 'To His Coy Mistress.' " In *On the Celebrated and Neglected Poems of Andrew Marvell*, edited by Claude J. Summers and Ted-Larry Pebworth, 47–69. Columbia: University of Missouri Press, 1992. [Argues for "grates," rather than "gates," in line 44]

Ray, Robert H. "Marvell's 'To His Coy Mistress' and Sandys's Translation of Ovid's *Metamorphoses*." *Review of English Studies* 44 (1993): 386–88. [Argues for the influence of the Echo and Narcissus story in general and in specific lines of the poem]

Roberts, John Hawley. "Marvell's 'To His Coy Mistress.' " *The Explicator* 1 (1942–43): Item 17.

Sasek, Lawrence A. "Marvell's 'To His Coy Mistress,' 45–46." *The Explicator* 14 (1955–56): Item 47. [Says that the last couplet implies that the lovers "can compress the activity of normal ages into one extraordinarily busy day"]

Sokol, B.J. "Logic and Illogic in Marvell's 'To His Coy Mistress.' " *English Studies* 71 (1990): 244–52. [Sees Marvell using both logic

and illogic "to disturb stereotypes, expose assumptions, and test the use of reason itself"]
Spinrad, Phoebe S. "Pall-Mall and the 'Iron Gates' in 'To His Coy Mistress.' " *Massachusetts Studies in English* 9:4 (1984): 71–74. [Relates several images in lines 37–44 to the game of pall-mall]
Taylor, Mark. "Marvell's 'To His Coy Mistress.' " *The Explicator* 53 (1994–95): 15–16. [Sees as important the change from "thy" in lines 25 and 26 to "your" in line 29 because it "makes the mistress impersonal without individual identity, unloved—as, the lover warns her, she is soon to be forever"]
Walker, Steven F. "Marvell's 'To His Coy Mistress.' " *The Explicator* 38, no. 1 (1979): 2–3. [Sees allusions to Virgil in some elements of the poem]

m. *Upon Appleton House*

Allen, Don Cameron. *Image and Meaning: Metaphoric Traditions in Renaissance Poetry.* Revised ed. Baltimore, Maryland: The Johns Hopkins Press, 1968. [Chapter 11 is "Andrew Marvell, 'Upon Appleton House.' "]
Barnard, John. "Marvell and Denton's 'Cataracts.' " *Review of English Studies* 31 (1980): 310–15. [Argues that "cataracts" in line 466 of "Upon Appleton House" refers to the floodgates at Fairfax's Denton estate, about thirty miles up the River Wharfe from his Appleton estate]
Brooks-Davies, Douglas. "Number Symbolism in Marvell's *Upon Appleton House.*" *Notes and Queries* 27 (1980): 336–39.
Canaan, Howard. "Meaning, Shape, and Number in *Upon Appleton House.*" *John Donne Journal* 7 (1988): 239–56. [Concerns "how Marvell's use of numerical symbology functions as a moral, structural, and aesthetic principle in the poem itself"]
Chambers, Douglas D.C. " 'To the Abbyss': Gothic as a Metaphor for the Argument about Art and Nature in 'Upon Appleton House.' " In *On the Celebrated and Neglected Poems of Andrew Marvell*, edited by Claude J. Summers and Ted-Larry Pebworth, 139–53. Columbia: University of Missouri Press, 1992. [Sees the poem supporting "a right kind of retirement as against its monastic perversion"]
Cousins, A.D. "Marvell's 'Upon Appleton House, to my Lord Fairfax' and the Regaining of Paradise." In *The Political Identity of Andrew Marvell*, edited by Conal Condren and A.D. Cousins, 53–84. Aldershot, England: Scolar Press, Gower Publishing, 1990. [Argues that, in contrast to previous royalist country house

poems, Marvell's presents the home's owner "as virtually embodying the Calvinist idea of moderation"]

Cummings, Robert. "The Forest Sequence in Marvell's *Upon Appleton House*: The Imaginative Contexts of a Poetic Episode." *Huntington Library Quarterly* 47 (1984): 179–210. [Concerns the importance of myths of Diana in the poem]

Cummings, Robert. "The 'Mose of Dust' in Marvell's *Upon Appleton House*." *English Language Notes* 24 (September 1986): 25–27. [Argues that line 22 should be emended with the word *mese* (meaning "mansion" or "house") in place of "mose"]

Erickson, Lee. "Marvell's *Upon Appleton House* and the Fairfax Family." *English Literary Renaissance* 9 (1979): 158–68. [Argues that Marvell's account of Isabel Thwaites is to justify dissolving Mary Fairfax's engagement to Philip Stanhope, thereby freeing her to marry the Duke of Buckingham]

Evett, David. " 'Paradice's Only Map': The *Topos* of the *Locus Amoenus* and the Structure of Marvell's *Upon Appleton House*." *PMLA* 85 (1970): 504–13.

Gray, Allan. "The Surface of Marvell's *Upon Appleton House*." *English Literary Renaissance* 9 (1979): 169–82. [Emphasizes the "surface excitement" of the poem and the fact that the poem "calls attention to itself technically," a "reflexiveness" which "is a key to the poem"]

Griffin, Patsy. " 'Twas no *Religious House* till now': Marvell's 'Upon Appleton House.' " *Studies in English Literature, 1500–1900* 28 (1988): 61–76. [Argues that the historical section of twenty-five stanzas is essential to Marvell's purpose, "representing the Fairfax possession as providential"]

Grossman, Marshall. "Authoring the Boundary: Allegory, Irony, and the Rebus in 'Upon Appleton House.' " In *"The Muses Common-Weale": Poetry and Politics in the Seventeenth Century*, edited by Claude J. Summers and Ted-Larry Pebworth, 191–206. Columbia: University of Missouri Press, 1988. [Argues that Fairfax's choice to end his military career and his choice to settle the Nun Appleton estate on his daughter's heirs are paired choices and that Marvell's poem mirrors these choices]

Grundy, Joan. "Marvell's Grasshoppers." *Notes and Queries* 4 (1957): 142. [Notes that lines 371–72 of "Upon Appleton House" allude to Numbers 13:32–33 and establish a parallel between the Israelites who were brought only within sight of the Promised Land and the Puritans who similarly hoped for a promised land in England]

Healy, Thomas. " 'Dark all without it knits': Vision and Authority in Marvell's *Upon Appleton House*." In *Literature and the English*

Civil War, edited by Thomas Healy and Jonathan Sawday, 170–88. Cambridge: Cambridge University Press, 1990. [Argues that "Marvell constantly subverts his poetic narrator's vision, intruding into the text to render its organisation unstable and suspect"]

Heumann, J. Mark. "Prophecy, Casuistry, and Epideictic in Marvell's *Upon Appleton House* XXVI–XXXV." *Cahiers Elisabéthains* 44 (October 1993): 33–43. [Sees the account of William Fairfax as a defense of Thomas Fairfax's choice to retire]

Jaeckle, Daniel P. "Marvell's Dialogics of History: *Upon Appleton House*, XI–XXXV." *John Donne Journal* 6 (1987): 261–73.

Jaeckle, Daniel P. "Marvell's Reformed Theory of Architecture: *Upon Appleton House*, I–X." *John Donne Journal* 4, (1985): 49–67.

Lewalski, Barbara Kiefer. *Donne's "Anniversaries" and the Poetry of Praise: The Creation of a Symbolic Mode*. Princeton, New Jersey: Princeton University Press, 1973. [Pages 355–70 concern the ways in which "Upon Appleton House" is influenced by Donne's "Anniversaries."]

MacCaffrey, Isabel G. "The Scope of Imagination in *Upon Appleton House*." In *Tercentenary Essays in Honor of Andrew Marvell*, edited by Kenneth Friedenreich, 224–44. Hamden, Connecticut: Archon, 1977.

McClung, W[illiam]. "The 'Real' Appleton House?" *Notes and Queries* 26 (1979): 433–34. [Argues for Marvell's poem referring to Lord Fairfax's newly built home]

McClung, William A. *The Country House in English Renaissance Poetry*. Berkeley: University of California Press, 1977. [Pages 157–74 concern Appleton House.]

McGaw, William D. "Marvell's 'Salmon-Fishers'—A Contemporary Joke." *English Language Notes* 13 (1975–76): 177–80. [Sees the last stanza of "Upon Appleton House" as good-natured humor, playing upon a contemporary misconception by some that those on the other side of the world walk on their heads]

Miller, Clarence H. "The Misprint 'Not Compare' in Line 303 of Marvell's 'Upon Appleton House.' " *English Language Notes* 25 (March 1988): 26–28.

Molesworth, Charles. "Marvell's 'Upon Appleton House': The Persona as Historian, Philosopher, and Priest." *Studies in English Literature, 1500–1900* 13 (1973): 149–62. [Argues that the triple role of the persona serves to show Mary Fairfax as illustrating "the results and possibilities of the historical values that fostered her," to mythologize her and thus vindicate her father and his estate's virtues, and to show how she "vitrifies nature"]

Norford, Don Parry. "Marvell's 'Holy Mathematicks.' " *Modern Language Quarterly* 38 (1977): 242–60. [Argues that "the emblem of the circle in the square is the key" to the poem, in which Marvell treats the "transmutation of matter to spirit by means of a holy art that perfects and complements nature instead of corrupting or destroying it, as do the nuns and mowers respectively"]

O'Loughlin, M.J.K. "This Sober Frame: A Reading of 'Upon Appleton House.' " In *Andrew Marvell: A Collection of Critical Essays*, edited by George deF. Lord, 120–42. Englewood Cliffs, New Jersey: Prentice-Hall, Inc., 1968.

Røstvig, Maren-Sofie. " 'Upon Appleton House' and the Universal History of Man." *English Studies* 42 (1961): 337–51. [Argues that the aesthetic design of the poem is grounded on the theological concept of the contrast between innocence and corruption and that this contrast is pursued through regional history, family history, and universal history]

Roth, Frederic H., Jr. "Marvell's 'Upon Appleton House': A Study in Perspective." *Texas Studies in Literature and Language* 14 (1972–73): 269–81. [Concerns Marvell's uses of perspective and disorienting the reader purposefully in order to "make men recognize the inherited curse of myopia and the perils of living in a topsy-turvy world, where everything appears inverted to our perverted vision" and his attempt to "bring the world back into focus"]

Schwenger, Peter. " 'To Make His Saying True': Deceit in *Appleton House*." *Studies in Philology* 77 (1980): 84–104. [Argues that the poem is informed by a sense of "potential self-deceit" that is detected in allusion, technique, and tone]

Simons, John. "Marvell's Tulips." *Notes and Queries* 36 (1989): 434. [Notes that the tulips referred to in lines 335–36 of "Upon Appleton House" might well allude to a gaudy and relatively cheap variety of tulip called the Switser, along with other political and theological implications]

Skulsky, Harold. "*Upon Appleton House*: Marvell's Comedy of Discourse." *ELH* 52 (1985): 591–620. [Sees the speaker of the poem as a loquacious guide on a tour of the estate, entertaining his listeners with jokes and play of wit]

Thomason, T. Katharine Sheldahl. "Marvell, His Bee-Like Cell: The Pastoral Hexagon of *Upon Appleton House*." *Genre* 16 (1983): 39–56. [Argues that Marvell adopts the conventions of six types of pastoral in order to give his poem "emblematic perfection and permanence"]

Turner, James. "Marvell's Warlike Studies." *Essays in Criticism* 28 (1978): 288–301. [Sees Marvell encouraging the Fairfaxes "to see life at Appleton as a beginning and not an end, to use these warlike studies to defeat the legacy of war"]

Turner, James. *The Politics of Landscape: Rural Scenery and Society in English Poetry, 1630–1660.* Cambridge, Massachusetts: Harvard University Press, 1979. [Pages 61–84 concern "Upon Appleton House," which Turner calls "the longest and most complicated topographical poem in English."]

Turner, J.G. "Upon Appleton House." *Notes and Queries* 24 (1977): 547–48. [Argues that the Appleton House of Marvell's poem is not the structure newly built by Lord Fairfax and that the new structure was still in progress in 1658, about six or seven years after Marvell probably wrote the poem]

Warnke, Frank J. "The Meadow-sequence in *Upon Appleton House*: Questions of Tone and Meaning." In *Approaches to Marvell*, edited by C.A. Patrides, 234–50. London: Routledge and Kegan Paul, 1978.

Wilding, Michael. *Dragons Teeth: Literature in the English Revolution.* Oxford: Clarendon Press, 1987. [Chapter 6 is "Upon Appleton House, to my Lord Fairfax."]

3. Restoration Satires

Benet, Diana Trevino. " 'The Loyall Scot' and the Hidden Narcissus." In *On the Celebrated and Neglected Poems of Andrew Marvell*, edited by Claude J. Summers and Ted-Larry Pebworth, 192–206. Columbia: University of Missouri Press, 1992.

Chernaik, Warren L. "The Heroic Occasional Poem: Panegyric and Satire in the Restoration." *Modern Language Quarterly* 26 (1965): 523–35. [Includes a discussion of "The Last Instructions to a Painter," arguing that its central theme is "a rigorous diagnosis of the illness of the body politic"]

Chernaik, Warren L. "Marvell's Satires: The Artist as Puritan." In *Tercentenary Essays in Honor of Andrew Marvell*, edited by Kenneth Friedenreich, 268–96. Hamden, Connecticut: Archon, 1977. [Emphasizes "The Last Instructions to a Painter"]

Farley-Hills, David. *The Benevolence of Laughter: Comic Poetry of the Commonwealth and Restoration.* London: Macmillan Press, 1974. [Chapter 4 is "*Last Instructions to a Painter.*"]

Fisher, Alan S. "The Augustan Marvell: 'The Last Instructions to a Painter.' " *ELH* 38 (1971): 223–38. [Sees the poem as "an attempt to bring the major lyric vision to bear on a scattered heap of public events"]

Gearin-Tosh, Michael. "The Structure of Marvell's 'Last Instructions to a Painter.' " *Essays in Criticism* 22 (1972): 48–57. [Sees Marvell giving "low portraits" and "high portraits" that lead to the portrait of Charles II, the betrayer]

Lynch, Denise E. "Politics, Nature, and Structure in Marvell's 'The Last Instructions to a Painter.' " *Restoration: Studies in English Literary Culture, 1660–1700* 16, (1992): 82–92. [Analyzes the poem in terms of three "movements," arguing that the "symmetries of these movements add unity to the poem and accomplish Marvell's partisan ends"]

Messina, Joseph. "The Heroic Image in 'The Last Instructions to a Painter.' " In *Tercentenary Essays in Honor of Andrew Marvell*, edited by Kenneth Friedenreich, 297–310. Hamden, Connecticut: Archon, 1977. [Sees Douglas as "the superior human being against whom many other characters and their actions are measured"]

Miner, Earl. "The 'Poetic Picture, Painted Poetry' of 'The Last Instructions to a Painter.' " *Modern Philology* 63 (1965–66): 288–94. [Argues for unity in the poem in large part because of its consistent anti-royalist, anti-court, pro-Parliament, and pro-country attitude]

Power, Helen D. "The Unity of 'Last Instructions to a Painter.' " *Satire Newsletter* 8 (1970–71): 98–100.

Quivey, James. "Marvell's Couplet Art: 'Last Instructions to a Painter.' " *Essays in Literature* 1 (1974): 28–36.

Riebling, Barbara. "England Deflowered and Unmanned: The Sexual Image of Politics in Marvell's 'Last Instructions.' " *Studies in English Literature, 1500-1900* 35 (1995): 137–57. [Argues that "the poem's governing pattern of metaphors represents the country's domestic and international plight by linking abuses of sexual power with abuses of political power and a collapse of gender norms with a collapse of political norms"]

Todd, Richard. "Equilibrium and National Stereotyping in 'The Character of Holland.' " In *On the Celebrated and Neglected Poems of Andrew Marvell*, edited by Claude J. Summers and Ted-Larry Pebworth, 169–91. Columbia: University of Missouri Press, 1992.

Zwicker, Steven N. "Virgins and Whores: The Politics of Sexual Misconduct in the 1660s." In *The Political Identity of Andrew Marvell*, edited by Conal Condren and A.D. Cousins, 85–110. Aldershot, England: Scolar Press, Gower Publishing, 1990. [Concerns "The Last Instructions to a Painter"]

4. Miscellaneous and More Than One Type of Poem

Abraham, Lyndy. *Marvell and Alchemy.* Aldershot, England, and Brookfield, Vermont: Scolar Press, Gower Publishing, 1990. [Emphasizes relevance of the study of alchemy, especially to "Upon Appleton House," "The Nymph Complaining for the Death of Her Fawn," and "To His Coy Mistress"]

Bennett, Joan. *Five Metaphysical Poets: Donne, Herbert, Vaughan, Crashaw, Marvell.* Cambridge: Cambridge University Press, 1964. [The chapter on Marvell first appeared in this 1964 publication: the book was previously published as *Four Metaphysical Poets.*]

Berek, Peter. "The Voices of Marvell's Lyrics." *Modern Language Quarterly* 32 (1971):143–57. [Focusing upon "A Dialogue between the Soul and Body," the Mower poems, "The Nymph Complaining for the Death of Her Fawn," and "The Picture of Little T. C. in a Prospect of Flowers," Berek argues that "Marvell's lyric poems articulate a complex and tentative vision of man's fate by presenting us with a series of brilliantly drawn but limited speakers."]

Berthoff, Ann E. *The Resolved Soul: A Study of Marvell's Major Poems.* Princeton, New Jersey: Princeton University Press, 1970.

Bradbrook, Muriel C. "Marvell and the Masque." In *Tercentenary Essays in Honor of Andrew Marvell,* edited by Kenneth Friedenreich, 204–23. Hamden, Connecticut: Archon, 1977.

Bradbrook, Muriel [C.] "Marvell Our Contemporary." In *Andrew Marvell: Essays on the Tercentenary of His Death,* edited by R.L. Brett, 104–18. University of Hull Publications. Oxford: Oxford University Press for the University of Hull, 1979.

Brogan, Hugh. "Marvell's 'Epitaph on -----.' " *Renaissance Quarterly* 32 (1979): 197–99.

Brooks, Cleanth. *Historical Evidence and the Reading of Seventeenth-Century Poetry.* Columbia: University of Missouri Press, 1991. [Contains two chapters on Marvell]

Carey, John. "Reversals Transposed: An Aspect of Marvell's Imagination." In *Approaches to Marvell: The York Tercentenary Lectures,* edited by C.A. Patrides, 136–54. London, Henley, and Boston: Routledge & Kegan Paul, 1978.

Carscallen, James. "Marvell's Infinite Parallels." *University of Toronto Quarterly* 39 (1969–70): 144–63. [Concerns the "interplay of contraries" in Marvell's works]

Chambers, A.B. *Andrew Marvell and Edmund Waller: Seventeenth-Century Praise and Restoration Satire.* University Park: Pennsylvania State University Press, 1991.

Chaudhuri, Sukanta. *Renaissance Pastoral and Its English Developments.* Oxford: Clarendon Press, 1989. [Chapter 22 is "Andrew Marvell."]

Clayton, Thomas. " 'It Is Marvel He Outdwells His Hour': Some Perspectives on Marvell's Medium." In *Tercentenary Essays in Honor of Andrew Marvell*, edited by Kenneth Friedenreich, 46–75. Hamden, Connecticut: Archon, 1977.

Colie, Rosalie L. *"My Ecchoing Song": Andrew Marvell's Poetry of Criticism.* Princeton, New Jersey: Princeton University Press, 1970. [Examines Marvell "working in and beyond his traditions" and as both creator and critic]

Cook, Elizabeth. *Seeing Through Words: The Scope of Late Renaissance Poetry.* New Haven and London: Yale University Press, 1986. [Chapter 7 concerns Marvell.]

Craze, Michael. *The Life and Lyrics of Andrew Marvell.* London and Basingstoke: Macmillan Press; New York: Harper & Row, 1979. [A brief biography precedes comments on forty lyrics.]

Creaser, John. "Marvell's Effortless Superiority." *Essays in Criticism* 20 (1970): 403–23. [Examines Marvell's combined somberness and gaiety, with primary emphasis on the Mower poems, "To His Coy Mistress," and "Upon Appleton House"]

Cullen, Patrick. *Spenser, Marvell, and Renaissance Pastoral.* Cambridge, Massachusetts: Harvard University Press, 1970.

Davidson, P.R.K., and A.K. Jones. "New Light on Marvell's 'The Unfortunate Lover'?" *Notes and Queries* 32 (1985): 170–72. [Raises the possibilities that a Latin poem by Sir Richard Fanshawe was an influence on Marvell's poem and that a political level of meaning exists in Marvell's poem]

Delany, Paul. "Marvell's 'Mourning.' "*Modern Language Quarterly* 33 (1972): 30–36.

Dubrow, Heather. "Marvell's Gallery of Art Revisited." *Concerning Poetry* 13 (Spring 1980): 61–64. [Concerns "The Gallery"]

Dubrow, Heather. "Teaching Marvell." In *Approaches to Teaching the Metaphysical Poets*, edited by Sidney Gottlieb, 144–49. New York: Modern Language Association of America, 1990.

Duncan-Jones, Elsie. "A Reading of Marvell's 'The Unfortunate

Lover.' " In *I.A. Richards: Essays in His Honor*, edited by Reuben Brower, Helen Vendler, and John Hollander, 211–26. New York: Oxford University Press, 1973.

Dundas, Judith. " 'All Things are Bigge with Jest': Wit as a Means of Grace." In *New Perspectives on the Seventeenth-Century English Religious Lyric*, edited by John R. Roberts, 124–42. Columbia and London: University of Missouri Press, 1994. [Discusses "A Dialogue between the Resolved Soul and Created Pleasure," "A Dialogue between the Soul and Body," and "On a Drop of Dew"]

Ellrodt, Robert. "Marvell's Mind and Mystery." In *Approaches to Marvell: The York Tercentenary Lectures*, edited by C.A. Patrides, 216–33. London: Routledge and Kegan Paul, 1978.

Empson, William. "Natural Magic and Populism in Marvell's Poetry." In *Andrew Marvell: Essays on the Tercentenary of His Death*, edited by R.L. Brett, 36–61. University of Hull Publications. Oxford: Oxford University Press for the University of Hull, 1979.

Empson, William. *Seven Types of Ambiguity*. 2nd ed. London: Chatto & Windus, 1947. [Comments on "On a Drop of Dew," "A Dialogue between the Resolved Soul and Created Pleasure," "An Horatian Ode upon Cromwell's Return from Ireland," "The Unfortunate Lover," "The Nymph Complaining for the Death of Her Fawn," "Upon the Death of Lord Hastings," and "Eyes and Tears"]

Enterline, Lynn. "The Mirror and the Snake: The Case of Marvell's 'Unfortunate Lover.' " *Critical Quarterly* 29 (Winter 1987): 98–112. [Argues that "the narcissistic predicament of the Marvellian lyric turns the lover into he who takes pleasure in his own wounds"]

Everett, Barbara. "The Shooting of the Bears: Poetry and Politics in Andrew Marvell." In *Andrew Marvell: Essays on the Tercentenary of His Death*, edited by R.L. Brett, 62–103. University of Hull Publications. Oxford: Oxford University Press for the University of Hull, 1979.

Ferry, Anne. *All in War with Time: Love Poetry of Shakespeare, Donne, Jonson, Marvell*. Cambridge, Massachusetts: Harvard University Press, 1975. [Chapter 4 is titled "Marvell" and presents readings of several poems.]

Friedenreich, Kenneth. "The Mower Mown: Marvell's Dances of Death." In *Tercentenary Essays in Honor of Andrew Marvell*, edited by Kenneth Friedenreich, 153–79. Hamden, Connecticut: Archon, 1977.

Friedman, Donald M. "Andrew Marvell." In *The Cambridge Companion to English Poetry: Donne to Marvell*, edited by

Thomas N. Corns, 275–303. Cambridge: Cambridge University Press, 1993.
Friedman, Donald M. "Marvell's Musicks." In *On the Celebrated and Neglected Poems of Andrew Marvell*, edited by Claude J. Summers and Ted-Larry Pebworth, 8–28. Columbia: University of Missouri Press, 1992. [Concerns Marvell's interest in and uses of music in various poems]
Friedman, Donald M. *Marvell's Pastoral Art*. Berkeley and Los Angeles: University of California Press, 1970.
Friedman, Donald M. "Sight and Insight in Marvell's Poetry." In *Approaches to Marvell: The York Tercentenary Lectures*, edited by C.A. Patrides, 306–30. London: Routledge and Kegan Paul, 1978. [Emphasizes the importance of detailed visual elements in Marvell's poetry]
Gent, Lucy. "Marvell's Games with Teleology." *Renaissance Quarterly* 32 (1979): 514–28. [Emphasizes design and purpose in Marvell's treatment of nature]
Goldberg, Jonathan. "The Typology of 'Musicks Empire.'" *Texas Studies in Literature and Language* 13 (1971–72): 421–30. [Argues that the poem is typological and concerns final fulfillment in Christ]
Gransden, K.W. "Time, Guilt and Pleasure: A Note on Marvell's Nostalgia." *Ariel* 1 (April 1970): 83–97. [Traces Marvell's nostalgia for the old order in England and for unfallen Eden in the Mower poems, "The Garden," "Upon Appleton House," "An Horatian Ode," and others]
Greenfield, Stanley B. "Ellipsis and Meaning in Poetry." *Texas Studies in Literature and Language* 13 (1971–72): 137–47. [Looks at ellipsis in "To His Coy Mistress" and "The Garden"]
Griffin, Patsy. "Structural Allegory in Andrew Marvell's Poetry." *Journal of English and Germanic Philology* 91 (1992): 325–43. [Emphasizes Marvell's allegorizing of the "fortunate fall" pattern over a spectrum of poems, including "Upon Appleton House," the Mower poems, "The Garden," the Cromwell poems, and "On Mr. Milton's *Paradise Lost*"]
Guild, Nicholas. "The Contexts of Marvell's Early 'Royalist' Poems." *Studies in English Literature, 1500–1900* 20 (1980): 125–36. [Concerns the poems on Villiers, Lovelace, and Hastings]
Hartman, Geoffrey H. "Marvell, St. Paul, and the Body of Hope." *ELH* 31 (1964): 175–94. [Readings of "The Garden" and the Mower poems]
Hartwig, Joan. "Tears as a Way of Seeing." In *On the Celebrated and Neglected Poems of Andrew Marvell*, edited by Claude J. Summers and Ted-Larry Pebworth, 70–85. Columbia: University

of Missouri Press, 1992. [Examines motif of tears in "Eyes and Tears," "The Garden," "On a Drop of Dew," "Mourning," and "The Nymph Complaining for the Death of Her Fawn"]

Heninger, S.K., Jr. "Marvell's 'Geometrick yeer': A Topos for Occasional Poetry." In *Approaches to Marvell: The York Tercentenary Lectures*, edited by C.A. Patrides, 87–107. London: Routledge and Kegan Paul, 1978. [Places Marvell in the context of other poets who view a human's life as comparable to a year within the eternal cycle of time]

Hill, Christopher. "Society and Andrew Marvell." *Modern Quarterly* 4 (1946): 6–11. [Reads several lyrics as pointing to Marvell's personal growth toward endorsing Cromwellian and parliamentary government]

Hinnant, Charles H. "Marvell's Gallery of Art." *Renaissance Quarterly* 24 (1971): 26–37. [Concerns "The Gallery"]

Hodge, R.I.V. "Marvell's Fairfax Poems: Some Considerations Concerning Dates." *Modern Philology* 71 (1973–74): 347–55.

Hyman, Lawrence W. "Politics and Poetry in Andrew Marvell." *PMLA* 73 (1958): 475–79.

Kalstone, David. "Marvell and the Fictions of Pastoral." *English Literary Renaissance* 4 (1974): 174–88. [Treats some of Marvell's classical models, ambiguity, and puns in the Mower poems, "The Coronet," and "The Garden"]

Kaufmann, U. Milo. *Paradise in the Age of Milton*. English Literary Studies Monograph Series, no. 11. Victoria, B.C.: University of Victoria, 1978. [Chapter 3 is "Herrick and Marvell: The Paradisal Quest"]

King, Bruce. *Marvell's Allegorical Poetry*. Cambridge, England, and New York: Oleander Press, 1977.

Klause, John, Ann Baynes Coiro, and Michael C. Schoenfeldt. "The Achievement of Andrew Marvell: Excerpts from a Panel Discussion." In *On the Celebrated and Neglected Poems of Andrew Marvell*, edited by Claude J. Summers and Ted-Larry Pebworth, 233–47. Columbia: University of Missouri Press, 1992.

Klawitter, George. "Sexual Imagery in Marvell's 'Daphnis and Chloe.'" *University of Dayton Review* 20 (Summer 1989): 51–56.

Korshin, Paul J. *From Concord to Dissent: Major Themes in English Poetic Theory, 1640–1700*. Menston, England: Scolar Press, 1973. [Chapter 4 is "Marvell: From Loyalism to Satire."]

Leishman, J.B. *The Art of Marvell's Poetry*, edited by John Butt. London: Hutchinson & Co., 1966.

Lerner, Lawrence. "Pastoral *Versus* Christianity: Nature in Marvell." In *Seven Studies in English for Dorothy Cavers*, edited by Gildas

Roberts, 20–43. Capetown, Johannesburg, and London: Purnell & Sons, 1971.
Lewalski, Barbara Kiefer. "Marvell as Religious Poet." In *Approaches to Marvell: The York Tercentenary Lectures*, edited by C.A. Patrides, 251–79. London: Routledge and Kegan Paul, 1978.
Lord, George DeForest. *Classical Presences in Seventeenth-Century English Poetry*. New Haven, Connecticut: Yale University Press, 1987. [Chapter 4 is "Andrew Marvell and the Virgilian Triad."]
Lord, George DeF[orest]. "From Contemplation to Action: Marvell's Poetic Career." *Philological Quarterly* 46 (1967): 207–24.
Low, Anthony. *Love's Architecture: Devotional Modes in Seventeenth-Century English Poetry*. New York: New York University Press, 1978. [Chapter 8 is "Andrew Marvell: The Soul's Retreat."]
Marcus, Leah Sinanoglou. *Childhood and Cultural Despair: A Theme and Variations in Seventeenth-Century Literature*. Pittsburgh: University of Pittsburgh Press, 1978. [Chapter 5 is "Beyond Child's Play: Andrew Marvell."]
Marcus, Leah S. *The Politics of Mirth: Jonson, Herrick, Milton, Marvell, and the Defense of Old Holiday Pastimes*. Chicago and London: University of Chicago Press, 1986. [Chapter 7 is "Pastimes Without a Court: Richard Lovelace and Andrew Marvell."]
Markel, Michael H. "Perception and Expression in Marvell's Cavalier Poetry." In *Classic and Cavalier: Essays on Jonson and the Sons of Ben*, edited by Claude J. Summers and Ted-Larry Pebworth, 243–53. Pittsburgh: University of Pittsburgh Press, 1982.
Martin, Christopher. "Flecknoe's Cabinet and Marvell's Cankered Muse." *Essays in Criticism* 40 (1990): 54–66.
Martz, Louis L. "Marvell and Herrick: The Masks of Mannerism." In *Approaches to Marvell: The York Tercentenary Lectures*, edited by C.A. Patrides, 194–215. London: Routledge and Kegan Paul, 1978.
Meilaender, Marion. "Marvell's Pastoral Poetry: Fulfillment of a Tradition." *Genre* 12 (1979): 181–201. [Concentrating on the Mower poems, "Upon Appleton House," "The Garden," and "The Coronet," the essay argues that "the Fall darkens all human experience and that within time one can dispel its shadow only for golden moments from the garden of the mind."]
Miller, Edmund. "Marvell's Pastoral Ideal in 'The Gallery.' " *Concerning Poetry* 8, (Spring 1975): 49–50.
Miner, Earl. *The Metaphysical Mode from Donne to Cowley*. Princeton, New Jersey: Princeton University Press, 1969.
Nardo, Anna K. *The Ludic Self in Seventeenth-Century English Literature*. Albany: State University of New York Press, 1991.

[Concerns theme of play in literature. Chapter 6 is "Andrew Marvell Recreating the Self."]

Nevo, Ruth. "Marvell's 'Songs of Innocence and Experience.' " *Studies in English Literature, 1500–1900* 5 (1965): 1–21. [Focuses upon "On a Drop of Dew," the dialogue poems, "The Nymph Complaining for the Death of Her Fawn," "Daphnis and Chloe," and "Damon the Mower"]

Norford, Don Parry. "Marvell and the Arts of Contemplation and Action." *ELH* 41 (1974): 50–73.

Patrick, J. Max. "Marvell's 'The Unfortunate Lover.' " *The Explicator* 20 (1961–62): Item 65. [Discusses the emblematic nature of the poem and its heroic picture of the unfortunate lover]

Patrides, C.A. " 'Till Prepared for Longer Flight': The Sublunar Poetry of Andrew Marvell." In *Approaches to Marvell: The York Tercentenary Lectures*, edited by C.A. Patrides, 31–55. London: Routledge and Kegan Paul, 1978.

Patterson, Annabel. "*Bermudas* and *The Coronet*: Marvell's Protestant Poetics." *ELH* 44 (1977): 478–99.

Patterson, Annabel. "Miscellaneous Marvell?" In *The Political Identity of Andrew Marvell*, edited by Conal Condren and A.D. Cousins, 188–212. Aldershot, England: Scolar Press, Gower Publishing, 1990.

Patton, Brian. "The Dubious Victory of Conscience over Courage: Marvell on the Retirement of Lord Fairfax." *English Language Notes* 33 (December 1995): 24–31. [Notes that Marvell's celebrations of Fairfax's retirement are somewhat ambiguous and embody mixed feelings]

Pequigney, Joseph. "Marvell's 'Soul' Poetry." In *Tercentenary Essays in Honor of Andrew Marvell*, edited by Kenneth Friedenreich, 76–104. Hamden, Connecticut: Archon, 1977.

Rajan, Balachanra. "Andrew Marvell: The Aesthetics of Inconclusiveness." In *Approaches to Marvell: The York Tercentenary Lectures*, edited by C.A. Patrides, 155–73. London: Routledge and Kegan Paul, 1978.

Ray, Robert H. "Ben Jonson and the Metaphysical Poets: Continuity in a Survey Course." In *Approaches to Teaching the Metaphysical Poets*, edited by Sidney Gottlieb, 89–95. New York: Modern Language Association of America, 1990. [Argues for the importance of Ben Jonson's classical style in shaping Marvell's poems, beyond the influence of Donne and the "metaphysical" characteristics]

Reedy, Gerard, S.J. " 'An Horatian Ode' and 'Tom May's Death.' " *Studies in English Literature, 1500–1900* 20 (1980): 137–51.

Rees, Christine. *The Judgment of Marvell*. London and New York: Pinter Publishers, 1989. [Critical commentary on about the first half of *Miscellaneous Poems*, 1681]
Rees, Christine. " 'Tom May's Death' and Ben Jonson's Ghost: A Study of Marvell's Satiric Method." *Modern Language Review* 71 (1976): 481–88.
Revard, Stella P. "Intertwining the Garland of Marvell's Lyrics: The Greek Anthology and Its Renaissance Heritage." In *On the Celebrated and Neglected Poems of Andrew Marvell*, edited by Claude J. Summers and Ted-Larry Pebworth, 29–46. Columbia: University of Missouri Press, 1992.
Ricks, Christopher. " 'Its own resemblance.' " In *Approaches to Marvell: The York Tercentenary Lectures*, edited by C.A. Patrides, 108–35. London: Routledge and Kegan Paul, 1978. [Examines Marvell's use of reflexive imagery in his poetry]
Rielly, Edward J. "Marvell's 'Fleckno,' Anti-Catholicism, and the Pun as Metaphor." *John Donne Journal* 2, no. 2 (1983): 51–62.
Rogers, John. "The Great Work of Time: Marvell's Pastoral Historiography." In *On the Celebrated and Neglected Poems of Andrew Marvell*, edited by Claude J. Summers and Ted-Larry Pebworth, 207–32. Columbia: University of Missouri Press, 1992. [Concerns primarily "Upon Appleton House," "The Nymph Complaining for the Death of Her Fawn," and the Mower poems]
Rosenberg, John. "Marvell and the Christian Idiom." *Boston University Studies in English* 4 (1960): 152–61. [Illustrates Marvell's underlying Christian suggestions and language in "Clorinda and Damon" and "The Mower Against Gardens"]
Røstvig, Maren-Sofie. "*In ordine di ruota*: Circular Structure in "The Unfortunate Lover" and "Upon Appleton House." In *Tercentenary Essays in Honor of Andrew Marvell*, edited by Kenneth Friedenreich, 245–67. Hamden, Connecticut: Archon, 1977.
Salerno, Nicholas A. "Andrew Marvell and the *Furor Hortensis*." *Studies in English Literature, 1500–1900* 8 (1968): 103–20. [Emphasizes the Mower poems, "Upon Appleton House," and "The Garden"]
Salerno, Nicholas A. "Marvell's 'The Unfortunate Lover,' VIII." *The Explicator* 18 (1959–60): Item 42. [Argues that "banneret" means "a small banner"]
Schwenger, Peter T. "Marvell's 'Unfortunate Lover' as Device." *Modern Language Quarterly* 35 (1974): 364–75.
Smith, A.J. "Marvell's Metaphysical Wit." In *Approaches to Marvell: The York Tercentenary Lectures*, edited by C.A. Patrides, 56–86. London: Routledge and Kegan Paul, 1978.

Spinrad, Phoebe S. "Marvell and the Mystic Laughter." *Papers on Language and Literature* 20 (1984): 259–72. [Argues that the key to Marvell's poetic ambiguity is his ability to see the "mixture of divine importance and human silliness that makes up the essence of man"]

Spitz, Leona. "Process and Stasis: Aspects of Nature in Vaughan and Marvell." *Huntington Library Quarterly* 32 (1968–69): 135–47. [Discusses "On a Drop of Dew," "Bermudas," the Mower poems, and "The Garden"]

Stocker, Margarita. *Apocalyptic Marvell: The Second Coming in Seventeenth Century Poetry*. Athens, Ohio: Ohio University Press, 1986.

Summers, Joseph H. "Andrew Marvell: Private Taste and Public Judgement." In *Metaphysical Poetry*, edited by Malcolm Bradbury and David Palmer, 181–210. Stratford-Upon-Avon Studies 11. London: Edward Arnold, 1970.

Summers, Joseph H. "Marvell's 'Nature.' " *ELH* 20 (1953): 121–35.

Summers, Joseph H. "Some Apocalyptic Strains in Marvell's Poetry." In *Tercentenary Essays in Honor of Andrew Marvell*, edited by Kenneth Friedenreich, 180–203. Hamden, Connecticut: Archon, 1977.

Swardson, H.R. *Poetry and the Fountain of Light: Observations on the Conflict between Christian and Classical Traditions in Seventeenth-Century Poetry*. Columbia: University of Missouri Press, 1962. [Chapter 4 is "Marvell: A New Pastoralism."]

Tayler, Edward William. *Nature and Art in Renaissance Literature*. New York and London: Columbia University Press, 1964. [Chapter 6 is "Marvell's Garden of the Mind."]

Toliver, Harold E. *Marvell's Ironic Vision*. New Haven, Connecticut: Yale University Press, 1965.

Toliver, Harold. "Marvell's Songs and Pictorial Exhibits." In *Tercentenary Essays in Honor of Andrew Marvell*, edited by Kenneth Friedenreich, 105–20. Hamden, Connecticut: Archon, 1977.

Wallerstein, Ruth. *Studies in Seventeenth-Century Poetic*. Madison: University of Wisconsin Press, 1950. [Part 2 (including Chapters 7, 8, and 9) is "Marvell and the Various Light."]

Wanamaker, Melissa C. *Discordia Concors: The Wit of Metaphysical Poetry*. Port Washington, New York: Kennikat Press, 1975. [Chapter 5 is "Andrew Marvell: Unity in Multiplicity."]

Warnke, Frank J. "Play and Metamorphosis in Marvell's Poetry." *Studies in English Literature, 1500–1900* 5 (1965): 23–30. [Concentrates on "The Gallery," "The Picture of Little T. C. in a

Prospect of Flowers," and "A Dialogue between the Soul and Body"]
Wilcox, Helen. " 'Curious Frame': The Seventeenth-Century Religious Lyric as Genre." In *New Perspectives on the Seventeenth-Century English Religious Lyric*, edited by John R. Roberts, 9–27. Columbia and London: University of Missouri Press, 1994. [Discusses "The Coronet" and "On a Drop of Dew"]
Williamson, George. *Six Metaphysical Poets: A Reader's Guide*. New York: Farrar, Straus & Giroux, 1967. [Chapter 9 concerns Marvell and presents general paraphrases of some poems.]
Wilson, A.J. "Marvell, 'Upon the Hill and Grove at Bill-Borrow': Symbolic Form?" *Notes and Queries* 24 (1977): 126–27.
Wilson, A.J.N. "Andrew Marvell: *Upon the Hill and Grove at Bill-Borow* and *Musicks Empire.*" *Bulletin of the John Rylands Library* 51 (1968–69): 453–82.
Wiltenburg, Robert. "Translating All That's Made: Poetry and History in 'Tom May's Death.' " *Studies in English Literature, 1500–1900* 31 (1991): 117–30.
Young, R.V. "Andrew Marvell and the Devotional Tradition." *Renascence* 38 (1986): 204–27. [Argues that Marvell's religious poems are inconsistent, enigmatic and that they ultimately subvert the English devotional tradition]

D. Prose

Anselment, Raymond A. " 'Betwixt Jest and Earnest': Ironic Reversal in Andrew Marvell's *The Rehearsal Transpros'd.*" *Modern Language Review* 66 (1971): 282–93.
Anselment, Raymond A. *"Betwixt Jest and Earnest": Marprelate, Milton, Marvell, Swift, and The Decorum of Religious Ridicule*. Toronto: University of Toronto Press, 1979. [Chapter 5 is *"The Rehearsal Transpros'd."*]
Anselment, Raymond A. "Satiric Strategy in Marvell's *The Rehearsal Transpros'd.*" *Modern Philology* 68 (1970–71): 137–50.
Campbell, Heather. "Burlesque in Marvell's *The Rehearsal Transpros'd.*" *English Studies in Canada* 6 (1980): 263–76.
Condren, Conal. "Andrew Marvell as Polemicist: his Account of the Growth of Popery, and Arbitrary Government." In *The Political Identity of Andrew Marvell*, edited by Conal Condren and A.D. Cousins, 157–87. Aldershot, England: Scolar Press, Gower Publishing, 1990.

Coolidge, John S. "Martin Marprelate, Marvell, and *Decorum Personae* as a Satirical Theme." *PMLA* 74 (1959): 526–32. [Concerns *The Rehearsal Transprosed*]
Jaeckle, Dan. "De-Authorizing in Marvell's *The Rehearsal Transpros'd*." *John Donne Journal* 10 (1991): 129–42.
Keeble, N.H. " 'I would not tell you any tales': Marvell's Constituency Letters." In *The Political Identity of Andrew Marvell*, edited by Conal Condren and A.D. Cousins, 111–34. Aldershot, England: Scolar Press, Gower Publishing, 1990.
Legouis, Pierre. "Marvell and 'the two learned brothers of St. Marthe.' " *Philological Quarterly* 38 (1959): 450–58. [Identifies the "two learned brothers" in *The Rehearsal Transprosed* as twins who contributed to revising *Gallia Christiana*]
Schmitter, Dean Morgan. "The Occasion for Marvell's *Growth of Popery*." *Journal of the History of Ideas* 21 (1960): 568–70.

VI. GENERAL BACKGROUND

Alexander, H.G. *Religion in England, 1558–1662*. London: University of London Press, 1968.
Cirlot, J.E. *A Dictionary of Symbols*. New York: Philosophical Library, 1962.
Comito, Terry. *The Idea of the Garden in the Renaissance*. New Brunswick, New Jersey: Rutgers University Press, 1978.
Heninger, S.K., Jr. *A Handbook of Renaissance Meteorology, With Particular Reference to Elizabethan and Jacobean Literature*. 1960. Reprint. New York: Greenwood Press, 1968.
Jones, Richard Foster. *Ancients and Moderns: A Study of the Rise of the Scientific Movement in Seventeenth-Century England*. 1936. Reprint. Berkeley and Los Angeles: University of California Press, 1965.
Meadows, A.J. *The High Firmament: A Survey of Astronomy in English Literature*. Leicester: University of Leicester Press, 1969.
New, John F.H. *Anglican and Puritan: The Basis of Their Opposition, 1558–1640*. Stanford, California: Stanford University Press, 1964.
Ruthven, K.K. *The Conceit*. London: Methuen, 1969.
Tillyard, E.M.W. *The Elizabethan World Picture*. London: Chatto & Windus, 1943.